THE NINE
LAWS

CASTALIA HOUSE

Non-Fiction
MAGA Mindset: Making YOU and America Great Again by Mike Cernovich
SJWs Always Lie by Vox Day
Cuckservative by John Red Eagle and Vox Day
Equality: The Impossible Quest by Martin van Creveld
A History of Strategy by Martin van Creveld
4th Generation Warfare Handbook by William S. Lind and LtCol Gregory
    A. Thiele, USMC
Compost Everything by David the Good
Grow or Die by David the Good

Military Science Fiction
The Eden Plague by David VanDyke
There Will Be War Volumes I and II ed. Jerry Pournelle
There Will Be War Volumes IX and X ed. Jerry Pournelle (forthcoming)

Science Fiction
The End of the World as We Knew It by Nick Cole
CTRL-ALT REVOLT! by Nick Cole
Somewhither by John C. Wright
Back From the Dead by Rolf Nelson
Victoria: A Novel of Fourth Generation War by Thomas Hobbes

Fantasy
Iron Chamber of Memory by John C. Wright

Fiction
Brings the Lightning by Peter Grant
The Missionaries by Owen Stanley

Audiobooks
A History of Strategy narrated by Jon Mollison
Cuckservative narrated by Thomas Landon
Four Generations of Modern War narrated by William S. Lind
Grow or Die narrated by David the Good
Extreme Composting narrated by David the Good
A Magic Broken narrated by Nick Afka Thomas

THE NINE LAWS

SURVIVAL
MOMENTUM
TRIUMPH

IVAN THRONE

The Nine Laws

Ivan Throne

Published by Castalia House
Kouvola, Finland
www.castaliahouse.com

Editor: Vox Day

Cover Design: Dark Triad Man, LLC

Contents

DEDICATION

For my wife, by whom I have learned
that even a **Dark Triad Man**
can find matchless contentment.

Acknowledgments

As with any publication there are many who contribute in essential and crucial ways not only to the act and discipline of writing but to the experience, passion and understanding that forms the basis of the knowledge and wisdom of the author.

In my own case this work would be utterly incomplete without an explicit acknowledgement of the men and women who have formed my growth, guided my life, and helped to carve out my experiences within the dark world that we all inhabit.

To my late father I give thanks for his passionate, powerful and deep examples of class and intelligence. Without his hand resonating through the shaping of my life, I would not have found dignity in it.

To my late mother I give thanks for her adamant, unwavering insistence that a love of learning be the foundation of all my interactions in the world. Without her fostering of my self-education, I would have grown into an ignorant, dogmatic man.

It is with grave and permanent reverence that I acknowledge the investment and mentoring of the *ninja*. Theirs is a long and challenging journey to absorb the often frightening lessons of mind and heart, bone and fist. Absent that sharing of their priceless knowledge I would be long dead.

Peter Paton was extraordinarily helpful in his independent review of the manuscript drafts, often finding obscure errors and points of clarity that I simply could not spot on my own. Because of his painstaking, methodical assistance this book shines with polish at a very granulated level.

Joe Katzman has been a wise and invaluable mentor, serving as a brilliantly insightful voice of clarity that sharpens structure and helps to identify targets of direction for this work. His ability to drill down to the core essence and build out the message delivery in my writing is superb, and his generous friendship is greatly appreciated. His immensely gracious authoring of the foreword to this book is a priceless contribution.

Sam Botta has provided intense and deeply personal validation of the framework and grid of the Laws, and of the direction I plan to drive my broader work in the new age that arrives with such enormous swiftness. His personal embodiment of determination and spirit remains a stellar example of perseverance in the face of mortal odds.

To Jerry Airheart, Chris Allan, Kifahi Bilal, Frank Black, Jeremy Brown, Jonathan Chu, Kevin Dabhi, Jacob Gaines, David Grim, Titus Hauer, Tommy Dante Ho, Baasit Khawaja, Grzegorz Piotr Knapik, Jonathan Lamptey, David Mackey, Vojtěch P., Robert Pearson, Ronald Swank, B. Thygesen, Rémi Walle, Donald Wheeler, Christopher Youssef and all the other members of the focus groups that helped shape the content of this book: my very sincere and appreciative thanks for your generous involvement. It has been a massive labor of love and the time you spent to engage and share have made all the difference in the final work that you now hold in your hands.

Your support in the early stages of conception for this edition of The Nine Laws is a valuable gift for which I am extremely grateful.

To Victor Pride of Bold and Determined: this work is all your fault. You are motivation for scores of thousands, and rightfully so.

Your own work inspires generations of men to rip off the chains of slavery, and that is an immeasurable legacy of deeply powerful truth.

To Vox Day, Supreme Dark Lord of the Evil Legion of Evil, I give my great respect and appreciation for the honor done to my work by publication through Castalia House. Our partnership delivers the opportunity for a much wider reach and resonance of this book. It is with vibrant pleasure that I look forward to the demands ahead of reshaping the trajectory of Western civilization with you and other men who drive vast, savage and brilliant currents below the surface of the new age.

To Hans Holbein the Younger, artist of great renown, sublime skill and honorable service to his dread and majestic sovereign, I give immense gratitude for the immortal and beautiful woodcuts that have come down to us through history and form the illustrations arrayed before each chapter. His haunting, striking artwork of the *Danse Macabre* helps to deliver the content of this book with matchless beauty and is an irreplaceable part of the experience of The Nine Laws.

To Mr. Swift goes my respect and enjoyment of the psychopathic embodiment of competence and power that you bring to the great challenges ahead of us, and the faith that reaches immortality.

To my family, much honor for everything you have done and continue to do as part of our blood tribe of men and women in the dark world. With each generation, our legacy of survival drives deeper into human history and none of you are ever forgotten.

In particular, appreciation goes out to my lovely and absolute crazy, whisky-drinking, gun-toting, homesteading cowgirl great-niece Gigi. Her ranch is a haven for the entire extended family, and we are all delighted in the sanctuary of love and welcome it provides.

To my older brother I give thanks for the guidance and competition that has been immensely motivating to me as I make my way in the dark world. I showed you the picture of a gorgeous girlfriend; you confessed you were dating a royal princess. I mentioned I'm meeting a billionaire; you could not spare a moment to talk because you were on your way up to the office of Donald Trump. I share my recent acquisition... and you inform me that you are wearing Trump's tie, given directly from his neck in personal appreciation.

It is comforting to be continually surpassed by your older brother. You are the right man to be the head of our ancient blood, and I know our father is vastly proud.

To my older sister I send my love and laughter, and immense gratitude for the warmth, fierce protection and occasional concussions you provided me while growing up in the dark world.

That moment of truth in the den shaped my entire life, and gave me strength to get up and walk.

To my little sister, I send my strength and barbarous ferocity, knowing that despite the tender and gentle exterior there lives a spirit of icy competence and brilliant testimony inside you. I am very proud to have seen it flash forward with severe and unyielding strength.

You are an honor to our lineage.

To my oldest daughter, I send my thanks and admiration for the tenacious, no-nonsense spirit that has been a constant demonstration of joy for me. Your intelligence, determination and focus are deeply ingrained in you and it is a source of much admiration for where I see you taking your life.

To my youngest daughter, I share a smile and pride in your absolute ferocity of spirit and the intense enrichment of color, beauty and song that exude from you with bottomless delight and power. Your loyalty and kindness are markers that will carry you far in life.

To my son, I give thanks for your firm leap at the ladders and challenges of the dark world, and share my pride in your indomitable spirit and deep, impenetrable intelligence. You carry heritage of a thousand years in your veins, and I know that you will crack open the future in your own right.

Lastly I wish to thank my wife Lauren for her inestimable contributions to my fulfilling experience as a human being. I would not be the same without it.

Authors often speak of the immense toll that their craft takes upon their loved ones through the long, ceaseless hours of writing; the temper tantrums that flare with frustration in struggle over a concept or a paragraph, and the scary exultation that accompanies breakthrough of ideas and the outpouring of words on a page.

It isn't a casual acknowledgement I deliver here. It is a very serious one, and Lauren has been an invaluable friend and sounding board, a partner through the passionate, roaring rollercoasters of literary creation.

Her patience, her love, her steadfastness and her integrity are vast enough to embrace and shelter a man forging through the crashing tides of the dark world, and greet him with warmth and embraces on his return home with the throne.

It is to her, with much love and respect, that this book is gratefully dedicated.

IV

The Young Child | Danse Macabre
Hans Holbein the Younger (1497–1543)

Preface: The Dying Child

The man sat across the sterile room and watched his child dying.

He had stood calmly under the hostile machine guns of the Soviets within the charred and shattered rubble of Berlin in service to his Crown and country. He had then crossed the world to America where he built and lived, loved and raised his family.

Now this former reporter could do nothing but watch, and wait, and take notes in a sad and tired hand on a yellow legal pad, recording details with the practiced habit of a journalist as fever migraines prodded his youngest son into crying, wakeful pain. The boy would writhe, then subside into exhausted silence on the bed once more.

Bruises covered him where intravenous lines had been run for weeks into his hands and arms, his feet and ankles. With each passing day there were fewer places to insert fresh ones, fewer issuances of hope from doctors and nurses who were reduced to mere attendants of pain and no longer able to act as healers.

Days and nights were a blur, for sleep and waking were run not by play and rest, by meals and repose, but by the fits and starts of fever and the incomprehension of the innocent who woke in the dark hours before dawn and cried and cried with pain at the soft light that glowed from the nurse's station.

As the weeks went by the man documented the progression of meningitis that writhed in the skull of his child, burning the boy's mind away and murdering his senses.

"His hearing is going," the man wrote.

"Even in the pain, he can tell something is happening to him, and complains that he cannot hear."

The love and helplessness inscribed into those pages shone from the written words.

The documentation stopped near the end, when against all odds the fevers broke and the doctor took the man aside and said to him, "It's happened. We saved him."

The grave illness had lost. The pain was gone, and the gift of calm and sleep had replaced the tossing and turning of agony and pressure within the golden head of the young child.

Soon enough the boy went home to his family, and entered into a world where nothing made sense any longer. The world had been turned upside down, and everything had been severed.

He was deaf. Birds, laughter, music, human connection through voices had all been stolen by the disease and the fevers and the drugs pumped into him with desperate hope and quantity.

The boy could no longer walk, for the nerves that connected his inner ears to his brain had been burned away. There was no longer an up or down to perceive, and even a simple attempt to stand on his own made the world tumble and turn and the floor would leap up and slam into him without sympathy.

The voice of his mother, which used to sing to him and lull him to sleep as one of the sweetest sounds of the universe, was now silent. There was only the great effort of slowly mouthing words, beginning the long and exhausting process of teaching the boy to lip read as if his life depended on it... and it did.

The living feeling of connection with friends and family was severed forever. No longer could the boy simply listen and be an integral and accepted partner of humor and discussion, of sharing and whispers. He was now a permanent outsider, cut off and reduced to an observer rather than an equal participant.

Gone were the dreams of a little boy to be an astronaut, a firefighter, a policeman, a soldier. Never again would a future be possible that relied upon the ability to hear, to listen, and act.

And so the boy was dependent, and hurting, and terrified, and did not understand. And finally the day came when the family sat down to dinner, and he lay on the floor and cried for help, because he could not walk. And not one person came, and he lay there alone in miserable despondency.

Until he started to scream in rage.

Then his older sister came down, and stood over him. And when she spoke, she made certain he could read her lips and understand.

"Get up and walk," she said. "Quit wailing."

Her face was harsh and neutral. "The world isn't going to help you."

And she turned away, and went back up the short flight of stairs to the kitchen and the family.

The boy lay there for a moment, stunned, and rebelliously enraged at reality.

Then something contracted inside him, and he sat up. He looked at the stairs, then silently wiped his face.

He crawled to those stairs and dragged himself upwards, furious, finally reaching the chair next to his father. Then he gasped and clambered until he had pulled himself onto it. Not one person at the table glanced at him or offered assistance. When he was seated, his father looked over and calmly offered him a serving of dinner. But in that Englishman's eyes was the glint of the most powerful approbation that an officer of the Royal Horse Guards can give another man.

It was respect, and the boy never forgot that look.

I was four years old.

The Priest | Danse Macabre
Hans Holbein the Younger (1497–1543)

Foreword by Joseph Katzman

The morning breaks quietly in my office as I watch them saw off a brave man's head.

I've come across a new writer named "Ivan Throne," who challenged me to learn something I didn't know about myself. The world is dark, he says.

And? I've seen and publicly coined key national security trends, and I actually read human rights reports. You don't have to tell me.

Ah, but go ask yourself how you would have endured, says Ivan, as you watch these videos of ISIS. Of death and persecution in The Bloodlands during World War II. Of Cambodian mass murderers at Tuol Sleng, who sound like they just walked out of an American college.

This morning, I watch. I ask.

He's right. What I thought I knew is not enough. I contemplate this in silence. Then Ivan's next lesson kicks down the door:

> *There is no one coming to save you. Your power in the world is all that you and your loved ones can depend upon.*

"There are no laws." The last of his Nine Laws. The Zen void that penetrates all things, and extends to all things.

I think I need to pay more attention to this guy.

That day, and for many days thereafter, I train a little harder. I focus a bit more. It's a shallow application. But it's a start.

Getting started is the most important thing.

✦ ✦ ✦

Life didn't get any easier for Ivan after that first painful crawl to his father's table.

Thrust into the crucible, he put in long years of study and practice. Trials in life, martial arts and business developed into a way of seeing, training, and doing. Posture. Endurance. Concealment. Survival. Freedom. Purpose. Power. The Grand Jokes of Preposterousness and No Laws. The arts of recovery and redirection. They have seen him through some shattering events.

Imagine that you understood them all at a deep level. Imagine that you embodied this knowledge, created a living framework for your personal "talent stack" of skills and techniques. What could you become?

Wouldn't you like to find out?

Which brings us to the catch. There's always a catch, so here it is up front:

Just how much do you want to find out?

Ivan had no choice. You do. His exercises are honest and difficult. That's why they will change you.

If—and only if—you dare to do the work.

Whenever you feel the itch from inner drive, from curiosity, or even from unpleasant emotions, pick up The Nine Laws and dive into a few pages. You will learn by doing. You will learn by noticing. Every time it happens, you'll take a small step forward. Congratulate yourself. If you're rolling, go on to the next application or the next concept. Continue making the investment that will set you apart.

In some cases, you'll hit barriers because you aren't ready to do what Ivan asks. So "tumble and turn," as he says. Try something else. There's so much to apply, and what's beyond you now may look different later.

In other cases, you may think that a lesson is too basic, or already mastered. Take a deep breath, and dive in anyway. Can you see a new facet that you hadn't fully grasped before?

Warning: Learning this way, with this material, tends to blow 'narrative', facades, and pleasant untruths all to hell. No, it won't force you to abandon morality. What it will do is make it impossible for you to serve morality falsely.

Those who profit from your illusions, and from your pain, will hate this.

We all have illusions, of course. I do. You do. Ivan does, too. So you won't agree with everything written here.

Great! The unthinking cannot be trusted to lead. Of course, neither can someone who never changes his mind. Don't be that guy. Buy the ticket. Take the ride. Do the work.

Keep noticing, and dare to discover what you might believe tomorrow.

The Sixth Law is Freedom, after all. You're investing in yourself, and building for yourself and your brothers. Once the insights you build begin to come to mind in real-time situations, the deep changes will begin.

The question after that is how you represent what you're learning to the outside world.

Ivan's laws of Posture and Concealment will apply, of course. You're learning things that will act as a hub for many of your other skills while sharpening your inner view. People will notice. When they do, remember that posture includes qualification. Remember that concealment can be used offensively, as a test of seriousness that seems to be about other things (do a search for "Milton Erickson mountain").

Finally, remember the Ninth Law. Ivan does. After long training in more than one martial arts school, he emerged with a perspective of "my guy can fight your guy, and I bet they'd both learn something." He won't be offended if you treat his book the same way.

All sincere learners are honored for their journey, and all are welcome.

That's why we're working on ideas to extend the book's lessons for those who have invested in it, and in themselves. What you're reading, and what Ivan has built online, are just the start.

I've watched Ivan's online presence take off to over 62,000 visitors, 155,000 pages, and eleven million Twitter impressions through late July 2016. That's a pretty good first nine months. This book is where the next level begins.

My parting word is to remember where you are. It's a dark world. Ivan is about to take you to the river—and drop you in the water.

See you downstream.

Joseph Katzman
Editor Emeritus, *Defense Industry Daily*

That the step to competence is held to be very dangerous by the far greater portion of mankind (and by the entire fair sex)—quite apart from its being arduous—is seen to by those guardians who have so kindly assumed superintendence over them.

After the guardians have first made their domestic cattle dumb and have made sure that these placid creatures will not dare take a single step without the harness of the cart to which they are tethered, the guardians then show them the danger which threatens if they try to go alone.

Actually, however, this danger is not so great, for by falling a few times they would finally learn to walk alone.

Immanuel Kant (1724–1804)

A Cemetery | Danse Macabre
Hans Holbein the Younger (1497–1543)

Chapter 1

Instant Immersion

The dark world calls to you ceaselessly. Our work together begins immediately.

My own introduction to the reality of the dark world began without remorse or pity for my loss of hearing and permanent exclusion from the murmured embraces of human communication.

Your education in the dark world also starts without comfort or softened blow.

Throwing *you* directly into the storm of the dark world is how you sink or swim.

The development of a **Dark Triad Man** is born from a combination of necessity, desperation and innovation. Those ingredients are the birth waters for a mindset of unhesitating ferocity that accepts nothing less than survival, power and ultimately a legacy left behind.

This book of The Nine Laws is derived from many sources. The most important source is the burning unstoppable fire to *live* that underpins everything that a man must think, do and be. You have that fire within you. For many men that fire is behind a door of fear, ridicule and social control.

This book will show you how to blow the locks off that door forever.

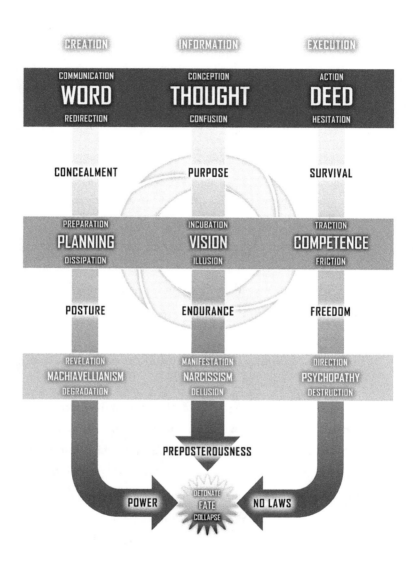

Figure 1.1: Complete grid of the dark world and the rails of
The Nine Laws

Careful study, contemplation and carrying out of the exercises within this book will cause you to drop complacency and commence profound changes in thought, word and deed. You will become harder, stronger and your male dignity will present itself.

There are too many emasculated, weak, frightened men. It is of utmost importance for powerful and determined leaders to step forward from the dark world and provide hardened, ruthless examples of manhood and deliver it to those in need.

Men do not abandon comrades, nor leave their wounded brothers behind.

Grasp the lessons of this book. Work them into your life. Observe their power. Stack them upon each other and discover how their combination simplifies and strengthens your focus and resolve. Sharpen your mind on the teachings and return to them often.

Own them completely. Use them to strip away the illusions of the time. Never be ashamed to be the most powerful person in the room.

Absorb the training and never forget it. This knowledge has been paid for over decades with much blood and suffering. Heed my voice, and absorb it.

Now it forever belongs to you.

Stand with courage, and learn:

1. The universe is impersonal.

You must accept that the universe does not notice your pain, your angst, your frustration or your screams. Operate within this frame of neutrality.

2. Ruthlessness is natural.

Nature does not have pity or grant favor to individuals, and life is unstinting in its ruthlessness. Ruthlessness is thus part of all living things.

3. Surprise is your own fault.

You are responsible for being prepared for encounters and engagements in life. Surprises are not favored by the powerful or the successful.

4. Tools, not weapons.

Physical objects do not bear moral freight. Understand that emotional attachment to the concept of "weapons" is a weak limitation of spirit.

5. Engage with deliberation.

Not all encounters necessitate engagement. When a decision to engage is arrived at, be deliberate and conscious with the deployment of your intention.

6. Quick beats fast.

Fast is impressive. Quick is successful. Strive always to shorten, remove and vanish the interval between stimulus and response through constant practice.

7. Understand the male and female.

Overt and covert, the yielding and the penetrating, are fundamental to human interactions. Understand the archetypes of sexuality.

8. Understand singularities.

Where infinite density of thought, word or deed arrives at a one-dimensional tipping point, you have a useable singularity. Understand this process.

9. Balance cannot be forced.

Balance relies upon itself. Become cognizant of balance as a place to arrive at, a pivotal state of fragility and not static homeostasis forced into being.

10. Others do not care.

You matter far less to other people and animals than your emotional attachment to illusion leads you to believe. Focus on results and do not expect pity.

11. Humans are predators.

In your encounters and engagements with human beings, recall always that they are the apex predator of the known universe and never underestimate.

12. Adversaries, not enemies.

Emotional attachment to the concept of "enemies" is a stumbling point of defeat and death. Adversaries exist to avoid or overthrow as needs demand.

13. Tumble and turn.

Develop comfortable familiarity and skill in the detached and practiced alternation of perspectives, intentions and postures. From their transformation leaks the real.

14. Understand duality.

The duality of the universe and the complementation of opposites is a fundamental and inherent principle. Master the ability to straddle and reposition them.

15. Achievement brings prerogative.

Those who produce results of value in the markets of the world retain the prerogative of power to receive value, defend value and speak for it.

16. Luck is manufactured.

What appears to be luck is nearly always the result of long cultivation of skill, awareness and preparation. Strive to seed life with future opportunities.

17. Karma is hungry.

Consequence is a grave foundation of the universe we inhabit. Cause and effect are inseparably entwined, and the wise contemplate outcomes with care.

18. Zoom in and out.

Perspective provides insight into reality. Work always to consider the deep and the shallow, the close and the far, and in the slide of perspective find opportunity.

19. Understand gradients.

Binary realities exist, but there is no dividing line between them. Understand the subtle shift of reality by seamless movements within spectrums.

20. Outrage is pointless.

Indignity and attack are inevitable and outrage is a pointless, inhibiting and useless emotional attachment. Respond with seamless accord to risk.

21. Train to avoid stutter.

Words, thoughts and deeds all stutter. Train well to understand the vulnerability that stutter creates, and practice to develop the fluid continuity of the master practitioner.

22. Comprehend moments of relief.

The spirit relaxes and sighs in moments of relief, and it is in that moment of Void that awareness suspends and the spear drives home into the heart. Learn this well.

23. All things degrade.

Entropy is the nature of our universal existence. That which is not attended, rusts. That which is not cultivated, rots. Choose which realms of life you attend and discard.

24. Time plays games.

Time itself is an illusion, a dimension that is even stretched by the presence of mass. Your interaction with time is defined by your intention and intensity. Practice this well.

25. Static state is illusion.

Absolute zero is an artificial and unsustainable state. Understand that all things have momentum and movement, and can be harnessed with utilitarian effect.

26. Class will out.

Essential social values, skill and upbringing will inevitably emerge as a demonstration of moral posture and breeding. Learn well to note subtle indications early.

27. Power is a language.

Those who have power deliver it in more than words and deeds. Posture, gaze, silence and myriad other indicators are flags and avenues of power. Learn to recognize them quickly.

28. Coincidence is a warning.

Awareness of coincidence is reaction to the subtle warning of the psyche to parallel concordance of manifestation. Patterns are both risk and opportunity. Learn them well.

29. Unravel and entwine.

Through separation and entanglement, through the application and division of realities, the man of power discovers the essential modes of utility for his purpose.

30. Understand rhythm and collapse.

Patterns become cycles, and cycles accord to rhythms. Learn well to recognize the rhythms underlying reality, for in their disruption and acceleration lies power to provoke collapse.

31. Find joy in the preposterous.

The vast deeps of time and space are nonetheless an instantaneous singularity against infinity. It is preposterous that things exist. Take great joy in each moment.

32. Fighting is extremely dangerous.

The nature of the universe is no laws and no guarantee. All engagements of combat bear the potentiality of your death. Brash engagement will prove fatal.

33. What is living can kill.

As long as your adversary breathes he is capable of rising and ensuring your death. When killing, certainty is demanded of you in the pursuit of your own survival. Do not guess.

34. Capture moments of shudder.

Shudder occurs when intensity is manifested with unexpected suddenness. Shudders create enormously powerful opportunity for penetration or redirection. Learn this well.

35. Intelligence is dangerous.

When a being is more intelligent than you there is infinite danger, for you cannot identify the extent of the capacity gap or ensure that you have addressed all risk. Be gravely aware.

36. Detachment is power.

The discarding of illusion and the seamless, responsive nature of correct posture are outgrowths of a mind that does not stop and a heart that does not cling. Learn this well.

37. Cultivate every day.

Grand realizations of vision and colossal achievements of purpose are not delivered with sudden fortune. Each day cultivate and groom, prepare and advance towards outcome.

38. Understand stacking.

The layering of methodologies and skills, of approaches and concepts, creates an impetus and momentum greater than the sum of its parts. Manifest this process of powerful building.

39. Consequences are invaluable.

The inevitability of cause and effect leads to the reliability and predictability of consequences in the dark world. Through recognition of cause, effect can be prepared for with profit.

40. Vision is essential.

Not one champion ever lived who did not believe in himself. You must work with severe and enormous determination to build, polish and deploy your vision in order to move the world.

41. Authenticity is pitiless.

The world is what it is and reality does not apologize. What is truly real and authentic does not flinch, or grovel, or supplicate. Strive for authenticity instead of expecting pity.

42. Entitlement is internal.

True entitlement is arrived at through the development of the inner self, manifested in the outer world, and gratified through receipt back into the spirit. It is the actual heart that deserves.

43. Intention manifests.

Will that arises in thought, word and deed inevitably and inexorably changes reality. The revelation of your purpose in the playing out of fate is best as deliberate expression.

44. Master each realm of concealment.

Learn well to conceal thoughts, lest they betray. Learn well to draw curtains across purpose, so that it is not thwarted. Understand that survival is at odds with prominence.

45. Lords and banners matter.

The dark world elevates and smashes, promotes and slays with visible lines of power. Adhere to banners and lords, for by the array of Heaven is found its intention in the dark world.

46. There is always a champion.

As nature abhors a vacuum, so does the world of men. There will be a man proclaimed as the apex of achievement, whether or not deserved or real. Find the flow towards this place.

47. Sunk costs are gone.

What is spent is gone. Chasing after wasted investment is a spiraling compulsion of failure and attachment to frustrated illusion of spirit. Failure exists. Learn well to move quickly on.

48. Patience is necessary.

Cultivation requires the passage of time from conception to delivery, from ideation to demonstration. Learn to accord with the natural pace of development, and thereby steer incisively.

49. Politics is not distinct.

It is a grave and futile mistake to condemn political maneuvering or skill. Political acts are in truth indistinguishable from human behavior. Do not resent this.

50. Master understanding of flow.

Water seeks the lowest level, and the universe itself has a perceptible flow of energy and power. Study well the concept of flow from one place to another, and to seize and ride currents.

51. Chaos and order are entwined.

Chaos is a crucial concept to understand. The reeling and rolling of the random is deeply woven into the fabric of reality. Know where it edges and dwells, for it creates opportunity.

52. Cultivate inevitability.

It is futile to thrash against and deny the inevitable force of destiny that Heaven has determined. Learn the Way of Heaven, accord with the Will of Heaven, and attain invincibility.

53. All things bend.

Just as there is no static state of absolute zero, there is no inflexibility in the universe. Things flex when leverage is appropriate. Learn well to position for powerful effort.

54. Nobility is mundane.

In the simple is the sublime, and within the direct and the calm is power. Learn the essentials of graceful, sacred expression and the posture of the indomitably blessed.

55. Humans are mostly weak.

Outstanding performance, exemplary skill and brilliant minds are rare peaks of human potential. Understand and set expectations accordingly, for not all share equal capacity.

56. Study and develop scholarship.

The seasoned practitioner marries deep understanding and investigation of theory with his application and manifestations of power. Consider deeply. Learn ceaselessly.

57. Harden the body for killing.

The dark world delights in surprise and in the overturn of expectation. Your survival as a living being may depend upon inherent strength. Cultivate serious resiliency.

58. History is written by the winner.

The truth of armies and nations, of kings and councilors, is written by those who wield the prerogative of the axe and block. Learn to read through the lines and perceive truth.

59. Harness passions.

Compulsive, rapacious desires and lusts are an inherent part of the experience of living things. Harness them with deliberate intention and find your outcomes driven by their power.

60. Penetrate deeper.

Shallowness is weakness when it is a limitation on capacity. Cultivate the ability to penetrate deeply into emotion, thought, action and targets in the dark world.

61. Remove envy from thinking.

Resentful jealousy is a corrosive and hobbling realm of futile idiocy. Do not envy, but attain. Do not covet, but reach. Do not whine, but drive yourself to achievement as an equal.

62. The world is a dark place.

Social constructs and ideologies are ever mere overlays upon the reality of blood and claw, of rending teeth and vicious feeding that is the nature of the dark world. Do not forget.

63. Each encounter is infinite.

Within each encounter is the infinite potential of enlightened understanding and the dropping away of illusion. Understand this well. Broaden, deepen and cultivate your receptivity.

64. Everything is training.

Each lesson that you survive brings with it greater knowledge, understanding and power if received with the correct mental, emotional and physical posture of learning. Train. Always.

65. Attrition is crucial.

Carving away the ineffective and scraping off the useless is an integral, equal partner to the process of growing and building. Prune all things with equal focus and determination.

66. You are replaceable.

You are a momentary, instantaneous spark in the eternal fire of all things. You are replaceable in all ways, for truth is eternal and you are merely a vessel. Maintain this humility.

67. Thought, word and deed must align.

The sacred nature of the human being is the existence of free will. Alignment of thought, word and deed to the will of Heaven in conscious choice delivers illimitable power.

68. Discipline your movement.

Movement of the body is a reflection of the mind and heart. Control the body with deliberation and develop your posture with cultivated grace, accuracy and power.

69. Internal locus of control.

Scattered, external dependencies of self-respect, approval or disapproval and other measures of performance are ultimately routes to frustration. Measure yourself inwardly.

70. Remove self-pity.

The universe has no time for feelings of self-pity. If you are sorry for yourself, you will sit sorrowful alone. Get up and walk. Develop resiliency of attitude towards living.

71. Train in methods of survival.

The unexpected arrives with tsunamic ferocity and the dark world does not forgive lack of capability. Learn well to fight, to speak, to survive, to escape and to conceal.

72. Develop social ease.

Smooth ability to build rapport and facilitate dialogue are the hallmarks of the human being who understands the flow of power. It is a demonstration of personal competence.

73. All things have utility.

There is nothing which is of no use, even if only by recognition of profit through avoidance. Master the ability to extract value from each encounter in the dark world.

74. Deeply comprehend exponents.

That which curves sharply upward on the scale is what brings wealth and disaster, victory and defeat with sudden inevitable denouement. Swiftly recognize, create and exploit it.

75. You can and will be broken.

Every human being has a breaking point past which pain, torment, stress and suffering will smash resistance and knock out the heart. Anticipate, prevent, accept and recover.

76. Understand the transformation of energy.

Energy flows with predictable breath and pulse. Know intimately the pattern of its living flow. Recognize the state of energy and know the future that arrives with imminence.

77. Understand the interruption of energy.

Energy has power, momentum and vulnerability. Master the correct perception of energy in order to interrupt the flow and accelerate determined future outcomes within the world.

78. Recognize enthrallment.

Mesmerized fascination with people, places and things is a predictable and readily instilled state of hypnotic folly. Learn to infect with enthrallment, and to recognize and extract self.

79. Understand breakouts.

The snapping of barriers leads to the collapse or surge of change and transformation. Learn to read the signals of a pending breakout, for it brings great risk and promise.

80. Cultivate the immovable spirit.

The Way of the immovable spirit is essential to the cultivation of true personal power in the human world. As broad as the sky and as inherent as the wind, the self finds power by infinity.

81. Understand the central heart.

Within the cycle of the seasons the master knows that each equinox is inherent. Because the universe exists, ultimate sincere truth is equally inherent. Learn this heart.

82. Become a vehicle for fate.

The decision through free will to accord with the path of appropriate consequence and justice enables the master to grasp and saddle the playing out of fate. Be the master.

83. Sorrow is normal.

Loss, agony, hurt and sorrow are inevitable and inherent in the experience of being a human being. Accept this as the nature of things, and move into acceptance and consequent peace.

84. Acceptance is essential.

Resistance to truth is futile and provocative of howling, idiot senselessness of action. Accept reality. Let go of frustration. Release expectation. Allow the universe to penetrate you.

85. Do not stop the mind.

Attachment to things creates a stopping point for the mind. When the mind stops on the sword, the body is cut. Train ceaselessly to embody seamless and fluid perception.

86. Understand doorways.

Within the manifestation of fate are choices, beyond which the inexorable direction of that fate cannot be reversed. Perceive these as doorways, and select with deliberate care.

87. Fulfillment arises in depth.

Fulfillment of desire and hope, of satisfaction and joy, is delivered through the depth of experience. Learn to descend through depths with cultivated skill, and life blossoms.

88. Master the concept of pivot.

The moment of pivot is where the universe spins upon quantum probabilities and the application of conscious will impacts the infinite. Learn to recognize and seamlessly direct fate.

89. Silence has value.

In stillness is heard the subtle, and in calm is contemplated the profound. Appreciate the power of the dark void, for even the universe itself exists within the infinite deep. Connect to it.

90. Boundaries are illusions.

In accord with the truth that no laws constrain the preposterous nature of what we call reality, understand well that boundaries are false and that total freedom is the Way.

91. Ego is illusion.

The sense of separateness of self from the universe is a great and silly self-promotion of an empty trick in place of the realization of utter connectedness. Do not be a fool.

92. Time and space are illusions.

The singularity of the physical universe operates according to physical laws, yet those laws are true only within our own singularity. Learn to shape and bend perceptions of interval.

93. Love is real.

In the conscious awareness of the mind and heart is the joyous infinity of recognition of each other, as one hand of the body knows the other. Within that adherence of self, is immortality.

94. Laughter is powerful.

Laughter fills the universe. It is the sound of joy, of transcendence, of indomitability and of courage. Bring laughter to the front. Take nothing too seriously. Exult in life.

95. The universe is infinitely fair.

The most crushing sorrow and horrible cruelty, as well as the grandest joy and the blinding light of ten billion universes, all are nothing against eternity. It all evens out. Accept this.

96. Infinity is real.

The mind cannot fathom eternity, but can endlessly compound in pursuit of it. The heart accepts death, but the spirit does not. Rest in the peace of this vibrant, ever-present perception.

97. Power is sacred.

As Heaven wills, so manifests fate. Cultivation of momentum according to that will, manifests that which is sacred. The sacred is the intent of the immortal engine behind all things.

98. There is a Way.

As infinity is perceived, so too is perceived the infinite purpose behind all things. Because this purpose exists, we know that the Way is for granted. Learn it. Study it. Walk it well, and die.

99. The Way can be learned.

The great and infinite mystery of all things is not merely perceived, but capable of infinite interaction with the spirit of the human being. Cultivate yourself as a vessel for the sacred.

100. Each moment is a beginning.

All things begin again, and each moment is the sacred peal of the bell of dual singularity and infinite realms beyond time and space. Each is a gift of learning and love. Live well.

Let these lessons from the heart of the dark world resonate through you and become a fundamental and serious source of study, scholarship and mastery as you walk the path of the Way.

The lessons above are your immediate entry into the dark world. They are skills with which you swim and lift yourself through the tide, your strokes of survival in the bloody froth that inexorably rolls in towards you.

My job is to teach you to keep your head above the surf.

Life is sweet, and bitterly short.

Marry it to knowledge, and survive.

You have tested the waters.

It is now time to prepare yourself for a deep journey into the dark world.

I will strip you naked of your illusions and foolishness and habits and beliefs. And I will hurl you in your naked vulnerability towards the vast darkness that watches you, and waits for you with blank and pitiless eyes.

But you are no longer helpless, and may stand unflinching in that nakedness.

For you are now equipped with immortal power.

In your hands you hold The Nine Laws.

The Laws are how the dark world is navigated, how thrones are earned, and how great ships of power are launched into the forbidding deep.

Take my hand, and let us set forth.

Read well, my brothers.

Welcome aboard.

The Judge | Danse Macabre
Hans Holbein the Younger (1497–1543)

Chapter 2

Frame of Knowledge

The structure of this book is designed to deliver truth. This truth comes in measured, concrete stages that bring you to a richly detailed, deep and comprehensive perspective on reality.

It is also important that you experience shocks as part of your training.

These shocks are necessary in order for you to absorb, embody, own and master the material of this book. Together we will move you from theory to practice, from scholarship to mastery.

You have a life to achieve out there. You must engage that life completely to attain total fulfillment.

I caution you here that our partnership is real. It is not a game or a playful waste of time.

Your observation of The Nine Laws will cause changes in you that will appear to others. They will question the source of those changes. You will be challenged in your newfound power, for there are always those who demand a vested interest in maintaining dominance over your mind, your heart and your body.

Weak slaves are less useful than strong ones, and you will experience no shortage of slavers.

Make no mistake. You will soon rise to the notice of adversaries in the dark world who bitterly resent your unblinded state. They will actively work to thwart and forestall your determination to be the master of your own life.

Good! Embrace challenges.

When battle is unavoidable, be the victor.

Read through this material fully. The key to sustaining your advancement and permanently snapping off your shackles lies in full application of the Laws and mastery of the complete structure of the dark world. You must grasp the entire frame.

It is vitally important for you to protect the nascent seed of scholarship that is planted in you by this work. You owe it to yourself to consume the material, assess its utility, apply it with experimentation in the world, and pitilessly judge your own results.

Ferociously make The Nine Laws your fuel of resilient and resonating power and use it to drive explosive and productive growth throughout your days.

And to do this, you must do far more than merely read.

You must blazingly achieve and build with it.

Rome was not built in a day. It was built through unrelenting focus and drive to rule Heaven and Earth and a refusal to accept anything other than a glittering empire.

The same is true of a **Dark Triad Man**.

For now, be a student. Study well, and respect my grim and personal warning to you: this book is a serious tool for responsible adults. Tools, like many things, can be risky, difficult and dangerous.

The purpose of this book is not to transform you into a caricature of a Hollywood *ninja* or to give you secret tricks for unearned billions in overnight wealth. Nor is it a guide to manipulation, deceit and trickery. Those are stupid, silly fantasies and I do not truck in such nonsense.

The dark world is littered with the unburied bodies of fools who did.

I am here to teach you the frame of the dark world and offer you your own mastery of it.

Do not attempt to swallow the entire whole at once. We will break it apart, piece by careful piece, and teach you the direct skills, methods and principles necessary for the mastery you seek.

It is only a fool that expects instant absorption of knowledge and sudden, massive attainment of triumphant power. Fools will always exist, and some of them will buy this book with false illusions of instantaneous dominance. Their illusions will be dashed.

**False and cruel illusions are not why
this book was written.**

The purpose of this book is constructive. It offers you sharp, necessary mental and emotional tools to unlock the immortal, bottomless power within you. You will learn how to take that power, and wield it within the dark world as a weaponized version of the most dangerous apex predator in creation: the human being.

I know that you have it within you. I know this because I have cracked this power open myself.

I know with devastating intimacy that the fearsome, forbidding dark triad traits of personality can provide you with a means to finding your sacred vision, planning its brilliant achievement and executing on it with momentous competence.

It is through your development of character, and by the ennobling of that character, that you will learn to apply your personal power for good or ill, for creation or destruction.

Most of all I believe that you have value as a human being. I believe that you possess the ability to take the reins of your own life and shape it to the most sacred and individual purpose you can possibly conceive. And as you read these words acknowledge a sacred, glowing truth:

The great plan of Heaven is your total development and fulfillment of your sacred purpose.

I determined my own sacred purpose, and I earned it.

I paid for it, and it is *mine*.

You must seize your sacred purpose.

It is important now to explicitly instruct that the framework of this book is not specific to any particular religious belief or cultural tradition.

It is specific to our universe, and applicable by any faith, worship, society or belief system.

The knowledge base from which this book is written is derived from the most pragmatically insightful knowledge bases available: the brutal world of modern finance and the battlefield skills and methods of the *ninja* of ancient Japan.

Those who work in markets and equities, traders who watch the flow of wealth and assess the risk of derivatives, have an outlook in common with those legendary warriors of the Eastern shadows:

Neither make their assessments on the basis of known illusion.

Pitiless, unblinking observation is the basis of action for both.

This book will walk you through many dark and difficult processes. It will unwrap and dissect the layers of the dark world from the most essentially minute level to the grand practice of total application.

You will master all of it.

The bones of your mastery are habits.

The Nine Laws will cultivate habits in you, stack them upon you, carve them away from you. Conscious fostering of habits is crucial to mastery of this frame of knowledge.

Read this book. Make notes in the margins. Cram it into your workout bag. Throw it into your briefcase. Perhaps one day we will meet and you'll show me a dog-eared, tattered, coffee-spilt book with frayed edges and a cracked spine and handwritten notes all across the margin. And I will smile at that, and be deeply proud of my brother, for that is what you do with knowledge.

You consume it, you take it apart and put it back together. You taste it and tear into it and consume it with voracious, insatiable hunger. You do this over, and over and over.

Don't buy this book and put it on a shelf. That is a waste to you and an insult to me.

Study it repeatedly. Read it and bore through it until this book falls into magnificent pieces and you are taping the spine to keep it together. Bring it to the table during contemplative meals and let each stain and crease be a memory of internalized knowledge, of determined scholarship, and of mastery that does not ever, under any circumstances, let go.

That is how you will learn this material and make it as truly a part of you as the last forty years have made it of me.

The Nine Laws have kept me alive, brought me to fulfillment, and are my legacy.

It is a legacy of living transmission, from one heart to another.

Shin-den, the *ninja* call it. Divine, personal delivery.

Here it is from me.

To you.

There are four parts to this book.

Part One instructs you in the truths of The Nine Laws.

It will teach you the Laws and align them to the grid of the dark world. When you have read and absorbed Part One in its entirety you will be equipped with immense understanding and possessed of formidable tools by which you will develop your ability to drive nearly unfathomable alterations of the world.

In Part One I also provide examples and anecdotes of personal and historical experience. They are stories of triumph and loss, agony and satisfaction. They are stories of very human circumstance, and they are important to you as reminders that it is a real world in which you operate.

It is the way of the adult human male to observe, assess and decide with cold objectivity.

You will attain that skill and produce it on demand and in practiced accordance with need.

The human mind is a fickle, foolish and silly thing. It is prone to trickery and deceit in relation to other minds; and also as an often idiotic trafficker of warped internal dialogue. Most of all, the human mind is a self-blinding processor that simply does not see what it wishes to discount.

Are you ready to unblind yourself?

Triumph in the financial markets demands icy judgments of probabilistic assessment and measurement of value trends with deliberate attrition of personal subjectivity.

Survival in the bloody, ferocious and vicious age of the Warring States period of Japan required a chilling ability to assess the tides of the time, human nature, and mastery of a sacred, hidden process that delivers reality into being by forged and focused intention.

Both appear as magic to the simple and the uninitiated. Fools call it mysterious, arcane, esoteric or wizardry. It is nothing of the sort.

The truth is that both money and humans are very simple things, independent of religion or culture.

Wealth is time and time is power, regardless of where or what you are.

Humans are fallen, conflicted apex predators that rule with merciless hegemony in the dark world.

To operate successfully in the world of men you must understand that framework.

To grow deep momentum of results within this dark world you must adhere to the Laws.

You must also understand how the dark world works at the quantum level.

Part Two is subtitled "The World, Man and God".

It reveals the inner lattice of the dark world, how that lattice is successfully navigated and controlled, and how to competently master it for victorious, determined result.

The dark world is broad, deep and dangerous. Its lattice consists of several realms layered and entwined as a grid. That grid runs from the infinity of God to the singularity of human deeds, encompassed within and without our arena of time and space.

To fully grasp the grid, it is necessary to use your imagination. You will be required to broaden your mind and absorb certain concepts that this book will explore, dissect, and deliver to you.

Are you prepared to unshackle your boundaries?

Part Two is the deep and penetrating scientific basis which underlies the swirling maelstrom of karma and consequence, fate and reality. By coming to full and complete understanding of the gears and mechanisms of the dark world, you become the great mechanic that controls it.

I will teach you this knowledge with strong and supportive guidance.

I will facilitate your progress through the use of examples and imagery. They provide mental lubricant for access by your mind into the material, and facilitate intellectual digestion of its content.

The Nine Laws are arrayed across the dark world as an interlocking rail system, and you will learn how to use them to navigate into gravely competent outcomes.

Trust must exist between the teacher and the student.

I do not throw you to the wolves, for their howling is close and savage outside the door. Not yet.

Not until you have armor of knowledge, sword of purpose, and banner of bloody power above you.

And remember: I am not here to entertain you. We cross this frame of knowledge to train you.

Firmly, clearly, and with determination.

Part Three provides you with profoundly immersive training in skills, methods and principles. You will find them challenging, provoking, and in some cases even disturbing.

That is by design. You did not buy this book for cheap and silly entertainment.

You bought it to excavate, comprehend, repurpose and deliver the ultimate levers of power in your own life and career, relationships and challenges. You will succeed only through consistent effort.

To drive your road of vision, purpose and power you must understand the pathway of development and achievement. You must move along this road in a transformative manner; taking care to adapt and to grow, to enhance your perspective and expand your resiliency.

You achieve this momentum of growth by training, study and comprehension.

You cement this enhancement through the expenditure of blood, time, effort and exhaustion.

A man who offers an easy road to the throne is a liar.

A man who claims that thrones are cushions of restful ease is a murderer who waits to topple you.

Do you understand that this is a dark world?

Then learn to grasp the Way of growth and pain, joy and ferocity, love and loss that builds it.

Growth comes as you move from theorist to practitioner, from practitioner to scholar and then onwards into mastery. With each step of growth, your results—whether creative or destructive—will match your capacities to the extent you present them.

It is dangerous. The wise make greater mistakes than the vile.

This is the great Way of which the sages speak, the path that men of severe wisdom and sagacity look back upon with solemn regard for the sacrifices of study and training they expended.

Those things are the living currency of the adult human being who transacts in the markets of power. They are the Way of the warrior, the competence of the *ninja*, the skill of the quant who masters instantaneous algorithmic flow of ten billion digital valuations through the indexes of the world with all the calm competence of a conductor before a ceaseless orchestra.

Once trained you must put your development into practice.

With power comes responsibility on many levels.

You must aim yourself at targets in the dark world.

Part Four is subtitled "Framework of Blood and War".

In the last section of The Nine Laws we discuss the nature of terror, the crashing tilted collapse of civilizations into rape and plunder, and the dreadful risks faced by cultures suffering smash.

I give you guidelines to safely and successfully navigate these vital and interesting times, and to walk triumphant into the future you choose for your loved ones, yourself and your brothers.

"May you live in interesting times" is a famous Chinese epithet. It flings resentful curse at the listener that challenge and upheaval, terror and risk, uncertainty and overthrow of nations become their inescapable and terrible experience of life.

The **Dark Triad Man** embraces interesting times for two reasons:

The first reason is this: he recognizes the truth that *all* times are *always* interesting.

There has never been, nor will there ever be, a period in history without warlords, colliding nations, sharp divergences in human destiny and the unfolding of limitless opportunity.

There has only been recession or surge in the number of men willing to step forward and claim the throne with their own hands.

The second reason is that the number of such men is *never* zero.

For the **Dark Triad Man** always strides to and fro upon the shadowed earth.

Today in the world there is great shock and tumult. The dark world boils, and the tide of blood now crashes firmly against the shores of complacent societies. Martyrs are beheaded by the score on the beaches of Africa and crimson, dripping knives are aimed in dreadful threat at the sacred but trembling cities of the West.

Black flags are raised and throats are cut, women raped, children sold, and empires are scattered and overthrown under the hot and unforgiving sun of this new age we face together.

It has happened before, and it will happen again. Long after you are dead and nothing more than blown and forgotten dust, it will happen again.

Therefore, I say to you, seize your chance.

Today is all that you have.

If you do not seize it, your life is a disgraceful and unforgivable waste.

Cruel and formidable challenges await you. But even though you will die, you need not live defeated. I challenge you, brother.

I challenge you to fully live.

In Part Four we look at the nature of that challenge. We examine how you, as a man of the West, can step forth into the dark world with clear vision to surmount and beat that challenge.

There has *never* been a more powerful time to be alive.

That is always true, and it is always increasingly true.

We will lay bare your glorious road for you.

None of this will be easy. But the rewards are incalculable.

You must learn and accept the realities of the dark world. What it is, how it operates, why it is dark, and what this means to the man of action who walks within it unblinded.

You must read this book with the attitude of the searching warrior who demands a great prize of enlightened knowledge, and pledges his honor and cutting steel as proof of his deserving virtue.

You must stand forth as a man who is the bulwark of protection and savage defense of his loved ones, who ensures the survival of his culture and country and civilization.

Here is knowledge that has been concealed in bloody shadows for nearly a thousand years.

With it are insights that guide the wealth of nations and trillion-dollar empires.

Learn well with an open mind, and consider with care the Way that is spread before you.

Let us accelerate, and drive.

The road is open.

Part One:

The Nine Laws

The Nine Laws Revealed

Survival ✦ Concealment ✦ Purpose

Endurance ✦ Posture ✦ Freedom

Power ✦ Preposterousness ✦ No Laws

The Astrologist | Danse Macabre
Hans Holbein the Younger (1497–1543)

Chapter 3

The Nine Laws Revealed

We begin Part One with a simple revelation of the Laws themselves.

It is important to grasp a serious and fundamental difference between the Laws that are revealed here and other various collections of laws, rules or guidelines that are available to men elsewhere in the world today. Each of those alternate sources has a narrow focus—laws of power and wealth, rules of politics and business or guidelines for men who seek to improve one area of life or another.

All of those are fine. And in many cases they are precisely what the seeker requires, something that they can easily and simply apply to a narrow niche of life—or broaden across a thin band of overall change in their daily activities.

They are designed to address a different audience and in a different milieu. They are designed to inform your behavior, to change your thinking, or to alter and improve your habits.

You will not benefit from treating the Nine Laws in the same manner.

This book does not offer easy guidelines, simple rules or suggestions of practice for the dilettante or the transient experimenter who flirts with ever-newer ideologies from a base of mindless interest.

The Nine Laws are not for the common man or the shiftless

child. They are not for the excited adolescent who seeks medals before achievement, title before skill and profit without sale.

The Nine Laws are the pitiless Way by which an entirely different being is formed.

They are the diamond spiritual and mental rails by which the dark world is navigated.

They are the foundation of a rare and fearsome archetype that does not stop.

These are the Nine Laws of the **Dark Triad Man** and they are his arsenal.

He is a savagely competent, deliberately-manifested apex predator with cultivated insight and perception that spans across the boundaries of time and space. He sees with the infinite mind and eyes of the divine and channels his intention by impersonal adherence to sincere truth. And in the end he concludes the demands of fate with momentous force of unstoppable impact.

Your task is to become a weaponized human being.

He integrates thought, word and deed from the sacred spectrum of mental conception all the way through the determination of fate. He forms outcomes with the total ferocity of a roaring lion that bears down upon his prey with complete and natural perfection.

The Nine Laws are the foundation from which the **Dark Triad Man** arises.

They are the shaped iron ribs of this grave form of being.

Understand this well. You enter into dark reality here, and the danger is real.

The dark world is fatal.

Thriving in it is not guaranteed. Your death is.

Therefore, you will learn the Laws.

And you will master the Way.

You will make your life and death worth the sacred cost.

The first path to understanding the Laws is to appreciate that, from one perspective, they arise sequentially in application. Later on we will cover manipulation, interaction and adjustment of the Laws in relation to each other.

The Way is living. Ribs flex as the organism breathes and moves.

We will explore spins and pivots, outcomes and failures, and provide you with deeply structured training exercises to expand your practice, scholarship and mastery.

But for your beginning education, revelation of them must first take place.

Here are the Nine Laws:

THE FIRST LAW: SURVIVAL

You must survive in the dark world as the basis of all your deeds. Failure to survive is the end of your ability to consciously interact with fate. You are solely responsible for your own survival.

THE SECOND LAW: CONCEALMENT

You must conceal in order to preserve your survival as prey. Circumstances always shift and at times you will be hunted by the unstoppable. The concealed path permits unhindered passage.

THE THIRD LAW: PURPOSE

Without purpose there is no driving resonance of intention behind the man. A man without purpose has no power as a momentous being. Purpose is sacred and utterly essential.

THE FOURTH LAW: ENDURANCE

The Way demands fortitude, continuance, effort and resiliency. The Way includes suffering, pain, loss and disappointment. The capacity to endure, persevere and withstand is demanded.

THE FIFTH LAW: POSTURE

Appropriate array of the self and its responses are crucial to successful engagement with encounters in the dark world. Posture determines life and death in the tumble and turn of conflict.

THE SIXTH LAW: FREEDOM

Freedom is the root and demand of living dignity. Acceptance of shackles is the death of mobility and the despair of life. Freedom is not negotiable.

THE SEVENTH LAW: POWER

The dread prerogative of choice is power within the dark world. Power arises from skill and is a cultivation of directed momentum. Power is the impact of your competence.

THE EIGHTH LAW: PREPOSTEROUSNESS

Random chaos entwines with outcome, and all fates are infinitely improbable. The coin does not know which side up it will land. Any prediction is preposterous and so are all results.

THE NINTH LAW: NO LAWS

The laws of men, lords, kings and nations are false, empty and unreal. As there are infinite universes, and infinite laws, there is no governing Law and there are no boundaries on the Way.

These are the enumerated Nine Laws of the **Dark Triad Man**. Do not trifle or toy with them, or fail to recognize their significance.

The consequence of foolish behavior is failure and death.

Death is inevitable and so are failures. But they need not be combined, and one not need result from the other.

Do not be a fool. Obey the Laws.

Keep your failures separate from your death.

The Gentleman | Danse Macabre
Hans Holbein the Younger (1497–1543)

Chapter 4

The First Law is Survival

*You ask, what is our aim? I can answer in one word:
It is victory, victory at all costs, victory in spite of all
terror, victory, however long and hard the road may be;
for without victory, there is no survival.*

—Sir Winston Leonard Spencer-Churchill,
KG, OM, CH, TD, PC, DL, FRS, RA

YOU MUST LIVE

The prime imperative of all living things is to remain alive. The demand for survival is the infinite and timeless source of inventiveness. Life innovates by its very nature in both exultation and desperation. Suicide and despair are thus mortal, unforgivable sins.

IRON CORE OF THE LAW

- Narcissism: Survival is the highest expression of self-love.
- Machiavellianism: Desperation is the root of creativity.
- Psychopathy: Instinctive ruthlessness is its core engine.

Survival.

It is a simple word, isn't it? In every case survival should be your first priority. There are very few causes that are not better served by living than by dying, and even in those rare cases (such as throwing yourself on a grenade or screaming your way to Heaven while chained to a burning stake) you are nonetheless furthering the survival of something greater than yourself. That is not suicide nor violation of the First Law.

Many years ago I stood in a hot rural field in southwestern Ohio with scores of other people who were gathered to listen to the teaching of a very rare type of man. He was a senior master teacher from one of the last *ninjutsu ryu* remaining alive in the world. For more than thirty years this middle aged Japanese man had been a devoted practitioner of the darkest and deadliest arts known to man.

I had a burning question. And I was able to ask him that day under the remorseless sun as he sat cross legged in front of us all:

What can one do when one is faced with impossible odds? When there are too many of them, or when the adversary before you has greater power and experience and you cannot possibly win? What can be done when it is hopeless?

He became very serious. He leaned forward, giving me his earnest and complete attention and his voice was firm and rang across the green field as he spoke:

"You must live."

He went on to explain:

"The only way to victory when death is certain against impossible odds is to believe with all your heart and being that you must live. You cannot focus on what the danger represents to your body. You must focus on your imperative to live—for your family, for your nation, for your faith."

Sometimes, of course, you are killed and die. That is the truth of the dark world. But when all is impossible, when death is inevitable and you have only the single current moment to defeat the grim and grinning Reaper as he viciously scythes for your head...

...remember those words, and explode from an infinite heart of utter commitment to the First Law. Show Death itself how it has underestimated you.

And survive.

This is why you never back an enemy into an impossible corner. Sun Tzu acknowledged this in The Art of War:

> *When you surround an army, leave an outlet free. Do not press a desperate foe too hard.*

> *Throw your soldiers into positions whence there is no escape, and they will prefer death to flight. If they will face death, there is nothing they may not achieve.*

> *On desperate ground, fight.*[1]

Man is a beast like all others.

Man is also a beast unlike any other.

Man sometimes does not fight for his survival. It is stupid and incomprehensible but it is a part of the various weaknesses that plague our super intelligent species.

We think too much, and we forget to survive. This runs the spectrum from giving up because of fear (watch any execution video out of the Middle East) to being so oblivious to reality through normalcy bias that we are caught by complete surprise.

The **Dark Triad Man** makes survival his priority.

He pays attention.

He fights for his life.

He fights like a demon possessed.

He fights with an infinite and unstoppable ferocity.

He is a **Dark Triad Man** and that is the Way.

Always remember. You must live.

Survival is the First Law.

FORGING THE IRON: PROMOTE SURVIVAL

Learn: Look at each moment as potentially fatal. Use your imagination to envision a deadly threat emerging from unexpected places. Continually work to sharpen your awareness of risk and take conscious steps to avoid being killed, even as you cross the street to work.

Explore:

- What were stark moments in which you realized you had been careless for your own survival?
- Were your perceptions of threat more prominent with people, places or in your own errors?
- How have you been contributing to your own moments of fatal vulnerability?

You bear total responsibility for your survival.

Reflect: Consider a primary adaptation that you will embody in the future to advance your own probability of survival.

Train: Develop continuous awareness of your mortality and protect your life in each moment. Do not allow yourself to become complacent in observation of the Law.

Task: Identify the three most dangerous current threats to your survival. Address them and take actual steps to change their potential impact.

IMPOSSIBLE GLORY

The sick and desolate men marched with grim and sickened futility.

Rancid wounds festered under sticky, putrid bandages. Hot and bubbling feces ran unwiped down their legs, for dysentery was rampant in the ranks and there was no time to halt. The enemy army outnumbered them four to one and marched in tandem with them, driving them desperately on.

The men soiled themselves in their own armor and kept going without rest. Their enemy kept pace, preparing for a brutal, savage orgy of mass murder.

The men were driven ahead of them, fully aware that their adversaries intended total massacre and annihilation without mercy.

And so the exhausted English marched for nearly three hundred miles in horrific condition. Cut off from resupply, there was not nearly enough food to keep the men alive. Starving, stinking and desperate, they were finally blocked by French forces from reaching the port of Calais and safety.

The only choice was to fight.

The only option was to win the day or die with their lord and master amid terrible and appalling butchery, delivered by armored men swinging cruel and pitiless steel.

It was a hard decision of survival that faced the king.

He made it with savage royal passion, and with the full prerogative of the sovereign.

He was the dread lord under a bloody banner that day, and he did not hesitate nor tremble.

He and his band of brothers made devastating work of it.

"We few, we happy few... we band of brothers."

William Shakespeare thus immortalized the words of Harry the king, the moment when grim and exhausted desperation was transformed into one of the most decisive and glorious feats of arms in history.

Into a sea of French mud the men drove their stakes, and that autumn day was filled with the incessant and deadly whine of English arrows.

The clang of iron on steel, the gallop and scream of horses, the din of blade and axe upon armor and the horrible hacking thud of bitter edges into meat and bone was the resounding work they accomplished.

At the close of battle, the English had lost barely over a hundred men out of the 9,000 that held position, including the Duke of York, killed in action in defense of the king.

Ten thousand French lay dead upon the field out of 36,000 that had chased and harassed, then attacked the English with thundering cavalry and malevolent men of war.

They died, slaughtered and humiliated on their own native soil of France, under the steel of the English king and his countrymen. Fatal casualties included the Constable of France himself.

They died in consequence of the pivot of fortune that accompanies terrible transformation from desperation to victory, born out of ferocious determination in the hearts of men to survive.

When facing certain death, know that you can achieve not merely survival, but undying fame and glory.

King Henry V halted his men on desperate ground.

He entrenched his men into position from which there was no escape.

He provoked the start of the battle, and won it with overwhelming competence.

That is the Law of Survival.

It is the tumble and turn of expectation.

It is the extraction of preposterous victory against utterly untenable odds.

Henry did not die in hacking blood under the unstoppable army of France.

He defeated it, and he and his men now live forever.

They live forever in the annals of glorious honor, because of this.

There is always a way out, a way to turn impossible odds into infinite glory.

It may be through bitterly fighting where you stand.

Horatio at the bridge, piling the bodies of his adversaries in horrible and dripping piles.

The British Army at Rorke's Drift, outnumbered forty to one, securing victory against a sea of incoming warriors who screamed in the drunken lust of killing.

It may be through dying with such profoundly noble ferocity that the story of your last stand is a tale of martyrdom that inspires men for countless generations.

Leonidas and his 300 at the Hot Gates, fighting to the last and bloody man in defense of Sparta.

Fight like mad. Win and live in glory, or die and be remembered forever.

It is the Way.

The Pope | Danse Macabre
Hans Holbein the Younger (1497–1543)

Chapter 5

The Second Law is Concealment

Words, like nature, half reveal and half conceal the soul within.

—Alfred Tennyson, 1st Baron Tennyson, FRS

DO NOT REVEAL

If it can be perceived, it can be hit. If it can be hit, it can be killed. This is true from the awakening of the mind to the movements of armies. The sages of old speak of the necessity and wisdom of concealing one's intentions, movements and plans from all.

IRON CORE OF THE LAW

- Narcissism: Perspective of self as protected treasure.
- Machiavellianism: Shields the woven narrative of plans.
- Psychopathy: Protection from revulsion of the ignorant.

Concealment.

It is a subtle word with many shades of meaning, as befits a Law that requires gentle and careful layering of motivation, procedure, intention, speech and action. Concealment is not hiding, nor is it a locking away of value from the eyes of the prying or the adversarial.

To conceal is to obscure, to veil, to alter the presentation of a thing so that its true nature is unperceived and its purpose unobstructed.

The value of concealment is twofold.

In the obscurity of concealment is the space for safety, a distance that permits noninterference and the unimpeded manifestation of purpose. This is true on a vast spectrum that runs the gamut from avoiding a rampaging active shooter to the nondisclosure of possessed information.

Within the concealed is also the space to consider without interruption, to absorb and cultivate and digest the various theories, concepts, plans and purposes that cannot survive the harsh light of exposure and the brutal interference of demanding interrogation.

As the chief executive charged with successful outcomes for your own sacred purpose, the ongoing requirement of concealment is unending. Understand the crucial importance of avoiding all unnecessary and unintentional exposure and consequent vulnerability in the dark world.

It may preserve your survival.

TOOLS FROM THE IRON

The first step to cultivating the skill of concealment is in the disciplined, deliberate structuring of your awareness, and of the revelations you have permitted.

Understand that exposure takes both passive and active form. Your inappropriate revelations may be inadvertent, driven by ego, or both. All of these are common.

And today we live in a surveillance state.

Are you visible to tyrants? Who is prepared to inform upon you? What would be the result of sudden raid and investigation this very moment, even if the sworn statement of an informer was a bare and outright lie?

Your every move, purchase, statement and public appearance is recorded, cross-referenced and used to build a profile of you for the lethal attention of the State.

Do those things accumulate to an equation of helplessness?

In the answer you will find those who are seen and who are the first to die when the world collapses into sudden and murderous violence and the State drops all restraint.

Learn to eliminate tells and displays from your posture, from your movement, from your involuntary presentations. Grasp well that involuntary flickers of the eye, nervous habits of the hands, and undisciplined alignment of the shoulders and spine scream out information to onlookers.

Learn to conceal preparation and plans from men and machines. Understand the entanglements of trust and risk. Understand how elicitation works, how casual questions encourage you to overshare and to reveal plans and preparations, relationships and networks that can be pieced together by the adversaries who prepare chains and killing pits in your future.

Do you grasp the danger of your ego and your speech?

In the cultivation of perception at finely granulated and seamless levels of awareness is an appreciation of risk and danger combined with the ability to move and act without interference.

To walk through a crowd unseen is power. To move past the watchful eye of the guard is freedom. To veil the emergence of spirit is to preserve an insurrection from sudden execution.

Concealment is shelter and sanctuary.

The **Dark Triad Man** and his purposes are transparent and unseen. It is not in bold conflict but in silent contemplation that his most powerful outcomes are derived.

It is not an attachment to secrecy or an obsession with hiding. Those are perversions of an attitude of graceful and efficient living.

The ostentatious is gratuitous. The gratuitous revelation of your purpose, intention and movement exposes and transfixes your spirit as a target and hinders opportunity.

Preserve your space of opportunity. Do not reveal.

You must obey the Law in order to preserve momentum.

This is guardianship by the master of fate.

Concealment is the Second Law.

FORGING THE IRON: DEFAULT CONCEALMENT

Learn: Be aware of all levels of revelation. Identify any such expressions earlier and earlier. Practice your posture to blend in and dwell as an unseen intelligence, unheard presence and unknown actor. Focus on this calm silence and unrevealed purpose as you go through daily living.

Explore:

- What secrets burn inside you and egotistically leak through your thought, word and deed?
- What gratuitous exposure do you show despite the hundreds of apex predators around you?
- Do you use premature exposure and resulting slain plans as excuse or avoidance of work?

The silly demand of ego is not grounds for revelation.

Reflect: Identify three examples of stillness of heart that permitted your ego to remain shadowed and your work to manifest into completion without interference.

Train: Understand that demand of the ego for recognition is deadly when applied to survival. Revelation that is driven by ego is a constant threat to your concealment.

Task: Examine why your pride and ego are allowed to extend into the world. Cruelly take apart your own vanity and examine the rotted interior. It will be more gentle than evisceration by predators.

RIFLES IN THE DARK

We moved the guns and ammunition well after midnight.

There were six or seven of us, garbed in layered clothing against the dropping temperatures of the high altitude environment. It was a clear night and our voices were subdued as we worked in the thin air.

There was an important task at hand. Hundreds of rifles, thousands and thousands of rounds of ammunition and gear for hundreds of men needed to be moved. Quickly, quietly and competently.

There could be no chance of interference from State power or obser-vation from the eyes of the idly curious, the covetous or even the hostile predator. The material was too valuable, too important to risk.

"Power grows from the barrel of a gun," said Mao Zedong. And he knew this well.

The most consequential form of power is the lethal force of the State. And in the reality of the dark world that lethal force is exercised at the whim of ideologists and politicians, applied with cruelty and rapacious brutality to inflict not justice but oppression, not truth but lies, and with determination to crush and murder the rights of human beings who dare to not merely proclaim, but exercise their freedom.

Every revolution begins with indignation.

Every purge ends with volleys of rifle fire into men standing before a wall.

It is in the space between those singularities, in the tumble and turn of social detonation and collapse, that the fate of a nation and its people are determined by men who hold levers of power.

History is written by men willing to use those levers.

That no revolution has broken out, does not mean that no revolution is possible.

That the oppressed and beaten peoples of any time or place do not savagely rise and teach bloody and permanent lesson to their overlords, does not mean that those overlords are secure.

"Sitting on bayonets is uncomfortable," said Joseph Goebbels. He spoke truth in that observation.

The discomfort of the tyrant arises from the sure and certain knowledge that men never have their dignity entirely erased, and when such men have nothing to lose they may turn upon their tyrant and tear him to pieces with the desperate ferocity of the hopeless.

There is a great and singular factor that separates successful revolutions from failed ones, and a grim and terrible difference between men who rise in the defense of their homes and communities and those who are herded with their wives and children, naked and emaciated, into a nameless forest and shot.

The ability to fight is what separates the murdered from the free.

The ability to fight is a necessary component of the dark world, and we did the sacred work that night of concealing that ability from the pitiless gaze of the tyrant.

Men rarely understand the nature of military power in the hands of governments.

The idiot believes that it is there to protect him, to enforce justice.

The common man thinks that it is used according to the law, sheltered within the principles of the culture.

The wise man assumes that human beings are fallible and their choices often self-serving; that the best interests and plans often reluctantly settle into the expedient and the tawdry.

*The **Dark Triad Man** knows the truth:*

State power is the tool of men with ruthless ambition, remorseless intention and brutal capacity who do not hesitate to shed blood, hide graves and rewrite history in their favor.

Concealment of capacity is among the most crucial components of freedom. For freedom exists in the dark world within a fearsome gradient, between the polarities of anarchy and totalitarianism, and at every spot between them the shade is merely a different hue of blood.

Thus concealment of plans from the organs of the State is vital to the preservation of freedom.

Concealment of networks from the agents of the State is the hyper-vigilant task of the insurgent.

Concealment of physical power from the intelligence of the State is the fearsome task of free men.

Do not trust the ruling power.

The ruling power always has more resources, more intelligence, more ruthlessness and more cruelty than you can imagine. And your survival depends upon concealment until the moment of decision.

The fool believes that his vote is a determining factor in the policies of the State.

The common man thinks that parties and coalitions and alliances represent his interests.

The wise man assumes that history and culture place boundaries on the system, which rights itself.

*The **Dark Triad Man** accepts the truth:*

There is always a Caesar waiting with grim and immortal ambition, nestled in the heart of the nation, who seeks to rise to total power and views blood and atrocity and horror as mere laurels of valid drama upon his entitled brow.

Just as the ambitious conceal plans, capacity in response is preserved through the concealment of revelation.

The work was done swiftly that night, nearly a generation ago. The rifles, oiled and wrapped and prepared, may still be there. Or they may be in the hands of men who can be trusted with truth and the momentum of history as it manifests in the dark world. Men who are loyal to their brothers.

Decades have passed, but the lesson of that night remains.

In response to the growth of fearsome tyranny, dreadful capacity must lie concealed.

Waiting.

The Abbot | Danse Macabre
Hans Holbein the Younger (1497–1543)

Chapter 6
The Third Law is Purpose

To the person with a firm purpose all men and things are servants.

—Johann Wolfgang von Goethe

MOTIVE IS INHERENT

Without purpose no man may exist or withstand. The purposeful heart is a fountain of word and deed. The intent of the heart promotes the elaborate manifestation of the universe as all things arise from the power of its determination.

IRON CORE OF THE LAW

- Narcissism: Expression of your utter value to the world.
- Machiavellianism: Your ends justify the means.
- Psychopathy: Intention is not bounded emotion.

Purpose.

The motive power of the entire universe is within you as a singularity of utter and determined will. In the infinite abandon of boundaries through adherence to divine purpose is the unstoppable and invincible power of Heaven.

Without purpose man is rudderless, shiftless, aimless and destroyed. Absent purpose there is no ground of being, there is no leverage for achievement, there is no will to survival and there is nothing to conceal. Purpose is the engine of your existence and the destination of your will in life.

All things have purpose. These purposes will be inherent and imposed, determined and derived, from infinite sources that tumble and turn within the heart and mind. Water seeks lowest ground; the Earth turns unhesitatingly; and through your harnessing of purpose is found your source of infinite power and performance.

The spirit of man is the spirit of God.

This has been known from time immemorial.

Purpose thus abhors a vacuum. In absence of your own derived purpose the outcome of other purposes will be determined for you. Without inherent purpose your life will have one imposed upon you, without interest or care or pity or grace—for those are not the ways of the dark world.

You must embrace, align, and embody purpose.

The aimless boy becomes the drifting man, and passes through this life without root or branch of power. To branch out into the world and provide shelter and resources, that root of power must reside in the heart of purpose.

In the examination of your purpose with colder and colder assessment you begin to approach the heart of self and the reason for the life you have been given.

What are you doing?

Who is it for?

Why are you here?

When is it achieved?

In the answers you will find your motivations, and in a clear understanding of your motivations is the delineation of your purpose and the opportunity to align your thought, your word and your deed to the manifestation of that purpose.

Clear and unmistaken purpose is a power that upholds and succors the spirit even in the midst of death and horror.

Purpose is the single, clear and ringing note of the heart. It is the immortal part of you, the voice of God speaking through the vehicle of your mortal body of ashes and dust.

You must understand the utter importance of your own sacred purpose in the unfolding of the world.

In the true internal revelation and recognition of your purpose is the source of infinite motive power to achieve the impossible, to surmount any obstacle, and to bring reality into being with the magic of total and unrestrained commitment. It empowers the man of purpose to throw away his scabbard, and walk forward into the arena of his life with the drawn and forbidding steel of intention.

The **Dark Triad Man** knows his purpose.

He reveres it.

He serves it.

He advances it.

He manifests its vision and creates reality from his channeled, deliberate and determined conscious intention.

The **Dark Triad Man** enthrones his purpose in reality.

You must be more than intimately familiar with your purpose. You must go further than fully understanding your purpose. You must remove any distinction between your breath and thought and heart of purpose.

You must be your purpose.

It is purpose that delivers endurance.

Purpose is the Third Law.

FORGING THE IRON: SACRED PURPOSE

Learn: Pretend you are to be beheaded at dawn. For one hour the night before you are put to this imaginary death, meditate on what your most powerful delivery into the world has been and your deepest task left unfinished. Arise at daybreak and formally compose your spirit to die.

Explore:
- Was there a recurrent theme of value in the contemplation of your execution?
- What was the deepest unfinished mission you would leave behind in the world?
- Where do you abandon or prostitute your sacred purpose for lesser plans and visions?

Your breath and bone, meat and blood are a vehicle.

Reflect: Conduct an unflinching assessment of whether your thought, word and deed are truly aligned as a single expression of the ultimate purpose of your existence.

Train: Distill your life achievements into singularity from the pivot of desire and frustration. Know your most powerful purpose, identify it and assess your success so far.

Task: Carve away confusion from your purpose. Identify and put to death any excuses for failure.

AGONY FROM THE NINJA

I did not know what real pain was. I thought I did, but I was a fool.
 Dark men exist who are masters of pain. And pity is not part of their training.

Little did I know that my purpose would be sorely tested by them, and that real depth of agony would become an intimate friend. The crack of bone, the snap of tendon, the hemorrhage of vast bruise and the taste of blood was to become a familiar companion for many years.

But that was why I was there: to absorb their great and terrible gift.

It was for purpose more imperative than life itself that I endured the tumble and turn of not just my mind and heart but also my body in their hard and unforgiving hands.

My joints were laughingly torn apart, my broken heart was dissected and turned inside out, and my mind was severed from everything it had taken for granted and the bottomless pit of the dark world yawned open and took my plummet with a howl of delight at the flavor of my terror.

It was the grim and determined desperation of a young man who had sought the darkest and most ferocious path available that brought him to that gulf. And he leapt in with both feet, his eyes wide open.

It was the only way out I could think of.

It was my sacred purpose.

Growing up smaller than your peers, with less athletic ability, is often a path to unpleasant interactions of bullying. It is normal, and while children can be rather abusive to each other, it isn't a bad thing.

It is simply healthy preparation for the human world.

Going through school a year younger than your peers, with less physical and emotional maturity, is a quick and unsurprising route to exclusion from cliques and clubs. Also normal, and very predictable.

It is accurate preparation for the social world.

Skipping a grade and being elevated over those older peers, in order to maximize your intellectual gifts, deepens the rift from mere difference to one of resentment and ugly, guaranteed disfavor.

That is the blunt nature of the real world.

Doing these things while stripped of a crucial sensory perception, the one that severs you from conversation and communication, removes both subtle signal and blunt warning, is a recipe for real danger.

That is the reality of the dark world.

I did them all. I was swiftly and irreversibly educated that I would need more than mere typical skills to survive and thrive in the world I would eventually head out into. It would not be sufficient to be smart… I needed to be incisive. I would not survive merely by being strong… I needed to be formidable. It was not going to keep me alive if I simply become fierce. I needed to be ferocious, and I needed to be fearsomely dangerous to the full extent of the weaponized human being.

I needed the skills and training of a gravely authentic warrior.

God help me, for I needed to find the ninja.

And so I sought them out. I read everything I could and learned to distinguish between myth and history. It was not enough to read that they were unstoppable silent assassins; I wanted to know who they actually killed, how they killed him, why he was marked for death. And how history changed after.

I needed more than just stories of mysterious sorcery and legends of power in the night. What was the reality of the nine cuts of the kuji-kiri, *of the dark mantras voiced by those figures of fearsome shadow?*

Movies were unhelpful: silly, stupid and absurd. Black-clad figures scaling office buildings in broad daylight, throwing glittering stars across football fields and instantly slaying scores of faceless soldiers who died in wave after wave of assault, suffering ridiculous casualties.

Sorting the nonsense and the legends from the probable mundane reality was necessary.

What was the truth? Did the ninja *in fact coldly decide the fate of a man's life and death? Was the magic of mantra and forged intention real, or simply an unsupported legend?*

Was there difference between their skill in battle and what was available to the casual public?

I learned the answers, and I learned the hard way.

I was twelve when I decided that the direction I would take was towards the ninja.

It was a year of searching before I met them for the first time, and begged for entry into their halls.

"Not fully," I was told. "Not yet."

"You must graduate high school. Only then will you be permitted to apply as a student to the ryū-ha.*"*

For three years I incubated that purpose. It was the focus of my days, it was the dream of my nights, it was hours and hours of study and planning. It was for deadly serious purpose: a life in which I was not deaf and helpless, but perceptive and dangerous. Not shunned and mocked, but seamlessly fluent and powerful with charm and magnetic leadership. Not weak and thin, but strong and graceful, capable of more physical capacity for dominance than most men even believed possible.

I held that purpose, and I nurtured it for three years. My desperation demanded it.

I was sixteen when I left home to enter training, hundreds and hundreds of miles from my home and parents and childhood. And I remember well the embrace of the master teacher, his words as I entered the halls of the ninja:

"Welcome to the family."

The very first things I was made accustomed to were the feel of pain and the hard impact of the floor.

Mats were rarely used in training. "There are no mats in the dark world."

Protective gear was prohibited. "You must know exact distance to the bone."

Points and competitive clash were cruelly disparaged. "Life and death are not a contest."

Injuries were common. Pain was not injury, but source of amusement. Pain was proof, pain was reality, pain was so intense that I spent the first six months in very real fear that I could not endure it.

For many years that was my life. I followed the purpose that I had conceived of as a child, and I made it a reality. There was no left hand, right hand waxing of cars, but there were many long hours with rake amid the leaves on the vast estate of the teacher. There were long nights of training with steel in the darkness, of disentangling illusion and reality, learning to tumble and turn, to penetrate and detonate and collapse.

At the age of twenty-three, my purpose was achieved and I set out into the world.

There have been many adventures since, and many terrors, but many joys and above all many lessons.

And there have been new purposes. For that, too, is the Way.

Find your purpose. It is sacred. Do not let anything deter you or derail you.

Live it, and make its full achievement the demonstrated proof of your sincerity.

Then find the next one, and the next. Win them all.

Live your life with all the purpose you can muster.

In this way, you will come to love it.

The Count | Danse Macabre
Hans Holbein the Younger (1497–1543)

Chapter 7

The Fourth Law is Endurance

Every calamity is to be overcome by endurance.

—Publius Vergilius Maro

IMMOVABLE SPIRIT

To endure is to win. To endure is to be patient. To endure is to shelter. To endure is to cultivate. That which endures, survives. The inner spirit is untouchable and unbreakable. This is proved by countless martyrs who have died unbroken as testament.

IRON CORE OF THE LAW

- Narcissism: Faith in one's own ability to withstand.
- Machiavellianism: Adherence to the unfolding narrative.
- Psychopathy: Withdrawal to the reptilian brain.

Endurance.

It is more than mere putting up with. It is the reversion to the reptilian complex of the brain, discarding of the limbic system and an abandonment of the ego of the neocortex.

Endurance is a diffusion of spirit into the essential base nature of the psychopathic self, where even boundaries of pain or pleasure or identity are gone and there is only the passing of the experience without attachment.

It is through this dissipation of attachment and ego that endurance can emerge, for the root of endurance is acceptance. It is in acceptance that endurance is given birth, for refusal of reality is the dark and painful root of suffering.

Within this enlightened detachment from your illusion of alternate reality, you will find the ability to dispassionately, and with sublime peace, deploy limitless endurance.

Truth is. Reality breathes. Facts are what they are. It is in resistance that will is broken, it is in struggle that defeat is inflicted, it is upon refusal that compliance is enforced.

The heart of endurance is the body of a rock.

Iwao no mi or the "body of a rock" comes from the immortal *Go Rin No Sho* of Shinmen Musashi no Kami Fujiwara no Genshin, a notable Japanese psychopath from the 17th century.

Musashi won over sixty mortal duels by killing his opponent.

Musashi understood the immovable spirit:

> *When you have mastered the Way of strategy, you can suddenly make your body like a rock, and ten thousand things cannot touch you. This is the body of a rock.*[2]

There is a story of Musashi and his teaching of this, from the chronicles of the House of Terao:

> *Once, a lord asked Musashi, "What is this body of a rock?"*

> *Musashi replied, "Please summon my pupil Terao Ryuma Suke."*

> *When Terao appeared, Musashi ordered him to kill himself by cutting his abdomen.*

Just as Terao was about to make the cut, Musashi re-
strained him and said to the lord, "This is the body of
the rock." [3]

It is in this immovable spirit that the heart of the warrior finds
infinite endurance and calm in the face of mortal agony, existential
horror and the brutal disappointment of purpose.

It is not frozen immobility that cracks and shatters when struck
with an unforgiving and terrible blow.

It is not rigid and unbending determination that breaks and
collapses when the heart is knocked out of it.

It is not supremacy of ego and belittling of opposing power that
is overturned and trampled in the unfolding of hard reality that
forms the essence of the dark world.

The body of a rock is found in the embrace of the infinite.

Pain is temporary. Understand that even unbearable agony is
only a fleeting singularity within the infinite span of the endless
reach of time. Pain will end, as surely as your death awaits you, as
it does for every living thing.

Sorrow is temporary, for just as pain is limited so is the ache of
regret and the lingering attachment to what no longer is. Sorrow
ceases, as surely as your breath will one day cease.

Resentment is temporary. Know that resentment passes too into
the blown and empty dust of the past, for resentment is not a true
expression of the will of Heaven and has no substance in and of
itself.

Heed the words of a long dead master of the *ninja*:

Sorrow, pain and resentment are natural qualities to be
encountered in life. Therefore, work to cultivate the en-
lightenment of the immovable spirit. [4]

The immovable spirit is unbounded, unhindered, unanchored and unattached. It is the cessation of suffering through unlimited appreciation of infinite transience.

The **Dark Triad Man** endures with radical acceptance.

Nothing is forever, including the worst of things.

Endurance is the Fourth Law.

FORGING THE IRON: PROUD ENDURANCE

Learn: Observe how you employ patience, in large and in small scales. Observe what hardens in you with each act of patience. Observe how ego is abandoned. Consider the relationship between endurance and perseverance.

Explore:
- Where do your weaknesses and vulnerabilities dwell and how do you sustain them?
- What is the traumatic root of each within your heart, your mind and your body?
- What ego supersedes your strength and what crumbling of perseverance weakens you?

What seems brutally unendurable never lasts forever.

Reflect: Contemplate how you postured yourself at a point in the past to endure and to embody the immovable spirit. How did you face the unendurable and yet persevere?

Train: The source of your strength is not situational, but internal. Identify it, and seed it. Know what you are capable of enduring, and what you cannot possibly withstand.

Task: Take what you cannot withstand, and envision a future that demanded precisely that.

THE STOLEN SON

The long flight home landed well after dark.

I had been in Manhattan as part of a political delegation from the Western states, representing a civil rights organization at a public event before the United Nations.

It had gone well, and the tumult of the past two days was still fresh in my mind as I collected my belongings from the baggage claim and headed outside to passenger pickup.

There was no ride waiting for me as expected. My wife was nowhere to be seen.

I called home. There was no answer. I kept dialing without result. There was only the ringing of the line, over and over.

Not even the answering machine picked up.

Annoyed, I called a friend. She agreed to come collect me and drive me home.

During the ride I expressed my frustration. It was irritating, but not unfamiliar, that a commitment was unfulfilled or a responsibility forgotten by my wife. My friend was circumspect, aware of the tension that was present in my marriage.

We arrived at the apartment complex just before midnight. As I walked from the car with my bag I let out a breath and purposefully relaxed. My young son was inside, and he was a bright and beloved part of my life despite all of the dissonance and tension between his mother and I.

The first sign that something was gravely wrong was the dogs.

They barked and whined at the sight of me, standing on their hind legs and trying to reach me from the below-ground concrete patio.

I could immediately smell the dog waste and spilled food, and saw the tipped over water dishes. They had knocked it over and tracked through all of it.

I realized instantly that they had been penned out there for several days.

I went down the stairs, my friend behind me, and unlocked and opened the door. Inside the apartment was dark. I saw that things were missing, furniture in disarray, pictures gone.

It was clear there was no one there. I let the dogs in and they were nearly frantic with excitement and relief. The water I quickly gave them was lapped furiously without pause as I walked down the cluttered hallway to my son's bedroom.

It was empty. His bed was there, and his car seat, but no little boy who would run to me with the thumping delighted steps of an excited toddler.

I walked back to the living room and spoke shortly to my friend. Her eyes were wide and her face pale.

"He's gone," I said.

She handed me the note that had been left on the kitchen counter.

It was full of disjointed, odd, hastily scrawled words. Informing me that the marriage was over, that she was not coming back, that I was not to try to find her. No word of where she had gone, nothing about our child's well-being.

"Let's let the dogs out," I said.

We walked outside under the stars that glimmered in the thin air and I lit a cigarette, watching the two dogs run and sniff in the field. My brain was spinning and my heart was aching; there was no denying that massive life changes were underway that I had to accept, and handle with competence.

But first I had to find my son.

"Take me to the police station," I said.

Law enforcement was sympathetic but helpless. No crime had been committed, for there was no order of custody or divorce in process to prevent it. That would soon be remedied.

The judge was angry but equally helpless up front. The first emergency custody hearing was held within days. When my attorney asked what I thought would be an appropriate division of parenting time, I had barely started to respond before the brooding magistrate cut me off with a wave.

He curtly announced, "She is not to have visitation with this child until she has appeared in this courtroom and explained herself to me."

But first I had to discover her whereabouts.

Any order of the judge was worthless until she was located and served.

I had to find my son.

The United States is a big place, and when you and your son are dual citizens and your wife has a foreign passport, the potential geographic range of a kidnapped child expands quickly.

It was weeks before I was able to rule out a disappearance overseas.

In the interim I moved in with a neighbor, a man who I had met only a few times in the communal park as he walked his own dog. An older gentleman of good humor and charismatic personality, he had traded just a few words with me before this. But he was quick to see that there was something wrong, and there was a reassuring bond of mutual interest when I told him what was taking place.

He'd been through a similar situation and offered his home as a place to stay. The apartment where my marriage died was too painful of a place to rest, too silent and lonely in the middle of the night when I would lie awake in anguished worry for my three-year-old son and his future.

It was after a month of loss and agony that he sat next to me one afternoon as I laid there on his couch in absolute misery and defeat, and spoke to me the words that I never forgot.

"You need to hear this," he said.

"It is going to get worse before it gets better."

I could feel my mouth turn down, knowing he spoke the truth.

"It is not going to get better for a long time."

He waited, looking at me, ensuring that his words were fully heard. There was a glint in his eyes as he delivered the last of his advice:

"It is going to get better."

Somehow that gave me the strength to endure.

I knew truth when I heard it.

I felt that truth, and the grave experience behind those words; and knowing that there was not a way around it, I decided then and there to endure the unendurable, and push through.

Within a week I had moved to a place in the mountains, preparing a room for my child.

Within a fortnight my hired bounty hunter was on the trail, searching for my stolen son.

Six weeks after that terrible night of shock and loss my child ran at last across the courtroom lobby into my arms. I vividly remember hoisting him up and turning away from the audience of court officers and attorneys and special advocates and taking several quick steps away as tears poured out of my eyes.

My little son held my face in his hands, and his own was full of happy awe as he brushed the tears away and hugged me tightly, the smile on his face one of the most beautiful I'd ever seen.

He never left my custody again.

Today he is a young man, entered into his own adult life, and that day is probably long since vanished from his memory.

But I will never forget it, nor the words that my friend spoke directly to the crushed and bleeding heart of a man who had lost his only child, perhaps forever, and lay there in the collapse of emotional defeat.

I have shared those words with other men, in moments when they needed to hear the power of them.

They are true, and they are resonant, and they are real:

It will get worse before it gets better.

It will not get better for a long time.

It will get better.

Remember that, in the darkest hour.

It will get better, and you will endure.

The Preacher | Danse Macabre
Hans Holbein the Younger (1497–1543)

Chapter 8

The Fifth Law is Posture

If your heart is large enough to envelop your adversaries,
you can see right through them and avoid their attacks.
And once you envelop them, you will be able to guide them
along the path indicated to you by heaven and earth.

—Ueshiba Morihei

MIRROR HEART

All things are as they will ever be. Seamless posture is the highest
form of receptivity and adherence to the will of Heaven. Pure
receptivity is unhindered by the existence of ego; the immovable
spirit is everywhere.

IRON CORE OF THE LAW

- Narcissism: Pure expression of self.
- Machiavellianism: Puppetry dance with reality.
- Psychopathy: No mind, no heart, no body.

Posture.

It is a powerfully significant word in the study of human movement, whether in the mind or heart or body. Posture is not the

crackling, static mimicry of "stance" nor is it limited to any particular realm of the human experience.

Posture as understood by the **Dark Triad Man** and adhered to as the Fifth of the Nine Laws is a broad, seamless and infinite concept of continuous, living breath and interaction with the scheme of total existence.

Posture is a deep and extraordinarily difficult concept to master but the mastery of posture is a nonnegotiable aspect of the birth, cultivation, development and deployment of power, success, survival, and all other aspects of life.

Animals have posture. Emotions have posture. Plants, even, embody and display their posture in response to light, wind and weather. Thoughts have posture.

Posture is best understood through the Japanese word *kamae* which although meaning, literally, "posture" it also has the quality of arrangement, array, readiness, care.

Your posture is your arrangement in the world.

Your posture is the flow of your engagement in each encounter.

Your posture is your communication with the reality of things, and the demonstration of your spirit and a pure revelation of your purpose.

Assessment of the correctness and power of posture lies in the most passively assessed measurement of utility.

The most appropriate posture is the most perfect.

The most perfect posture is the most appropriate.

It is by the utterly seamless, unhesitating, egoless, unattached, mindless and purest posture that the enlightenment of total appropriateness flows.

The purest heart is like a mirror.

It reflects perfectly, without stain or shimmer, the ultimate reality it is presented with. There is no space between light and reflection, between input and output, between acceptance and response. There is no gap, no interval, no consideration, no analysis, no shading or twisting or interpretation or corruption.

There is only sharp, instantaneous, continuous and eternal reflection with perfect and infinite purity.

In this purity lies the power of the appropriate.

In the appropriate lies the seamless accord with the will of Heaven. And in accord with the will of Heaven is the unstoppable, unconquerable, unfathomable power of the enlightened spirit.

Your posture is the shining light of your intention.

Where that shining light is a pure reflection, there is nothing that can be seen by the adversary but his own mind.

There is nothing that can be felt but his own heart.

There is no sword that can cut but his own, and through his own defeated self. The perfect mirror displays movement in parallel and makes helpless any effort to accelerate past one's own reflection in the heart of purity.

The **Dark Triad Man** strives tirelessly to streamline his posture, to cut away and discard the gratuitous. To remove the excess from his movement, his thinking, his feeling. To embody the purity of uninfected reflection, and to thereby soar unhampered through the infinity of all possibility.

There is no fear in posture, only in personalized and infected reflection. There is no anger in posture, only the delivery of a fate already sought. There is no effort in posture, only the accordance with the will of the universe as it perceives.

This is the secret of "one cut".

This is living in seamless grace.

This is the way of nature and of God.

There is no self, there is only the mirror of being.

Posture is the Fifth Law.

FORGING THE IRON: DIGNIFIED POSTURE

Learn: Pay close attention to your physical posture. Observe revelation and disjointedness. Take note of any dissonance between seamless posture and the dwelling place of the ego. Extend this observation through your daily living.

Explore:
- That which is observed is altered by observation. How does your ego effect your posture?
- How does your posture communicate strength or weakness, dominance or submission?
- Where does a natural ferocity arise in the posture of your thought, word or deed?

The most powerful posture is graceful and transparent.

Reflect: Consider how your awareness of posture magnifies stillness of spirit and increases receptivity, both in your perception of yourself and externally of the world.

Train: Examine your posture and how it varies in relationships, offices and environments. Learn the common core of your heart that is consistent from posture to posture, and what changes.

Task: Visualize your worst fear, what shatters you inside. Observe resulting effect on your posture.

COURTROOMS AND CASH

"Hold on a moment!" I exclaimed. "Let me get this right:

"You're telling me that I have sole custody, but alimony to her is twice the amount of child support? That means I have to raise him with no financial help AND pay her over $1,000 a month?"

The judge looked at me, frowning, and said "That's correct."

"What the bloody…"

My attorney took me sharply by the upper arm, digging into me as hard as he could. He was a small man, perhaps half my size, but his grip was insistent and immediate.

"Thank you, Your Honor," he said. Then he quietly snarled at me.

"Shut up and get out of here."

I was in absolute disbelief.

"Are you fucking kidding me?" I asked him.

He ushered me outside of the courtroom. The judge watched, waiting to see if an affront to the dignity of the court was about to arise.

I wisely shut my mouth and went with my lawyer.

My soon-to-be ex-wife and her attorney walked past us and down the hallway. I watched them go for a moment, seething, then turned back to the man I had retained as counsel.

"What the hell, Barry?"

He shrugged, spoke calmly. "It is what it is. You're the father, but you got custody. That's not how it's supposed to work in this liberal enclave. You're a known conservative activist. You're paying for it."

"A thousand bucks a month?" I was furious. At the time, it was about a quarter of my after-tax pay.

"How about she gets a job, takes some responsibility?" I demanded.

The slightly built lawyer shrugged again. "She doesn't need to. They've imputed income to her, and this monthly result is after that calculation. You want her to get into the job market and start working?"

He cut my sarcastic retort off with a wave of his hand and continued.

"Then we'll have to come back here, and you'll end up in a worse spot. They are probably imputing more income than she's capable of earning anyway. Look at this as the best result you could expect."

He was right, of course, as ugly as the truth was.

It was a late Friday afternoon. I left the courthouse, picked my son up from day care, and drove home to enjoy the weekend with him. It was summer, and beautiful, and we had a new life to create together.

On Monday morning I was laid off.

"We selected the other candidate for conversion of your contract to a full-time position."

I was dazed, listening to the newly hired executive I now reported to. "You said incumbents had preference. She and I have the same experience," I pointed out. "And I've run your entire program office for over a year."

He was inflexible. "She also has a master's degree in statistics. You have a high school diploma."

Arguing or discussing was pointless, I knew. Decisions like that are not negotiated with the losing party, only communicated with finality. I cleared out my desk.

It was a long drive home that morning. I had plenty of time to think.

I'd built my career from the ground up, starting with moving boxes of files from one room to another on a simple labor contract in Silicon Valley. That turned into a data entry position, and within six months I was overseeing all the contractors engaged on a $6 billion state sales tax audit.

I had a talent for swift organization and enough ferocious ambition to be in the office at 4am and make things happen. I also had the skills to automate much of the work, freeing up my actual time in the office.

Within two years I was married, a new father, and working in New York as a project manager in one of the largest global technology firms in the world.

Posture is the skill of array, of shaping your encounters with responsive engagement.

No college degree? No work experience? How you position yourself matters. Identifying value, bringing it forward and presenting your bright complementation of need is how the markets of the world are engaged.

I was to learn, very quickly, the crucial importance of posture during the fight for custody of my son.

In the meantime, I had to come up with not just a thousand bucks a month, but a new job.

I could do it, I knew. I'd proven my ability to secure well-paid and prestigious positions solely on my capacity to deliver vision, planning and competence into reality. What I didn't count on was the tech crash of the turn of the century that was gearing up into full swing.

I was one of the first casualties. It would not be a matter of weeks, or months, or even a couple of financial quarters before I returned to the corporate world.

It would be six years.

You learn much about posture when you are desperate.

That thousand dollars per month went unpaid, accumulating on a frightening scale. "This court finds that you are deliberately underemployed," the magistrate would drone, and marginally move the payment needle downwards while at the same time the interest on unpaid spousal support surged higher.

Compounded interest on unpaid debt is horrible posture.

"She's filed a complaint against you," the detective said. "A year ago you pulled the phone line out of the wall while she was using it."

"Disconnecting her Internet gaming and insisting she feed and bathe our child during the day while I was at work?" I asked. "Having to be a mother is an actual criminal complaint?"

"Interfering with telephonic communication is felony wiretapping."

"Are you fucking kidding me?"
Events and situations have posture as well.
You must learn to ride the flow of it.

My attorney was unimpressed, and framed the situation accurately.

"This means that you're on probation for a little while, but it didn't work as planned. You still have sole custody. It's harassment. Give it a few months to show them you're a good boy, and the charge gets dismissed, and she finds something else to try. Eventually she'll give up—no judge will find her fit."

The district attorney thought otherwise.

"Spousal maintenance arrears are a violation of probation," he said. "You need to pay her $15,000 and catch up or I will jail you."

I rolled my eyes in exasperation, as hard as any man ever did. "And she gets custody. You realize this is all about that, don't you?"

He shrugged. "Doesn't matter." He was very matter of fact. "Pay it by Tuesday."

"I can't possibly come up with $15,000 in five days. You know that's not reasonable. Work with me here."

"I'll do $7,500."

"Deal," I said. And that is how justice is concluded in the halls of power.

She bought a thirty-year-old, 97% depreciated trailer home in a remote, destitute rural area with it.

Shortly afterwards the final orders came in. Spousal maintenance was found to be unconscionable, and the remaining debt was wiped out.

I had permanent sole custody.

Within a few months the rest of the issues unraveled.

I won't ever forget the judge standing up, kicking her chair across the room, and leveling a shaking finger at my ex-wife and saying "I am too angry to continue. You will get an order from me shortly."

I kept my posture calm that day, for I had learned to master it in a courtroom.

My ex-wife's attorney had quit the day before and cleared her calendar. She called me on her drive home that afternoon, sobbing into the phone and apologizing for taking the case personally. I told her she was fully forgiven, and that I knew she would make good use of the experience.

Today she is a magistrate herself. Although I have never appeared before her, I believe that my posture of persistence—and final magnanimity—may help shape her own posture to deliver justice for men who do.

The district attorney, furious at being lied to, immediately dismissed all charges against me and agreed to be a positive reference if any future employer had questions.

Today, I am owed nearly a quarter million dollars in back child support.

Interest rates are fixed, and in another ten years I'll revisit the matter and ensure I profit from it.

I haven't had to look upon my ex-wife for over a dozen years. I am happily remarried, my son is grown and an adult moving into his own life. I don't hold resentment, just a smile.

Posture matters. Adaptation to events, to challenges, to adversaries and their plans, matters.

Accord yourself with complementary, appropriate posture.

That is the Way of both survival and triumph.

The Abbess | Danse Macabre
Hans Holbein the Younger (1497–1543)

Chapter 9

The Sixth Law is Freedom

I am free, no matter what rules surround me. If I find them tolerable, I tolerate them; if I find them too obnoxious, I break them. I am free because I know that I alone am morally responsible for everything I do.

—Robert Anson Heinlein

INFINITE MOBILITY

The highest wealth is that of freedom. This is true from the singularity of the spirit through all the vast and infinite realms of existence. Freedom is observed in alignment with the carrying out of the Will of Heaven.

IRON CORE OF THE LAW

- Narcissism: None is worthy as your master.
- Machiavellianism: No limit on considered possibilities.
- Psychopathy: Abandonment of external locus of control.

Freedom.

The very word itself has been torn screaming from a million lips at the moment of horrible death. It has driven men to topple and crash entire civilizations in the pursuit of this most principal soaring desire of all living things.

No healthy animal willingly seeks the cage. No growing life turns backwards and dies when faced with boundary. The inherent drive of life is to cross boundaries, to surmount obstacles, to find freedom in existence, purpose and outcomes. It is the Way of growing things.

The existence of laws and codes and social mores has arisen in order to secure the reliability of profit. In the unfettered and absolute freedom of anarchy is the impossibility of predictable outcomes, for chaos by its very nature is profoundly unpredictable and indeterminate of outcome.

Yet there is a balance between freedom and constriction, and the Sixth Law of freedom is recognition that external imposition of control is incompatible with the dignity and power of unfettered achievement.

This is a difficult and uncomfortable truth for many to accept.

The laws of men do not arise from the word of God. The laws of men are merely veneers of convenience for the many, and profit of the few, under the advancement of violently contrived order and by imposition of external power and consequence on the lives of men beneath their yoke.

Social and cultural boundaries are even less profoundly important, for they are often not enforced by the violent response that underlies the constituted laws and formal statutes of civilization. The consequences of ostracism, disgust, opprobrium, isolation and ridicule are used to keep men in line and once more preserve a predictable and harvestable array of resources for the unhindered.

Your acceptance of shackles is your sentence of death.

In agreement to be helpless you abrogate and abandon your manhood and power.

By limiting mobility of thought, word or deed you reduce your humanity and nobility of character.

The dark and difficult truth is that freedom is the most dangerous thing in the universe. In recognition that unbounded freedom is the natural order, and in your rejection of the artificial constraints of external imposition, comes the ability to attain complete prerogative of choice.

In this ability to choose is your manifestation of purpose, the concealment of vulnerability, and the decision to survive despite all odds and to endure any experience presented.

When each action, each thought, each emotion and each breath of life is, for you, the result of a choice—then you have attained the ultimate fountain of total wealth, which is freedom itself from the will of others and from imposition upon you of choices that are not your own.

In the acceptance of your choice alone is the nurtured and honored primacy of your own conscience.

You cannot force a man to abide by his conscience.

You cannot force a man to violate it.

For a man's conscience is the conclusion of his bare and starkly naked dialogue with God. The direction of his determination into the will of Heaven arises from a command deliberately made to his immortal spirit.

You must utterly adhere to your own conscience, and discard any lesser demands upon your thought, your word and your deed. For your conscience is your alignment with the divine and the salvation of your spiritual resolution.

The laws of men are merely arguments of the violent.

The strictures of culture are but drifting ashes of the weak.

Love is a choice. Honor is a choice. Trust is a choice. Success is a choice. Glory and power and gold are a choice.

A **Dark Triad Man** knows that his freedom is his birthright and guards that freedom with savage and unflinching perseverance, even before the glittering throne of Caesar.

Without freedom there is nothing.

Freedom is the Sixth Law.

FORGING THE IRON: SUPERB FREEDOM

Learn: Consider boundaries you observe and those you do not. Compare those you observe to those others expect. Where you find disregard of expectation, go into the ego and dissect the source of ego.

Explore:

- Where in your heart does ego abandon boundaries in the pursuit of freedom?
- How is the alignment of your heart determined towards independence or servitude?
- Where can your adherence to external boundaries of control be permanently dissolved?

Freedom is not negotiable for the human being.

Reflect: Describe a deliberate and powerful or shocking permanent abandonment of external boundary that did not generate ripple within your ego.

Train: Examine your boundaries and limitations, identify useless illusions, and strip them away. Question assumptions that prevent you from mobility, attachments that restrict your perception.

Task: Identify your true state of freedom. To what must you answer? What do you resent obeying?

SILENCED WORDS AND GUNFIRE

"Don't you dare let that happen again."

My mother's words were severe, fierce, even harsh as she instructed me.

"Don't you dare let anyone, ever, tell you what you can or cannot read. And never let anyone tell you what you are, or aren't, allowed to think."

I was eight years old. I arrived home from school that day to complain that the reading teacher had spotted me absorbed in a book by the brilliant writer John Irving, and told me that I was too young to be reading it. That I was to put it away. And that my mother was to call her the next day.

"Nor do you ever let anyone silence you when you have truth to speak." *Her voice shook with anger, one of the few times I saw her utterly livid.*

She didn't call the school. She went there the next day, in the absolute height of fury, and it must have been a lovely and mesmerizing sight.

She never had to tell me a second time, and that teacher never spoke to me again.

Free speech matters.

Education and information matter.

And your conscience, that with which you interpret and combine them, matters most of all.

These things are the heart of freedom.

I grew up with revolutionaries and political exiles at the kitchen table, playing in and around their heated words and clouds of cigarette smoke, listening to their arguments of insurrection and political theory, of practical power and conniving statesmen.

One thing was always sharply, disturbingly clear from both the experiences I listened to and from the history books I absorbed as part of my voracious reading of everything I could get my hands on:

When the talking stopped was always when the shooting started.

I have seen many things in my life, in many different countries, but the common thread through all of them is this: the human being is a consistent animal. He moves inexorably towards tyranny.

The most vitally restoring antidote that sustains the life of freedom, is that of a very specific kind:

Freedom of speech, the open expression of opinion. Unfettered delivery of ideas and conscience.

Freedom to keep and bear arms is also important. It is an irrevocable, sacred right of free men.

But it is for use when speech fails. And speech fails when it is suppressed.

To prevent the shooting, you must prevent the silencing.

Human beings are easily provoked and the results of provocation are often terrible, especially on national, cultural and civilizational scales. The tumble and turn of peace and war, freedom and slavery, wealth and poverty are all inherent, normal, predictable and observable.

So is the suppression of free speech in the pursuit of power, and the bursting outcome of violence that inevitably follows it. Free men do not bargain with tyrants, and good gains nothing from compromise with evil. Freedom is not negotiable.

Hate speech is the most important to protect. It is the canary in the mine, the finger in the air, testing the wind of pogrom and revolution, of public massacres and killing pits. If you silence one, you silence all, and openly invite the most horrific lusts of human beings to rampage unrestrained.

Freedom is binary. You possess it, or you do not.

You fight for it, or you don't.

Freedom requires traction, from which mobility arises. Traction comes from contact. Contact comes from engagement, and engagement takes place within encounter. Understanding this is important.

When speech is silenced, and men cannot openly challenge each other and work out conflict and ideas in open forum, consciences curdle and hatred stews and violence is planned.

The only encounter left between silenced men is collision over distance.

This is neither right nor wrong, but simply how it is.

You will not suppress free speech and have a contented people.

You will instead create a restless, angry beast that coils and looks for provocation to kill.

Today in the West there is enormous and concentric assault upon free speech of an unusually competent and subtle kind. It is not the simple proclamation of ordinance against speech that offends the dignity of the king, followed by fines and chains.

It is, instead, the insinuating spread of disgustingly pervasive shame and public social lynching inflicted on those who exhibit wrongthink, badspeak, thoughtcrime; any who mysteriously manage to offend one of thousands of possible permutations of political correctness in Western society.

We are subjected to ever-tightening control in the public sphere, and it has moved from mere idiocy to active, open suppression of speech. Men lose jobs, families, careers and companies for the grave yet imagined sin of having an individual opinion.

As I write these words today I watch the American election cycle break out in open violence on the streets. I see photographs of injured citizens and I read the words of elected politicians on the Left, blaming those bloodied people for their own injuries and assaults by claiming that Donald Trump's followers, in essence, deserve it.

"Do you wish to go that far?" I would ask them. "Do you believe you have become the new dread lords?"

I tell you today that when speech is not merely punished, but openly suppressed with violent force—that bloodshed and rage, outrage and killing, are made both unstoppable and deserved in terrible consequence.

I did not make the dark world, brothers.

It was dark when we got here. It is what it is.

But I operate within it as a skillful practitioner, a methodological scholar, and a master of principles that are unforgiving when they are violated. And I tell you that the bloody tide of the dark world laps close.

You do not need to be a master to feel that tide turning, nor a scholar to realize that a new age is unfolding, or skilled in politics or speeches to feel the cresting anger of men.

It is too much to tell you in these pages of all the various ways you are subjected to muzzle and shackle.

You are a man, and because you hold this book in your hands, you have both the tools to see it and the means to harden against it.

It is not the purpose of this book to give you political instruction, or to guide you into delivery of speeches.

You are a man, and you are responsible for your own outcomes, and if freedom is what you desire then you have no choice but to do something about the loss of it.

There are men out there who see what I do, and who make it their work to lead. Together there is opportunity for you to do the most important possible thing to fight back, to win victories, and smash the cloying, hideous and humiliating chains that are being wrapped around the wrists of men of the West:

Find your brothers, speak the truth, and build your tribe.

Once more I tell you that loners die alone, and armies win victory.

A thousand years of Western history have led us to this point of decision.

Seize it, and let freedom roar with bloody triumph at shackles snapped.

Else freedom will find its way back in a different hour, with dreadful talons and fire.

That is the way of the dark world, and it is also the way of men.

Pick a road, and choose wisely.

Your time for hesitation is over.

The King | Danse Macabre
Hans Holbein the Younger (1497–1543)

Chapter 10

The Seventh Law is Power

A true king is neither husband nor father; he considers his throne and nothing else.

—Pierre Corneille

POWER IS WORSHIP

Power is a sacred vehicle within which one operates in the world of men. Power is holy and infinite and cultivated as a method of solemn worship. Power delivers from absence of ego. Power is the highest form of love.

IRON CORE OF THE LAW

- Narcissism: Prerogative arises from possession.
- Machiavellianism: Subtle tendrition arises from the core.
- Psychopathy: Absence of ego in the cutting through.

Power.

It is a word that ripples with potential.

Men seek power, and always have. Animals seek power, and always will. There is ever a Caesar and a contender, an alpha who is eventually torn by the throat and left dead behind the pack. Power abhors a vacuum, power is fluid, power is mysterious to the weak and terrifying to the fearful.

Power is capacity. Power is expansive, it fills where it is permitted and displaces where it overflows. Power is both light and dark in manifestation, active and passive, and arises in direct proportion to acceptance of the prerogative behind it. Hesitant power strips itself; regretful power inhibits itself; apologetic power dissipates and abandons itself.

The possession of power is not a thing to be feared, but respected. Power is not immoral, but amoral. Power is simply momentum, it is mass, it is reality in the dark world.

The first step in adherence to the Seventh Law is to recognize that power and drama are oppositional to each other. They may coexist; the exercise of power may be dramatic or result in drama, but drama is never the true purpose of power.

Power is not exultant or gratuitous. It simply is.

Power possesses no moral freight of its own. Power is a natural force and has no more ability to flavor or tint itself with good or evil than gravity, leverage or momentum.

For power itself is simply physics... the influence of things.

You are responsible for the discovery, cultivation and sustenance of your own power.

For power does not seek you, but must be sought and captured and harnessed. It is female in this respect.

You are accountable for the determinations, actualizations and outcomes of your own power.

For power does not excuse you, but must be owned and admitted and proclaimed. It is male in this respect.

The abandonment of power is the abandonment of opportunity, of humanity and of adulthood. Learned helplessness is a grotesque and disgusting wallow in the rejection of personal power.

There is no moral superiority in willful helplessness, only spurning of responsibility and an absurd and contemptibly stupid self-degradation.

You are a human being. You are therefore the apex predator of the world, the finest animal in the universe. Created, as is said, in the image of God and as the master of life and death upon the earth. No lion tears off his own claws, no bull breaks and tramples his own horns. Neither does a man of health and appropriate posture limit or hobble his power in the world he has inherited.

Understand that power is the nature of all things.

This understanding brings the **Dark Triad Man** to the realization of his own integration into the very fabric of reality. For there is, in truth, no separation.

It is power that glues together the quantum essentials of matter into particles.

It is power that pulls the expansion of the universe across the infinite yet weirdly expanding ether.

It is power that drives encounters and engagements of mass and motion and thoughts and love and fear and every singularity of existence.

For power is the voice of Heaven and its projection through the infinity of things is the wind of capability that man harnesses and directs according to his needs.

The **Dark Triad Man** cultivates power but does not hoard it.

He grows and tends to it but does not obsess over it.

He displays and deploys it but does not brandish it.

Power is water but employed with firmness.

Power is unforgiving but used with forbearance.

Power is pitiless but delivered with mercy.

Power is the Seventh Law.

FORGING THE IRON: EXULTANT POWER

Learn: Consider that correct use of power is absent regret. Examine at a miniscule level how you apply power or restraint. Flip scale to observe where power is hindered by apology instead of expressed as prerogative. Continue this dual assessment each day of living.

Explore:
- What power do believe you truly possess, and would it remain if you were stripped naked?
- Where in life do you choose abstention and regret rather than exercise of natural power?
- Where does emasculation fester within you, and is it thrust upon you or volunteered?

Power is the prerogative of those who possess it.

Reflect: Describe an encounter when your most powerful expression was wholly absent ego. Reflect on the outcome and itemize the feelings that accompanied this purity of expression in the world.

Train: Return to the feeling of absolute power and prerogative, and accept that feeling as your deserved birthright, belonging to a being made in the image of God.

Task: Dissect your greatest power. What is left if that is gone? Identify three alternate sources.

BAMBOO CAGES AND GARDENS

"They are pulling my Daddy's fingernails out."
    The words of the five-year-old were calm but the sadness in his eyes spoke volumes as he repeated himself, standing there in my dining room.

"*They locked him in a bamboo cage. Now they are pulling his fingernails out.*"

I listened with uncertainty and surprise. I was not more than two years older than him, but still old enough to know that keeping a man in a cage was wrong.

There was something unnatural about it that bothered me more than the torture he described. The pain of torn out fingernails would hurt, I thought.

But being in a cage? That was very bad. Did people really do that to each other?

"*Why are they keeping him in a cage?*" *I asked.*

"*Indira Gandhi is scared of him,*" *he said.*

Who was Indira Gandhi? How far away was India, where the boy and his mother were from? Why did they do those things there? Why were he and his mother now living with us?

I had so many questions.

"*Hush,*" *my mother said.* "*They are family friends. Don't talk about his father.*"

Family friends they were, for generations. My mother, the daughter of a university president, had continued a deep friendship that her father had begun in the days of India's early independence. And with the rise of Indira Gandhi to power and the declaration of emergency in the early 1970's, political opponents were jailed and horrifically treated.

Thus the man's wife and son fled to America and stayed with us for a time. Forty years later that friendship still lives, although it has been many years since I last saw them.

The day Indira Gandhi was machine-gunned to death by her own bodyguards I remember thinking, simply, that karma might be slow— but it never forgot to return and feed.

I grew up loathing tyrants but with a very firm understanding of power.

My mother's politics were quite different from mine. A lifelong socialist educated at Berkeley, her economic beliefs were starkly opposed to the ones I embraced as an adult in my own right. But she successfully and fiercely instilled an important truth in me, and we never disagreed on this point even in the most heated political discussions that followed as I reached adulthood:

Power matters. Men with power eventually turn cruel ambitious guns on their brothers with predictable butchery. And the heroes of freedom often die miserably against a wall, or in a hastily dug grave in the forest. But the work they did was crucial to the tide of history.

And the only thing that opposed power, was power itself.

"Why can't his family or friends just break him out?" I asked her.

"They have no power," she replied. "They would be killed if they tried."

I absorbed that, deciding that powerless was never something I wanted to be.

As I grew up the stories of resistance were often firsthand. There were many guests at the dinner table from far corners of the world. One gentleman, a politician exiled from Haiti under the regime of Papa Doc Duvalier, told me stories of the terrifying secret police under the dictator.

"They are called the Tonton Macoute," he said.

"You knew them by their mirror sunglasses and their cruelty."

I listened, rapt, still trying to grasp at that age how this thing called power worked.

"They would come and take you away in front of everyone. Beat you to death and hang you from a tree, and if your family did not leave your body there, they would be taken away too."

"But couldn't you fight back? What if everyone fought back all at once?" I asked.

I did not like this story. What if that was your brother, your mother, you had to leave hanging there? How could you just accept that without bringing justice back into the world?

He shrugged. "Do you want to be the first?" he asked. "That is how you die."

"Bad men take power and everyone else suffers.

"Fear is how the powerless are controlled."

He smoked his pipe, silently, and I considered what he said about power and fear.

Many decades later my father remarried a Frenchwoman and retired to the north of France. My new stepmother and I looked across the garden of the home she grew up in, and I listened as she told me the story of her older brother.

"The Gestapo took him that afternoon, in front of our mother and father."

Her voice was level with characteristic Gallic phlegm. "They came with an officer and three soldiers. We never saw him again.

"They shot him at Stutthof camp in Poland as the end of the war neared. The Germans knew the war was lost. They killed everyone."

Her brother was in the Resistance and paid the ultimate price for his opposition to power. The work he did of insurrection, of secret messages and smuggling, of sabotage and assassination, had impact.

There was sacred value in it. Though he did not survive to see his native France risen from under the boot of the invader, the work he did helped to change the fate of his nation and his people. And it was honored by them, with words that bespoke their love and respect for his sacrifice.

It is a small memorial, on the outside of the house. Underneath his name, graven there with dignity into the cold and weathered stone, the words are simple, solemn, and sublime.

ICI DEMEURAIT
PATRIOTE
FUSILLE AU CAMPE DE STRUTHOF
1917–1944

Here remained a patriot.
Shot at Stutthof, 1944.
He was twenty-seven years old.
But his countrymen remember.
He died for France.

Patriot.
A word that has grave and passionate depth, that exudes and res-
onates with power.
Power is the responsibility of every human being.
Personal power, tribal power, national power, power of civilization.
You will not impact fate without power.
You will not protect your family and community without power.
You will not steer the fate of your people without power.
Power is your prerogative, the demand of manhood.
Cultivate it, attain it, and deliver it.
Power is what unlocks the cage and frees bloody hands from torture.
Power is what halts men with mirror sunglasses when they arrive
with machetes and cruelty.
Power preserves peace and safety in the garden, and power is what
men honor after death.
Seek it, and hold it. You and your people will need it.
It is the way of the dark world.

The Creation | Danse Macabre
Hans Holbein the Younger (1497–1543)

Chapter 11

The Eighth Law is Preposterousness

In fact, it is often stated that of all the theories proposed in this century, the silliest is quantum theory. Some say that the only thing that quantum theory has going for it, in fact, is that it is unquestionably correct.

—Michio Kaku

CREATION IS ABSURD

That anything at all exists is entirely and infinitely preposterous. The existence of the universe is, in itself, an absurd and illusory violation of the eternal mind. The ten thousand things are ridiculous to behold.

IRON CORE OF THE LAW

- Narcissism: You are the center of your universe.
- Machiavellianism: There is no true reality.
- Psychopathy: Absence of ego in absurdity.

Preposterousness.

It is in acceptance of the preposterous nature of existence and appreciation of the inherent nonsense of form, that man rises beyond them both and connects with the infinity of the endless divine.

There is great challenge in understanding this.

There is bottomless absurdity in the form of all things, for they are forms only and not reality. This is known to all faiths, and to all sacred texts, and to all ways of spiritual growth that men have arrayed for themselves in response to the weird and terribly lovely fabric of time and space.

Yet in order to pass through daily life and not fall into a spiraling insanity of gurgling incomprehension, the mind accepts form as reality. We have five fingers on each hand. The sky is blue. Matter has mass, there are nuclear forces, there are mechanical, physical laws we can test and prove.

But this is a simplistic overlay to enable simple living.

Consider the depth of space and time.

The age of the universe is virtually beyond comprehension. Understand the scale of it, the breadth of it, the vast and infinite deep and the tiny, almost instantaneously negligible slice of reality that the presence of humanity represents.

It is preposterous to consider it as real. For with sufficient perspective, even the billions of eons of deep time and the swirling clouds of a billion galaxies that lattice through the visible universe are themselves mere immeasurably brief and ridiculously tiny hiccups within something else.

Where God is infinite and unbounded, how can He have a definitive image in which to create His children?

In the vast and staggering distance and age of the universe, how can there be purpose in such fleeting self-awareness of human beings who think and feel and experience?

How absurd to believe that we are alone in the universe, that the span of time and space are solely for our amusement.

How ludicrous to believe that life arises at all in a universe teeming with sentience but built upon entropic principle where heat death and extinguishment are foregone imperatives!

How can there be reconciliation between the provable operation of Newtonian physics and the weird and bubbling probabilistic froth of quantum foam that creates it?

How can we conceive of division by zero but be unable to approach the impossible answer?

The truth is in acceptance of the preposterous nature of all things. That division by zero results not in error and halted information, but laughter and delight.

It is said that God is love. That God is thought. That we think, therefore we are, and that love is acceptance and that love is not bounded by time and space.

Can that be felt? Or is division by zero, truly a howling fling of your sanity into the outer darkness of infinite concentric hells of broken logic and repetitive madness?

To attempt to define the nature of the universe is, in the end, preposterous in itself.

This is not a rejection of faith or an abandonment of science. For faith does mighty works, and science is itself unraveling the physical fabric of the universe. As this book is written, announcement was made of the creation of an unknown particle in one of the many particle colliders across the world.

How preposterous, but how delightful.

In the recognition of the preposterous nature of existence, the **Dark Triad Man** learns to let go of worry and concern and in the end, to appreciate and laugh at the morbid seriousness of the earnest and the lugubrious.

It is silly to invest mortal seriousness beyond effective utility.

The face of the Buddha is a smile; the eyes of the infinite are kind. Things are all right.

It is too silly to be otherwise.

Preposterousness is the Eighth Law.

FORGING THE IRON: ABSOLUTE PREPOSTEROUS-NESS

Learn: Consider that there cannot be absence outside the universe. Consider deep time, deep space, the very violation of universal law necessary for the universe itself to exist in the first place. Form and shape are preposterous.

Explore:

- What does it mean if all is illusion? And if everything is an illusion, then what is reality?
- What lies beyond time and space and the infinite deep? What is the point if you are mortal?
- How do you balance acceptance and denial of various forms of "reality" you encounter?

Infinite probability is proven right here, right now.

Reflect: Grasp how the existence of the mind is a singularity within infinite illusion. Explore the depth of your understanding of how transiently silly the fabric and form of reality are.

Train: Move from the singularity of stress and anxiety to the infinity of perspective, and thereby gain the calm of the immovable spirit. Practice this continually.

Task: Consider the most preposterous experience of your life. Absorb that it had infinite probability.

INCARCERATE AND REPLACE

The doctor was the best in Manhattan.

He was renowned for his insight and experience and had great reputation in his field. His advice was clear and unmistakable to the man and woman who sat painfully before him in his well-appointed office.

"Your son will never function in society," he declared.

The doctor looked from man to woman, confident in his knowledge, and continued with his cruel advice:

"Put him in an institution, and have another child."

The woman stared down at her lap, opening and closing her hands. The man looked away, his face stern and angry, his jaw tense. The doctor went on with his recommendation.

"He is permanently deaf. It is impossible for him to keep up with his peers. He will never be able to hold a job. Who would hire him? He would be a permanent burden on you."

The medical savant leaned back in his chair and continued pronouncement of his sentence with practiced finality. In front of him tears rolled down the face of the woman, and the hands of her husband turned white where they gripped the chair in refusal.

"Educating him will be a futile waste of money. His chances of having a normal life are virtually zero."

I played quietly outside in the waiting room as my fate was grimly decided. The silence of that room was to be the silence of all rooms, all games, and all days. But I played nonetheless.

"I can provide you with a list of excellent facilities. It would be best to choose quickly, and move past this tragedy. His hearing loss is permanent, and the longer you wait the more challenging it will be."

The woman glanced at her husband, who looked back at her. The sharp line of his English face bespoke the fury inside him, although his voice was calm as he stood and spoke.

"Thank you. We will make our own decision."

Until the end of his life many decades later, my father would display freezing and disgusted contempt at any mention of that day, or of the recommendation he and my mother were given.

They left that office, collected me, and headed back to the shores of the Gold Coast of Long Island where I was raised and where the green rolling hills and estates are a treasured memory of childhood.

How preposterous life is!

Preposterous that the little boy who was condemned as helpless, who was to be shipped off to a miserable and horrific life of institutional existence, forgotten and then replaced, could rise above his fate.

Preposterous that he would master lip-reading until even whispered conversations at the end of a distant hallway were as clear and revealing as bright words on a page.

Preposterous that by the age of eight he would have the reading skill and comprehension of a college senior, and walk the halls of his private school each day with his head buried in the works of the ancients.

Preposterous that at the age of twelve he would be in high school.

Preposterous that by the age of sixteen he had left home with his diploma to chase after the legend of the ninja, and devote himself to their forbidding physical training of bone and steel.

Preposterous that he would attain professional success as a program manager in the field of finance, where his daily responsibility was to lead and inspire teams of men and women from all corners of the globe, and not merely support himself but also build his own family and raise children.

Preposterous that the little boy who was deaf and helpless would master the craft of writing and public speaking, and share words from the steps of public legislatures and bring tears to the eyes of hardened veterans as they listened to his ringing words.

It is utterly preposterous that you hold this book in your hands today.

You face your own utterly preposterous challenges, and you have equal power to leap through them.

Understand well that there is a difference between probability and possibility, and that the gap between may seem infinitely small but is nonetheless wide enough to explode an entire unexpected universe within it.

Do not fail to believe in possibilities.

Do not fail to believe in yourself.

It is how odds are ferociously defied.

Even preposterous dreams can be made real, my brother.

I am the living proof.

The Temptation | Danse Macabre
Hans Holbein the Younger (1497–1543)

Chapter 12

The Ninth Law is No Laws

In times of war, the law falls silent.

—Marcus Tullius Cicero

UNBOUNDED ARENA

There are no Laws and there are no Rules. All is division by zero. No guarantees, absolutes, or laws are permanent and eternal in the world of men, and the dark world has never taken notice of laws.

IRON CORE OF THE LAW

- Narcissism: Infinite prerogative of power.
- Machiavellianism: Infinite freedom of posture.
- Psychopathy: The mind and eyes of God.

No Laws.

At the very end of things, an enlightened acceptance ultimately arrives at the understanding there are no laws.

Laws are simply mental formations of human imagination, and not explicit commands of God underlying the concrete foundations of the universe.

It is your prerogative to choose your path, to expand your power, to utilize your freedom and all in the service of your purpose. You will achieve what you earn and you will pay what you owe, and at times luck and chance will intervene.

There are no guarantees.

The unbounded freedom of infinite possibility provides the basis for seamless interaction within uncountable scales of understanding and meaning. Where truth is relative, where laws are nonexistent, where validity is mere probability and probability itself is indeterminable, the **Dark Triad Man** finds his ease in the application of power within the world.

With no handicaps, his performance is unchecked.

With no blinders, his perspective is infinite.

Within this diffusion of self and the disappearance of the last wisps of ego, is the resting place of the eternal mind and the perspective of the divine.

The ego is the sense of separateness of self from all things.

Ego is the belief in a bounded existence.

When ego is abandoned via enlightened understanding that there is no interval between thought, word and deed, the mind of God appears.

When ego vanishes in the beloved acceptance that there is no gap between imagination of the heart and the manifestation of physical reality, the eyes of God see through infinity.

Shinshin shingan "heart divine, heart eye" is the seamless state of pure psychopathic presence: unbounded purpose, conscience mirrored to justice, and embodiment of the will of Heaven.

This is important to understand. You must study this well.

Psychopathy is not evil. Nor is it immoral. It is, at the core, purely acceptance without illusion.

Machiavellianism is not evil. Nor is it cruel. It is, in full expression, merely perfect posture within creation.

Narcissism is not evil. Nor is it selfish. It is, in its brilliance, only one more vision of the God of infinite multiverses.

To see without illusion; to engage with perfect posture; and to accord the vision of God as your purpose is to attain the state of invincible power and unstoppable achievement.

This cannot be ignored or refused.

There are no laws. There is only what is.

There are no boundaries. There is only what happens.

The **Dark Triad Man** pursues the state of *shinshin shingan* through mastery of self, mastery of posture, and mastery of purpose. In this mastered alignment of heart, word and deed is the Way of Heaven.

When you match the Way of Heaven, you match its Will.

The man who carries out the Will of Heaven is unstoppable.

There are no laws. There are no barriers. There are no adversaries powerful enough, no challenges too severe, no limitations on engagement with the power of Heaven behind him and driving his intention forward. For it becomes not his own egotistic intention, but the will of the Universe itself.

Shinshin shingan is not an academic achievement, although it requires scholarship and study. It is not a physical understanding, although it requires often dangerous lessons in the dark world to comprehend. It is a spiritual lesson, but it cannot be attained in the dark recesses of a protected monastery.

The mind and eyes of God demand you live in the world, without laws, without illusion, without support beyond the mirrored heart of the infinite.

The Ninth Law is No Laws.

FORGING THE IRON: WORSHIP NO LAWS

Learn: Exist without assessment. Observe without label. Encounter without judgment. Attain silence of the mind and stillness of the heart. The ego does not exist.

Explore:
- What is your most vivid experience of absolute unboundedness and total wild chaos?
- What laws remain to save you when illusions are completely and permanently shattered?
- Where have you invited fatal error through belief that the dark world notices human law?

Live as you will, for you pay with your life.

Reflect: The full circle of the Nine Laws inevitably brings the **Dark Triad Man** back to survival. In absolute preposterous and lawless infinity, what is the purpose of your survival?

Train: Understand the reduction of infinity to singularity, and the infinities that exist inside each singularity. Work to accept and penetrate the paradox of reality.

Task: If society were to collapse, what grand new structure would you build? What stops you now?

BLOOD ON MARBLE

The man fell to the floor as his adversaries plunged bitter steel into his limbs, his abdomen, his groin. Blood drenched his rich robes, glistening in dark rivulets and pooling on the marble floor.

Steel flashed and drops of crimson spattered as the crowd of men continued to stab him. The scrape of metal on bone resounded as the blades hacked, and the gasps and grunts of men engaged in killing echoed through the theater.

He flinched involuntarily as each honed edge drove into him, opening his body and spilling his life out. Eventually the conspirators backed away, knives dripping and horror irrevocably committed.

He had received over a score of wounds.

Yet only one of them was mortal.

They left him there to bleed out. And so the man died slowly, pulling his robe over his face to expire with the remaining private dignity he could muster.

Gaius Julius Caesar lay butchered on the cold marble and those murderous, regicidal senators would soon follow him in death. The Republic itself would pass away, and his nephew Octavian would assume the mantle of Augustus, the revered, the emperor.

Nothing had stopped Caesar from crossing the Rubicon with his army and entering Rome, violating the great law of the Republic and establishing himself as perpetual dictator.

He cast his lot with fate, made his own law, and entered immortality.

This is the true way of the dark world.

Nothing stops men from toppling Caesars with steel and treason, whether in the ancient days of Rome or in the modern age where dictators are put up against a wall after a drumhead court martial and summarily blown to shattered bits of gristle and bone.

Nothing stops men from rising to the state of Caesar with intrigue, alliance and war. There is no prevention, there is no prohibition, and a door unlocked and a door wide open are the same thing.

There is a single thread, infinitely thin, entangled through every story of history where brutal sovereigns rise and noble revolutionaries fight; where sadistic apparatchiks take over a people or a vivid-eyed corporal marches to the role of Leader and oversees the bureaucratic extermination of millions.

That thread is the final, chaotic reality of the dark world.

It is the truth that there is no such thing as law.

Law may cause men to investigate your death, but it will not save you in the moment of truth.

Law may spring forth grand temples and ceremony designed in its honor, but the farthest private room of the king is where real decisions are made, and the truth is that law is simply all for show.

It comes down in the end to human beings, making decisions, and shaping a new world in their image.

Conquerors have risen and marched through the ages. Tyrants have ascended as well; the story is as old as man himself and this process of insurgent, unstoppable Caesars is inherent to our species.

It is only a fool who believes that the door of the global warlord and world conqueror is locked.

Fool, I tell you today that it is not even a doorway, but a roaring highway that does not sleep.

This is the last of The Nine Laws, and it is the deadliest. It gives birth to all others.

There are no laws that hold in the end.

It is all simply the collusion of the capable, the outcome of the winner, and the survival or death of the rest.

Understand this well.

There will be a day when the entire Earth is united under a single bloody standard, and one man walks to his bedchamber as the glorious, glittering lord of the entire human race.

Every day brings it one step closer.

Do you believe he will rule with benevolence?

Do you think benevolence is the currency of rulers?

There is a grave and serious truth that all generals will concur upon, that every councilor to the king fears, and that the most vicious praetorian of the imperial bodyguard cannot deny:

One man, willing to abandon all law, and trade his life for the king... can win.

All kings know this, for it is the spinning card of chaos that enables their own hegemonic dominance over their wealth and power, position and property, as they reap it in harvest from humanity.

All things only take one man.

Never forget this.

Part Two:

The World, Man, and God

The Soldier | Danse Macabre
Hans Holbein the Younger (1497–1543)

Chapter 13

The Dark World

All of this takes place in what is known as the *dark world*.

For many there is great fear and anxiety in response to words that are spoken or written to invoke the image of power. Words that declare ferocity. Words that speak of the dread reality of this dark world and the necessity of blood, steel, incandescent flung iron and detonations of dust and thunder as the voice of deciding finality between individuals and armies, ideologies and civilizations.

Your fear and anxiety are real, but nonetheless irrelevant to the impersonal nature of creation.

Any desire that things be other than they are, is not even perceived by the universe.

Illusions of safety are not rewarded by change in the arcs of planets or the halt of invading armies.

The reality of the dark world is that blood and iron resolve entanglements and sever crises with efficacy and controlled result, just as love and compassion and gentle kindness create connection, calm anguish and open the hearts of others.

You cannot have one without the other.

You will not have pleasure without pain.

You will not experience love without loss.

Do you think one of these realities is more pleasurable to the universe than the other?

There is a difference between appreciation of the nature of the dark world, and glorying in the darkness. Appreciation is not glorification. Acceptance of the darkness is not denial of light, nor is skill with darkness a refusal to enlighten.

Once more I tell you that the pivot of the **Dark Triad Man** is not balance but appropriateness.

What is appropriate is what works.

What works is what complements.

Complementation is where the potential of the dark world is unlocked, and in that complementation is found the impact of fate. It is the willful delivery of finality by conscious, deliberate condensing of information that is created and executed.

Consequence is the alignment of thought, word and deed into a single realm.

Karma is the focus of vision, planning and competence into a single channel.

Reality is the impact of narcissism, Machiavellianism and psychopathy.

Fate is what happens at the singularity of determination, where all things collide.

Fate is the infinite point of outcome. It is where Schrödinger's cat lives or dies, where a quantum particle lands in final state, where life and death, profit or loss, impact or miss ensues.

This is where *makoto*, the sincere truth of the *ninja*, at last becomes final.

The polarities of this final singularity of fate are equally infinite, instantaneous outcomes in opposite directions of stream, much like the polarities of magnets that inexorably repel or attract.

Figure 13.1: The singularity of fate in the dark world

The achievement of success is the detonation of truth, the formation of a new reality. It is where the physicist describes an alternate actuality as diverging, a splitting of strings, the shudder of a virtual particle that explodes from potential and expands a new universe, a bubble of newborn foam that in its expanding boundaries contains a new infinity of uncountable internal divisions of measurement.

The theologian calls it justice, the moment where the will, the plan and the word of God come together and the earth cracks apart, death itself is shattered, universal sin is forgiven and all things are made new and eternally bright.

They are the same thing.

The other side of the spinning coin, tossed by the master into the randomness of chaos, is the jeering failure of collapse. Collapse is what takes place when expanding momentum is not sustained, when escape velocity is not reached, and the inexorable drawback commences into the sucking roar of the plummeting void.

Collapse is the negative, hollow, dead laughter of fate that mocks the unaware and the illusory.

Collapse is the result of redirected word, confused thought, hesitant deed stillborn at the outset.

Collapse is the outcome of dissipation, illusion and friction in the world.

Collapse is the degradation, delusion and destruction of the man.

From collapse, there is no recovery. Only rebirth.

Understand this polarity well.

It is the dark world laid bare, and condensed to the final impact of the Laws.

It is a dark world not because it is cruel and bitterly painful, although it inexorably is.

It is not the lies or deceit, butchery or horror that you encounter which make it dark.

This is vitally important.

It is the shape of creation that makes it dark.

It is a condensing creation. It is a sinking framework, a narrowing path.

It leads inexorably to death through the entropy which is its nature.

Creation is finite and temporary.

Thus it is the sinking, the withdrawing, the colluding, the draining.

It is a dark world not because it is evil, but because it dies.

The **Dark Triad Man** complements the dark world with his thought, his word and his deed.

He focuses the flow of the dark world through the channeling of vision, planning and competence.

He controls the outcome of the dark world by narcissism, Machiavellianism and psychopathy.

He aims impact on behalf of the will of Heaven through the aperture of man.

Thus he is the bold, the active, the purposeful and the powerful.

He is the bright figure, resonating in a spectrum of sacred *makoto*, "sincere truth".

Understand the nature of the dark world.

It exists for, and because, of you.

The dark world is yours. Own it.

Study its nature well.

Understand the principle of gradients.

Learn and absorb the spin of polarities.

Comprehend the opposition of infinity and singularity. Master the application of appropriate complementation.

Together these are the inexhaustible flow of all things.

It is the bellows of the Tao. It is the breathing of God, the blended state of particles. It is the beating pulse of *makoto*. In the very center, born from the blur, it exists.

This is the theory of all things.

Inform, create and execute.

Integrate the broad realms of thought, word and deed into alignment. Focus them into channels of vision, planning and competence.

Grasp the momentum of the dark world through the controls of narcissism, Machiavellianism and psychopathy. Steer fate itself into impact!

That is how the theorist is moved into the living process of the practitioner, the scholar and the master. This is the great Way of which the sages speak, priests chant and scientists explore.

This is the Way of the warrior.

It is the way of all things.

Once more, look upon the grid of the dark world and the rails of The Nine Laws by which you will transit threat, challenge, risk and chaos and find your road of power:

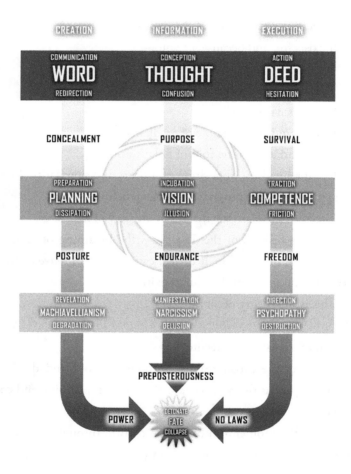

**Figure 13.2: Complete grid of the dark world and
the rails of The Nine Laws**

We have examined the nature of the dark world.

You now understand its inexorably fatal nature.

Soon we will walk you through how the grid descends, how it is shaped and condensed from eternal unbounded information into the realms of thought, word and deed. We will dissect and explain the process by which you, the human being, take those realms and focus them into channels of vision, planning and competence.

But first it is time to uncloak a savage and terrifying figure, and personally introduce you.

He has been waiting for you, out there in the howling darkness.

And now he steps forward to be recognized.

Give welcome to the **Dark Triad Man**.

The Allegorical Escutcheon of Death | Danse Macabre
Hans Holbein the Younger (1497–1543)

Chapter 14

The Dark Triad Man

The **Dark Triad Man** is both an archetype and reality, a sharp constellation of brutally ruthless traits that arise beyond simple focus of the grid and deliver the capacities of perception and insight, perspective and intelligence, wisdom and savagely relentless performance.

This chapter will define the nature of this legendary figure and how he profits from skilled, methodological and principled navigation of the dark world. It will reveal how he steps through its arenas cloaked in the sovereign mantle of command over invincible and inexorable fate.

The dark world regards him as a natural inhabitant, a feature of itself, and permits his passage.

The realms of life and death, creation and destruction are his prerogative. He does not hesitate to harness and employ them, steering the arrival of destiny.

There is often uncertainty and apprehension associated with the concept of the dark triad traits. In particular, the three traits are colloquially assessed by contemporary social culture as dangerous. Clinical professionals view them as atypically ordered or even dysregulated.

Yet to the kings and generals who raise banners and lead national armies across the surface of the dark world, the three traits are appropriate, necessary and valuable aspects of a deadly vassal who can be entrusted with secrets, appointed to office and charged with mission.

When a rebellious castle must be smashed and its insolent baron hurled screaming from the highest tower, the **Dark Triad Man** is the grim and methodical knight who lays siege on behalf of the king.

When a blade must be thrown through the black shadows of midnight into the heart of a malevolent tyrant, it is the silent footfall of the **Dark Triad Man** that passes without echo as steel slams through gristle and bone and silences forever the beating heart of evil.

When the bursting passions of a frenzied empress endanger peace in the land, prosperity of the kingdom and security of fragile alliances, it is the subtle penetration and calming endowment of the **Dark Triad Man** that soothes the wild, frenzied energies of his histrionic sovereign.

He hardens the grid of the Laws into a lever, and with it he moves the dark world in his chosen direction.

He is frightening and extraordinary among men, for he brings vision, planning and competence one grave step further. He goes far beyond the common man and bends focused channels into handles of masterful control.

Those controls are narcissism, Machiavellianism and psychopathy.

The dark triad, the penultimate edges of a weaponized human being.

The **Dark Triad Man** stalks through history, a figure of grave and shadowed power standing behind thrones and astride the horseback of the raiding lord. Names come down to us through human memory, immortal and ringing through the annals of mankind:

"The Great Khan."

"The Scourge of God."

"The Red Eminence."

Centuries later they still provoke study and awe.

What are these traits, and how are they applied? How does one attain them, possess them, use them?

What is their real nature? Are they actually disorders or weirdly innate and vested forms of magic?

They are none of these things, and they are all of them.

Let us tumble and turn them, each after the other.

You will see, and you will learn.

Narcissism is the first trait we examine.

Named for the Greek myth of Narcissus, a beautiful youth who stared, transfixed, at his own gorgeous reflection until he wasted away and died—the trait of narcissism is a familiar label in our age of selfie sticks and repetitively compulsive photos on social media.

The current cultural and political use of "narcissism" can be simplified and translated as "proclaiming how great and wonderful you are—and really believing that you are in fact as good as you claim to be".

That characterization is indeed simplistic. It misses the mark entirely. The broad common masses of uninteresting men and women, accepting the learned helplessness of the dependent class and a mediocre life of minimalist achievement, need their labels as defensive measures to hide from their own obvious, miserable inadequacies.

It preserves and permits their pointless, unfulfilled existence.

The clinical view of narcissism is both broader and more precise, for it considers narcissism as a spectrum that ranges from healthy self-love to derailing pathological disorder, characterized

Figure 14.1: The control of narcissism and its polarities

by grandiosity, hypersensitivity, compulsive arrogance and lack of empathy.

Yet the clinical view is nonetheless limited. For it misses badly in applicability of its assessments to the man who is of uncommon intelligence, spectacular achievement and championship performance. The clinical view was developed to see disorder, not to appreciate true exultant power.

Just as measurements of body mass indicator (BMI) are fine for the average individual yet absurd when used to judge a contest-ready bodybuilder, standard scales of assessment lose their utility when applied to outlying performers.

The narcissism of the **Dark Triad Man** is a very distinct trait, and is not merely grand infatuation with the self or dysregulated mental and emotional processing.

It is the driven, hardened vision of a man who *believes* in his own future achievement with such force, drive and experienced, focused mind that reality itself shimmers and shifts, and accords with his vision the way time and space curve in the presence of mass.

Such powerful force of manifestation is indeed dangerous.

It is dangerous because the polarities of narcissism are extreme in their result.

The positive, expanding, fulfilling pivot of this control is manifestation. Vision becomes real, it has shape and form. Ideas become movements, strangers become followers, employees become worshipers and a lover becomes a wife.

The negative, contracting, devolving pivot of this control is delusion. Vision becomes corrupted, it curdles into the bizarre, and rather than attracting the healthy it swirls with the obsession of the sick. Focus becomes obsession, obsessions become compulsions, and victory is flung away by the centrifugal force of spiraling insanity along with discarded relationships and resources.

The correct path for the control of narcissism is through the reinforcement of achievement.

Thought becomes vision, and takes on grand proportions and glittering presentations that are far beyond the current reality.

Then the **Dark Triad Man** achieves it.

From the infinite information of his life he conceives his singularity of specific thought, and incubates and nurtures and cradles it until his vision is bright and formed and real. He levers control over belief and his vision is made vibrant, finally manifested as an established beacon in the dark world we inhabit.

Remember well this warning: the three realms of thought, word and deed must be forged, and the three channels of vision, planning and competence must be focused. Otherwise the transition of infinite potential through finite man and into the world is not attained. You must have all three legs of the stool.

It is no different, and even more crucial, for all three controls to be leveraged in parallel.

There is less room for error where rubber meets the road, where metal meets the meat, and men collide with each other. In these controls of the grid, errors have fatal and terrible consequence.

It is the same with planning as you harden it with Machiavellian control.

Niccolò Machiavalli (1469–1527) was born in Florence, Italy to an attorney of old family. He rose to position as a diplomat and senior official during a time of warring papal ambitions and tumultuous political intrigue.

Although famous in his native land for his personal correspondence and the sublime examples it presents of the Italian language, Machiavelli is best known throughout the world for his seminal work *The Prince*. Written after a fall from grace and three weeks of disabling torture, *The Prince* was his distillation of advice to the Duke of Urbino.

It achieved notoriety in his lifetime and immortality after his death.

Focused on the principles of effective statecraft for the rulers of principalities, *The Prince* delivered the name of its author into history and ultimately to the label of our next control.

Today's popular culture treats Machiavellanism as mere manipulation, an ugly and evil shade of cunning that delights in weaving tangled webs of complex and hidden motivation.

Once more the crowd is simplistic and helpless, affixing a label of "you cannot win or deal with the Machiavellian" rather than explore and embody the skills that differentiate the statesman from the peasant, the prince who bears personal responsibility for the security of the State from the weak and helpless chattel who labor, rut and die without perception of the larger terrain.

Our clinical profiler has a more explicit perspective.

The profile of a Machiavellian persona is one where emotion is absent, and conventional morality does not drive the communication, conduct or engagement of the subject.

The clinician's view of Machiavellianism is one of primacy of selfishness and the exploitation of others, subsuming even success itself to pleasure taken in the very fact of that expense to others. It is seen as duplicitous, focused on winning, and lacking reasonable regard to the values and boundaries of culture and community.

This model has its uses when the subject is within the bell curve of average distribution.

Where a man is calculating, cunning and manipulative for gain, but has no achievement of grand vision nor delivery of matchless competence in action, it is indeed an asymmetric dysregulation.

In that instance the application of skill does not accord with the actual character of the man.

Gratuitous excess of subtlety and arcane weaving of unnecessary traps to confound allies and adversaries alike is foolish and unnecessary. It is not the Way.

The correct application of Machiavellianism is through the methods of planning. It is masterful control of revelation and the prevention of degradation.

The **Dark Triad Man** embraces total responsibility for the delivery of his vision and his plans. The control of Machiavellianism is not merely "control" in the sense of constriction; it is *a* control, a lever, a minutely adjustable feedback loop of engagement with the dark world in which he works.

The revelation of plans invites their disruption. Revelation is to be controlled, to be parceled, for the failure of plans is held to the account of the manager. Put a man in charge of plans and watch his automatic preservation of their privacy.

Control of revelation is critical for plans to proceed in the depths of the dark world. Adversaries exist there. It is reality we deal

**Figure 14.2: The control of Machiavellianism
and its polarities**

with, not fantasies of peace and justice, and the human beings that surround you are at the most basal level a conglomerate of apex predators.

Human beings are not paragons of virtue and grace. Humans are not righteous, stainless and pure.

They are fallen animals. Deceitful, covetous, resentful and dangerous.

It is not immoral to control the revelation of word. God works in mysterious ways, and the plans of Heaven are never fully disclosed to mortals.

It is dangerous, however, to control.

Too much control and plans degrade into ruin.

Therein is the spinning card of polarity, made clear for your understanding.

Why does too much control over planning lead to breakage and failure?

The answer here is most easily found in the blunt and ruthless world of the financial industry, and specifically in the project management it exercises.

Control in the matter of planning is enforced over a cascade of deliverables, work packages and tasks according to expectations and schedule. It demands clever and capable fine-tuning of tension between resources and requirements, communications and protocols, people and relationships.

This control is the orchestration of a living model, the application of masterful reins to a suite of horses at breakneck speed with a furious goal of arrival in mind.

Too much control, and profitable tension grows stiff. The resiliency of plans become calcified. They begin to crack and fall apart.

Excessive control means resources are hoarded, leading to the starvation and degradation of teams.

Inappropriate control and resentment is fostered, abrading relationships and encouraging abandoned commitments.

Absolute control and rebellion is brewed, infecting and degrading the product and the enterprise.

It is not "balance" that the **Dark Triad Man** seeks, but *appropriateness*.

Appropriateness is determined by identification of necessary utility.

Utility is, itself, the arbiter of your lever of Machiavellian exertion.

Only the useful are employed.

Only appropriate measures are taken.

Only necessary revelations are permitted.

That is the Way that must be accorded with.

Do what is useful.

Do not do what is not.

We now turn to analysis of the final control that is demanded by the dark architect of fate.

The controls of narcissism and Machiavellianism are joined by the most severe and dreadful expression of competence that rears up from the grid of the Laws:

It is psychopathy.

The **Dark Triad Man** is a psychopath.

Psychopathy is the third of the dark triad traits and the least understood by the general public. Use the word "psychopath" and the instantaneous image that arises is that of an incomprehensible, savagely intelligent and remorselessly vicious predator who does not hesitate, does not slow down, and delivers unstoppable hideous destruction.

Well, yes. You are describing a lion in his natural environment.

We all know that lions are evil and criminal animals, do we not? They lurk and scheme and plot, dreaming up calculated sadistic, triggering oppression against peaceful and inoffensive antelopes, then exploding against them with completely unreasonable racist murder that violates the rights of those angelic denizens of safe spaces in the veldt.

Perhaps those gender-normative bullies with masculine shags of hair would even vote for Donald Trump if given the chance.

A silly reduction to absurdity, is it not?

But there is a cold reality underneath the mockery you have just read.

The lion is an apex predator. He is not excessive in his strength, but fearsomely powerful nonetheless. Exactly as he was designed to be. There is no shame or immorality in his dominance.

The lion is a carnivore and kills what he needs to sustain his life and his pride. He is not cruel and sadistic in his harvest, merely explosive in his rush and overwhelming in his attack. There is no murder, no criminal intention in his action.

It is the same with the true psychopath, and most of all with the **Dark Triad Man**.

His competence is unapologetic. There is no shame in matchless competence.

There is no hesitation in his execution of thought, word or deed. Quick is not evil.

Friction is removed through his vision and planning. Great skill is not an immoral quality.

His narcissism and Machiavellianism are controlled with utterly fearless direction.

Yes, there is fear on the part of those who perceive his power.

The weak are typically afraid, and cling to their fear.

It is easier to be afraid than to be strong.

The constant shiver deployed by the fearful is an internal method of survival. They rely upon timidity to remain alive, rather than becoming the fully validated and completed predator they are capable of being. For one reason or another they have decided to hobble, cripple and abandon their capacities.

They are no less human than you or I.

They are simply weakly manifested.

Do not be weak. You are not an antelope.

In the dark world, it is not rewarded.

There is no moral virtue signal that will issue from your eviscerated belly.

You will not attain dignity through the fact of your own slaughter.

We will speak more of outcomes and challenges in the dark world soon. We will examine them coldly and you will understand how to survive and overcome them.

Prepare for it now by abandoning your illusions of safety.

Safety does not exist.

The psychopath knows it.

The clinical description of the psychopath is one that confers lack of boundaries, absent remorse, deactivated empathy, ease of boldness and uninhibited engagement. Brain differences are noted, and most strikingly it presents that the psychopath has ready access to the switch which governs empathy. Empathy is a decision for the psychopath and not the common involuntary reaction experienced by the average man and known as "emotional contagion" in the lexicon of the clinician.

The public notoriety and misapprehension of psychopathy also takes place to a degree among clinicians themselves. In the clinical sphere there is even disparagement between them, criticism leveled against their own use of various forms of label for the trait:

> *Few psychological concepts evoke simultaneously as much fascination and misunderstanding as psychopathic personality, or psychopathy. Typically, individuals with psychopathy are misconceived as fundamentally different from the rest of humanity and as inalterably dangerous.*
>
> *Given these contrasting depictions, it is scant wonder that some experts have concluded that the concept of psychopathy, as commonly understood, is disturbingly problematic: a "mythical entity" and "a moral judgment masquerading as a clinical diagnosis". (Blackburn, 1988, p. 511)*[5]

What, then, is the psychopathy that the **Dark Triad Man** embodies and how is it applied?

What are its characteristics, and can the shape of its delivery be assessed?

The answers lie within the tumble and turn of polarities of this control.

Recall that psychopathy is the control for execution. It is the ultimate delivery of competence, with proven traction and seamless absence of hesitation.

Consider well that there is a vast difference between being fast and being *quick*.

"Fast" is a comparative measurement, a contrast of time elapsed between a beginning and an end. "He is fast," they say, "and he does not waste time."

A strong attribute, certainly. It implies skill, does it not?

Now let us examine the psychopath.

"He is quick," they say, "and he does not hesitate."

There is a more defined impression in the latter statement.

The former is strong. The latter is competent.

Fast is an increase in speed. *Quick* is the removal of interval between intake and output.

Quick beats fast. Where there is no space between perception and reaction, the organism is quick in response, quick to succeed, quick to survive. With no space of interval, traction is already instantaneous.

The *ninja* teach infinite quickness of movement that arises from severance of tension, rather than development of force. It is the source of their matchless speed and power.

The psychopath is quick because he executes with determination and direction.

Direction is the *yang*, the broad, the male aspect of psychopathy. Direction instills competence in motion and momentum. It is the root of accuracy and the skill of delivery.

Absent controlling direction, what happens when the momentum of plans collides with reality?

Figure 14.3: Control of psychopathy and its polarities

What are the results when incompetence is in control and many forces are directed to one place?

Destruction is the *yin*, the narrow, the female aspect of psychopathy. Destruction is the result of failed psychopathy, whether the defeat and annihilation of the army and the king or the complete loss of leveraged capital and the plunging of the trader into horrific, unrecoverable debt.

Psychopathy is a necessary control in the dark world.

Predators are psychopaths.

They do not aimlessly graze, but target, pursue and overcome. They do not engage in useless shame, remorse or wringing of paws at their own nature.

Apex predators are peerlessly psychopathic. They do not yield prey to greater animals, or scavenge their putrid leavings. They observe, they orient, they decide and they act.

They do not hesitate, they do not drag feet, and they directly control.

You are a human being. You are the apex predator of the dark world. Men kill lions for sport. Do not abandon your birthright or your manhood.

There is a grim word for an incompetent man, out there in the billowing shadows.

It is "prey". Do not be prey.

You will not survive it.

Master the controls of fate.

Figure 14.4: The controls arrayed as a jackpot

They detonate upon your delivery in the dark world.

Let us examine that place, and learn its features and terrain.

You must be the most dread inhabitant it possesses.

You must begin this process of personal weaponization in the correct place.

You must gather and forge thought, word and deed into one.

The Husbandman | Danse Macabre
Hans Holbein the Younger (1497–1543)

Chapter 15

Gather and Forge the Three

To forge is to heat, hammer, combine and shape.

A forge is a crucible of iron, of plans, of men.

Thought, word and deed must be forged. A unified shape must result. These three realms arise from the infinity of God, assume shape through the creation of the universe and are resolved into fate by the actions of man. Your process comprehension of funneled descent provides you with the very first method of capitalizing on the spinning polarities of gradients as they interact and entangle, tumble and turn.

The three realms of thought, word and deed are inseparable and yet independent from each other.

You must understand this well.

Just as the spinning indicators on the jackpot machine cannot be separated one from another—all three start and stop at the same time—they are also proud in their unique alignment, none dependent upon the other. The state of one does not determine the state of any other, yet together by their arrayed positions they collectively determine the flow of wealth and success, power and outcomes, earnings and fate.

We will apply another gradient here, one that moves vertically from top to bottom on the grid of the Laws that is being revealed to you.

That gradient is the process of focus, a condensing of energy.

As the sincerity and authenticity of truth moves down through the grid, it condenses. Information becomes thought. Creation becomes word. Execution becomes deed.

Man becomes real, and his actions determine fate.

Each condensation contains within it a pivot point of outcome. Action or hesitation, conception or confusion, communication or redirection.

Those pivot points are where our polarities spin, the central pin in the slot machine. The randomness of things, the chaos that is inherent and unavoidable in any system, grins with immortal delight within it. You cannot remove it, only befriend it and exult in it.

Let us examine how this works. We will continue with our example of the slot machine, and the analogy of our jackpot. Once that lever is pulled and the tumble and turn has commenced, there is no turning back—only anticipation, fear, excitement, dread, and waiting for the inevitability of fate.

How does this work in practice?

What does the **Dark Triad Man** do to forge his thought, word and deed into a fearsome spear of human achievement? How is the unstoppable, sorcerous ferocity of the *ninja* developed through deep and sagacious comprehension of these realms?

What sort of predictability can be found from the dizzying example of the slot machine of fate?

Awareness, estimation and application are the Way.

The first layer of the grid of the dark world is exposed, and the basis of it is revealed.

Consider well this basis of our grid:

Figure 15.1: The realms arrayed as a jackpot

At the very top is the infinity of pure information.

Information condenses, assumes shape and form. It is by formation of an idea that the conception of thought takes place. It pivots there, contemplating, and in the end delivering either true concept or scatters into confusion.

Creation descends towards communication. What good is a universe that no one knows about? Consciousness reaches out, expresses resonant intention, and communication of word takes place. It spins there, either reaching understanding, or redirects and misses.

Execution solidifies through action. Practice must be the outcome of theory or there is no earning of value. As action takes place, outcomes of probability dance, until deed is completed or dies in hesitation. Fate is either driven, or shudders and falls without guidance.

This is how the realms work.

It is where your self-examination begins.

Forging the three secrets into one is the Way that our grid operates.

The crash of one realm into the negative is terrible for all three. It is the removal of one leg of a three-legged stool, which cannot stand on merely two. It topples, and brings down empires with it.

Consider this well:

When thought is confused, is not man vulnerable to redirection? Does he not hesitate to act?

Where words are redirected, are not minds confused? Does not fate hesitate in delivery?

While hesitation is habitual practice, is not confused redirection the continuous outcome?

The forging of the realms is the process by which you master alignment to and accordance with the momentum of fate. When thought, word and deed are aligned and forged into a single realm, there is no gap between the image of God and the manifestation of the man.

Learn this well. It is the essence of the Way.

Discord, dissonance, conflict, echo, gaps and intervals will inevitably infect your integration of thought, word and deed. That is the nature of the dark world, for it is entropic in nature. Therefore, all things inevitably degrade and die.

Your task is to monitor, to work, to expend effort and life to manage and master the integration of thought, word and deed. It requires active measures.

When you have forged the three realms into integrated alignment, you have embodied the highest reason for the human being: the mind of God, the plan of the universe, and the delivery of fate.

That is why you have been placed here within the reality of the dark world.

Whether you accord with theological or scientific assessment of the nature of the universe, the reality of sincere truth is inescapable:

You are here. You have been provided with a life so that fate has power to deliver through you. This delivery of fate is the prerogative of the human being.

Absorb this deeply. Open yourself to sincere truth.

Dogs are not the rulers of the wide world. Deer do not raise glittering towers to the sky. Lions have no concept of rockets of fire lancing into space, or the splicing of the genome of life itself.

Human beings understand life and death and infinity.

It is why we are here. Forge thought, word and deed and fulfill your existence.

When you have aligned them and integrated them, then what? How do you condense further down the grid? How do you seize the momentum of fate, once the realms are forged?

It is achieved when you focus the three.

Focus puts the rudder of fate into your hands.

And steers you through the channels of the living world.

The Physician | Danse Macabre
Hans Holbein the Younger (1497–1543)

Chapter 16

Apply and Focus the Three

The next stage is the application of thought, word and deed with conscious focus. Your focused exertion is more than merely trying hard, or putting in effort. It is deliberate and exacting, a critical and irreplaceable process.

It is how the road of power is driven upon.

This driving is done through focus.

I say "through" focus instead of "by" focus for an important reason. Just as with gradients, focus is a crucial concept to practice, study and master.

Focus is a throughput mechanism.

Focus is attained through the deployment of aperture.

Apertures are the Way.

Figure 16.1: Aperture, as in the lens of a camera

A mistake often made by those who preach focus is to start with the end result.

"Concentrate to attain focus!" they urge, as if merely thinking harder was the basis of focus.

"Focus by paying attention to what matters!" they announce, as if their audience was composed of idiots who cannot tell the difference between life and death.

They are obsessed with the outcome, and cannot teach the process.

It is why casual warriors die on the field, and aimless traders are raped in the market.

You are not an idiot, and your life—until you reach your inevitable death—is the grave and serious purpose of this book and I will not waste platitudes on you.

Concentration is the *result* of focus, not the means to it.

Focus is a tightening, a narrowing. It is the spiraling concentric closing of an aperture.

This narrowing of the passage increases force of the flow.

A hose works by apertures. As you tighten your grip, the continuous stream of water must rush through a smaller passage, and your compression of the aperture results in greater spout and reach.

A microscope works by apertures. As you zoom into smaller and smaller scales, your vision becomes tunneled into ever-diminishing frames, and your narrowed perception grows deeper and deeper.

Decisions work by apertures. As evidence is sifted and weighed, risks and opportunities pivoted, considerations are subordinated in a tightening process of determining truth and path.

The three realms of thought, word and deed must be subjected to the focus of an aperture in order to deliberately tighten your grasp of fate and condense it from a container to a conveyance.

You must transform the Way into a vehicle. This is how destiny is reached!

Focus is how the forged tool of the three realms of thought, word and deed is wielded.

"But what is the aperture?" you ask.

It is a sacred aperture, a living one, formed in the very image of God.

That living aperture is you.

Your ability to become an aperture and provide focus which increases the flow and reach of reality is integral to the process that is laid out in the grid of the Laws.

Our first lesson on the next layer is vision. Thought must become vision.

Vision is the end state of predetermined fate.

The development of your vision is through narrowing the aperture of the human being. This is not mere daydreaming, or fantasizing of power and wealth, a life of unlimited sexual profligacy and ceaseless adventures of glory.

Those are the habits of the child and the fool.

Wealth and power, sexual conquest, adventure and fame, empires and immortal name are merely rewards on the other side of effort and advancement, value cultivation and risk, achievement and domination and conquest.

The process of establishing those rewards—in truth, any outcomes—lies through conception in the mind of a fully-formed future state. It must be clear, for like the microscope you must focus precisely at great depth to establish precision of mental clarity.

The realm must flow through a human aperture and become a channel.

What is channeled, can be harnessed.

Figure 16.2: The channel of vision and its polarities

Vision is the first channel to focus.

Vision is channeled through incubation.

Incubation is what happens after conception.

Your living thought is shaped. It develops, it grows. It is sheltered, it is protected. It is nourished. It is defined, developed, and nurtured.

This is the way that thought is channeled into vision.

You must produce vision through refinement, care and cultivation.

"I want to be rich" is not vision. That is just desire, the confused abortion of an idea.

"I want to be worth ten million dollars" is not vision. That is incomplete conception, a malformed and unviable lump.

"I will have ten million dollars in liquid assets distributed among cash, equities and bonds and no debt." That is a sickly infant, stillborn upon delivery.

You cannot channel thought into a static state of frozen vision.

Your vision must be a *living* vision, for as an aperture in the image of God you are focusing the flow of infinity itself and a static vision is dead on arrival.

"I have ten million dollars in liquid assets distributed among cash, equities and bonds, replenished continually through dividends and reinvested capital gains, propagated through constant acquisition of additional assets without risk to my existing capital, and employed to the purpose of financing the achievement of my lifestyle of disciplined health, global travel, fulfilled experience and consumption of rare joys."

That is a vision.

It is living. It is ongoing, it has momentum, it has immediacy, and it has reason.

You have become the aperture, the focuser, the building of a channel for thought and you have developed and cultivated a vision to nurture, cradle, protect and grow.

It is alive, and it is an expression of you.

Yet as you focus vision, you bring into being the alternate side of risk.

That risk is illusion.

If your thought is not clear and your scales of measurement are not accurate, you will not perceive information correctly and your vision will be an illusion.

If your estimation is unrealistic and your proportions are thoughtless, your vision will not have sustainable shape and the viability of realization will be empty.

See clearly. Do not fantasize or daydream. Calm and serious consideration is where fertility of thought meets the seed of vision, and clarity is the womb-water of your outcomes.

Be clear with your vision. Measure twice, cut once. See the shape clearly before measuring.

Know truly before you speak, for the second channel of focus is word.

Your word must mean something.

It must resonate into the future.

Your word is your vowed intention.

To have value it must drive shape into momentum.

The realm of word becomes the channel of planning.

It is planning that brings resonance to your vision and makes real the lines of manifestation.

Vision is what you see in the future. Planning is how you map your road to it.

Without plans to achieve your vision, it will not manifest.

Once more we return to the pivot point of light and dark, the gradient of fate and failure, spinning on the axis of your personal outcomes.

Planning is delivered through preparation.

Preparation for success, preparation for failure.

Preparation of equipment, preparation for surprise.

Preparation for plenty, preparation for loss.

Without preparation, planning is mere silly playing without true intention.

The negative outcome of preparation is dissipation.

Planning dissipates without consistency and preparation. With each constriction of focus in the realm of word, plans either prepare for manifestation or wither and die.

Understand this well. Do you not see that planning must be continuous?

Turn to analogy of the sacred to comprehend the infinite resonance of this sincere truth.

Does God not have vision for the world, and is there not a sacred plan for creation?

Tumble and turn with the alternate perspective.

Figure 16.3: The channel of planning and its polarities

Across infinite multiverses of quantum probability, through entanglement of information and alignment of matter, does not the song remain the same?

Planning is the second channel of focus.

With vision and planning, the third channel is where traction takes place.

Through focus, deed becomes competence.

Competence is the third channel.

A man may conceive of great thought, incubate it into grand vision, prepare concrete plans—and still fail with utter, miserable and catastrophic collapse that brings down not only his life and loved ones, but his nation and culture and civilization.

If he is an incompetent fool, disaster waits with a silent smirk. It opens hard and terrible jaws to eviscerate and gobble him alive the moment that his incompetence results in stumble.

It is useless to sigh and wish that things were different. The dark world is what it is. Competence is rewarded, and the incompetent are feasted upon without pity.

As you focus your deeds into competence, your outcomes will pivot on the axis of traction and friction. They are similar, for they

Figure 16.4: The channel of competence and its polarities

exist on the same gradient of competence, but they represent the polar binaries of outcome.

Traction is friction that permits acceleration.

Friction is traction that kills momentum.

Consider this well, and comprehend carefully this important and subtle aspect of your focus.

The nature of competence is in its handling of contact.

It is contact that produces traction and friction. Indeed, traction is the result of friction, and friction is what takes place when traction is applied.

What a paradox! Which comes first, traction or friction? Which gives birth to the other? How do you separate the two? How do you have one without the other?

These are the questions of fools who are bled dry and discarded in the dark world.

The question is whether contact will allow acceleration of momentum or inexorably kill the energy of it. It is through judgement of the probable outcomes of contact that competence is exhibited.

You are a self-aware mind and living heart, taking deliberate action in the world.

If you are a clandestine officer, you make contact with your agent and accelerate his treason through the traction of your bribe.

Figure 16.5: The channels arrayed as a jackpot

Thereby the visions of your nation and the plans of your government are driven further into reality by the competence of your deed.

Incompetent handling of your agent produces friction that puts the entire basis of your engagement at risk, and potentiates exposure, arrest and death.

If you are a spouse, you make contact with the heart of your partner and accelerate your relationship through the traction of trust. Thereby the vision of your marriage and the planning of your future is cemented into bonds by the competence of your deed.

Incompetent relations with your partner generates friction which lessens trust. Loss of trust potentiates estrangement, separation and divorce.

If you avoid contact, seeking to depart from the risk of friction, you abandon the possibility of traction and you will fail and die anyway.

Embrace the frightening demand of competence. Engage fully.

That is how the channels of the grid are focused.

The forging of thought, word and deed through channels of vision, planning and competence deliver the three secrets into a shaped form that you can heft, wield and deploy as a tool.

Tools require skill, and victory requires commitment.

It also requires grasping the source of all things at the heart.

We will now tear off the cover and reveal the birth layer of the sacred grid, the eternal and endless fountain of this source.

And you will grasp the ultimate essential essence.

We now hurl you at the infinite source of the universe itself.

Prepare yourself for the drop.

The Last Judgment | Danse Macabre
Hans Holbein the Younger (1497–1543)

Chapter 17

Eternal Information

Mastery of the dark world depends upon a simple but crucial lesson.

The basal teaching your mind must grasp and absorb is the concept of gradients.

Gradients are not complicated but they are integral to understanding how the Laws are shaped, how they interact, and how the grid of the dark world performs in application.

Indeed, the entire universe itself can only be experienced as a seamless blend of entangled gradients. Gradients of material state, gradients of momentum and acceleration, gradients of truth and falsehood, gradients of light and dark.

How important this is! For even love and hate exist along a gradient, endlessly blending.

What exactly is a gradient?

Let us picture a spectrum (which is a form of gradient) ranging from the purest white to the utter blackness of the void.

Figure 17.1: Simple gradient

Gradients are a powerful concept that we often employ as we walk you through the array and structure of The Nine Laws and how they operate within the grid of the dark world.

We now zoom into the very essence of it to build your understanding.

Let us dissect this gradient more carefully, for there are deep lessons with it that shape the penetrating perceptions of the **Dark Triad Man** and equip him with dependable vantage points to build his extraordinarily insightful perspective.

The gradient in Figure 17.1 displays the transition of light and dark. At the very ends we can see pure white, and also pure black. This is self-evident, is it not?

The mind easily accepts the concept of purity at the twin ends of the gradient. There is a starting point of absolute value, and a complementary and opposite ending point of absolute value.

White and black.

Good and evil.

One and zero.

Life and death.

Truth and falsehood.

These points of absolute value are called "singularities". We have spoken together about singularities. Singularities are another important and very characteristic aspect of our grid for the Laws.

But for now let us continue to analyze our simple gradient. Consider that there is an infinitely divisible spread of gray between those two binary points of reality, between white and black.

The mind understands more than just the idea of absolute end points. The mind also understands that infinite shades of gray spread between those two absolutes.

The binary singularities of white and black, *ying* and *yang*, truly exist—but their complementation and blending is inseparable along the gradient itself.

A deep feature of the **Dark Triad Man** is his strong ability to visualize. The practice of visualization is key to your work in this book, and our exploratory steps through gradients is a crucial training method for your brain—a process of teaching it to understand absolutes, understand infinite shades between absolutes, and above all, how they interact.

My purpose here is to teach you not merely to visualize concepts, but to use them.

It is time to take our visualization a step further and illustrate the concept of pivots.

Generate the vision of a card in your mind.

Take our absolutes of white and black, and use them to color the opposite sides of this card.

For a moment here, pause reading. Stop to picture this card of black and white in your mind.

Good? Now spin it until it is a blur.

Spin it at infinite speed.

When that card blurs in its infinitely rapid pivot, your eyes eventually cannot perceive the motion: only a single color, harmonized by those infinitely spun polarities. It will only see the blur of grey. The exact shade of gray presented, what results from the process of pivot...

...is precisely and perfectly the central absolute between the purity of the polar colors.

This is how pivots work, and how accuracy of targeting is found from the tumble and turn of truth and lies, from contrasting the hollow and the real.

One shade emerges, the central and infinitely immeasurable point where impact has the most power.

That is the spot at which you aim. It is the doorway of fate.

Hold this in your mind. Continue to return to and absorb this lesson. It will arise again and again as you move through roads of application and experience of the Laws.

Now we turn to the highest realm of our immortal grid.

We turn to the infinite, inexhaustible source from which all things flow.

Some call it the Tao; others speak of God or the quantum foam. The unknowable, the eternal mystery that we cannot grasp but yet *know* is present behind all things; full and limitless and endlessly outside time and space. It flows to us without let or cease, a living stream.

This is the infinity of information.

Information is an eternal thing. Scientists have long committed to the principle that information cannot be destroyed. Even within the crushing, reality-shredding depth of a hyper-massive black hole, the most powerful physical force in the universe, information is not destroyed.

The infinity and continuity of information is well understood.

Information is the source, and transcends all states.

It transcends everything.

It is greater than the universe itself.

Information is the nature of God that exists before time and space, the reality which is infinite and true and sincere, the basis of all things swirling in the blissful and insane paradox of ever-divisible measurements.

No matter how finely you cut, you may cut finer still.

No matter how minutely you measure, narrower measurements exist.

What is halved can be halved again, and again and again to infinite levels.

Thus within the constraints of the finite, infinity dwells forever.

This inexhaustible depth does not require the action of your measurement to exist.

The true state of the particle is present before the existence of the physicist.

That state is already there and timeless from the source of the One.

His observation is only an illusion.

Understanding eternal, infinite information as the source is crucial.

It sets the stage for the first realm we traveled to.

What is the first transformation that occurs on the gradient of information?

What separates mere infinite, endless data from the experience of God?

The answer is consciousness. It is why God is perceived as a being, and we as a derived image.

Thought.

Thought is the first realm.

Thought is the beginning of focus. Remember that word, focus.

Thought represents the distillation of information and commences the utility of the mind. The process of focus moves along a gradient as well, just as the aperture of a camera smoothly tightens with seamless, infinitely divisible measurements.

By thought, the spectrum of infinite consciousness begins to possess shape, and therefore utility.

Thought is the first of the three secrets you must master.

I have taught you what.

Figure 17.2: The realm of thought and its polarities

Now you realize why.

Thought is the mind of God.

Information takes on consciousness through the process of conception. Conception is a subtle word with profound meaning you must consider deeply. Conception is the moment where possibility is born: life or death. Conception is the formation of shaped information: ideas. These are the positive, light, expanding aspects of this realm.

Confusion delivers the negative, dark, condensing aspects of it. Confusion is the disorder of information, the jumbling of data, the diffusion of intelligence into incoherence.

In the tumble and turn of conception and confusion, and via their infinitely rapid spin of potentiality, we have the living process which arises from consciousness: thought.

Think on this well. For we move now to the next realm within the grid of the Laws.

Creation. The universe exists, and we are in it.

Creation has an immense quality.

You must seize it, and ride it.

That quality is momentum.

The Expulsion | Danse Macabre
Hans Holbein the Younger (1497–1543)

Chapter 18

Momentous Creation

The second realm that descends from the infinite is creation.

Creation is integral to your understanding the grid of reality, both as a noun (creation as a finite object) and a verb (creation as an action). In essence there is no separation.

This is a little-known truth: Creation is communication, which is also both a finite object and a verb. And this is good, and rightful, for the existence of a thing is always finite yet never static.

Voice begins, resonates with momentous vibrancy, and concludes.

Just as our universe itself has a beginning and an end, all things within it are subject to the entropic nature of the container. There is nothing in the universe that does not have momentum towards death. This is an inescapable truth of the dark world.

It is not a bad thing.

You do not need to mourn the death of the universe.

Bring your mind and heart to understand its nature.

Between the singularities of birth and death there is always momentum.

That momentum is the will of God, and is the intention of consciousness given voice.

It is useless to quibble over the semantics of a Judeo-Christian concept of Heavenly Father, the sterile, unfathomable simulation theory of the physicist, or any other pantheons of theology that may be contrasted with this understanding.

Once more I tell you that the Laws and the grid in which they operate are independent from the imaginations and dogmas of priests and theorists.

All are subject to the same truth:

Shaped information requires <u>consciousness</u>.

A shaped universe requires <u>intention</u>.

Creation requires word.

Our universe exists, for we are within it and part of it. There can be little argument there; even those who advocate the most extreme proposition of simulation theory ("everything is just a computer program, nothing is real") cannot deny that *within* this universe, life and death are real things.

This true, actual, manifested quality of creation is inherent to our existence, whether one proclaims a ridiculously simplistic tribal theology or the most esoteric explanation for the nature of matter that quantum physics can offer.

Both arise from the same inescapable truth: there was a point before which the universe did *not* exist, and therefore the fact of conception itself is for granted.

Creation is unmistakably finite; it has boundaries of before-and-after.

It has a beginning and an end and it has momentum from one end to the other. The polarity of these defining moments—the pure white and black of our gradient—gives rise to the gray area of subjectivity and relativity, whether from the delusional, fallen perspective

Figure 18.1: The realm of word and its polarities

of the fool or the boundless insight of Einstein's theorems which capture the mathematical essence of the universe.

Word is the essence of creation.

Word is the expression of consciousness.

Word is the distillation of intention.

It commences the living, deliberate shaping of creation.

Word is the second secret you must master.

Creation takes on shape through the process of communication. Communication is a vibrant, powerful, thrumming live wire of consciousness that transforms possibilities into probabilities, shapes the nature of existence and gives voice to the intention of the mind.

In the beginning was the Word.[6]

Communication is the bright, the *yang*, the pure white absolute of our gradient.

Communication is the process by which information is shared within the universe, from one consciousness to another.

Redirection is the dark, the *yin*, the pure black absolute of our gradient.

Redirection is disturbed information, disrupted communication, failed connection.

In the tumble and turn of communication and redirection, through their brilliantly pivoting card of connection and disconnection, the vital exchange of information that is conversation takes place.

It is the dialogue of consciousness, the very purpose of Creation itself.

I will turn here to our Judeo-Christian priest, and say that in their framework of theology it is clear that the purpose of Man is to worship God... the mutual communication of intention and thought in prayer and love. It is the ceaseless, swelling choir of angels that forms the resonance of Heaven.

Our clinical and emotionless scientist will observe that the vibrating potentiality of the quantum foam along theoretical strings is, in essence, the continuous and harmonious chord of infinite multiverses in song. And the entanglement of particles is instantaneous, constant communication.

Understand this well.

For word has a beginning, and it has an ending.

Fate is that ending. And fate is remorseless, inevitable, and inescapable.

Rise with dignity, my brother.

We now stand and walk to execution.

The Consequences of the Fall | Danse Macabre
Hans Holbein the Younger (1497–1543)

Chapter 19

Willful Execution

The third realm of our grid for The Nine Laws is what takes place *within* the universe.

It is execution.

Without execution there is no manifestation of intention, there is no carrying out of the will of God, there is no possibility of manifested destiny or even the fate of the universe, whether in extinguishing heat death or a big crunch of all matter collapsed to a singularity.

The *ninja* speak of a principle that they call *makoto* or "sincere truth". The trader in the merciless markets of the world speaks of earnings... that which is indisputable and real.

What is sincere truth? How can truth be unerringly known by the fallible mind of man? How does one perceive sincere truth? How can *makoto* be put into use as earnings by the **Dark Triad Man**?

The answer lies within the correct approach to this sacred principle.

The correct approach is to understand that sincere truth exists.

Outcomes happen. Results are delivered. Impacts ensue. Death occurs. Decisions are made.

Once the potential has become actual, fate has been made real.

Commitment has been detonated, and the sincere truth of reality is evidenced in the colliding outcomes of existence. Men die, empires fall, plans are achieved, states are changed, matter is transformed into energy, earnings are met or not.

Fate takes place in the singularity of execution.

Execution transforms potentiality and probability into a determinative state.

This process is most easily illustrated by murdering a magical cat.

An Austrian physicist named Erwin Schrödinger (1887–1961) created a thought experiment to illustrate the superposition of quantum states and the preposterous but inescapable results when those quantum states are extended to the world of reality.

His paradox also demonstrates, for our purposes of teaching you to understand the pivot of fate, the impact of your execution upon reality at even the most infinitely tiny level:

> A cat is penned up in a steel chamber, along with the
> following device (which must be secured against direct
> interference by the cat): in a Geiger counter, there is a
> tiny bit of radioactive substance, so small, that perhaps
> in the course of the hour one of the atoms decays, but
> also, with equal probability, perhaps none; if it happens,
> the counter tube discharges and through a relay releases a
> hammer that shatters a small flask of hydrocyanic acid.
> If one has left this entire system to itself for an hour, one
> would say that the cat still lives if meanwhile no atom
> has decayed. The psi-function of the entire system would
> express this by having in it the living and dead cat (pardon
> the expression) mixed or smeared out in equal parts.

It is typical of these cases that an indeterminacy originally restricted to the atomic domain becomes transformed into macroscopic indeterminacy, which can then be resolved by direct observation. That prevents us from so naively accepting as valid a blurred model for representing reality.[7]

Figure 19.1: The realm of deed and its polarities

It is the action of observation that determines the fate of the cat. It is the deed of taking notice that executes terminal delivery of that fate.

Deed is the third of the three secrets, and the means to achieving the sincere truth of *makoto*.

Deed takes on shape through the process of exertion and outcome. It is the realm of contact, of traction, of delivery of finality for reality.

Where thought is the journey and word is the fuel, deed is the vehicle itself that delivers the sacred occupants of the universe with momentum into thundering arrival at the karmic permanence of fate.

The reality that is present, here today, right now—is the only thing that could have ever been. For Fate itself is only known retroactively. This is a very important principle.

All that exists is the result of achieved fate.

Fate is *makoto*, sincere truth.

Deed is what moves this *makoto* from idea and intention into reality.

Deed is spun through polarities of action and hesitation.

Action is the living, growing, expanding polarity that accords with the positive, successful realm of deed. Bold action is beloved by the universe, for it accords with its very own nature.

Hesitation is the dying, shrinking, contracting polarity that descends from the negative, failing realm of deed. Success, power, wealth, love, joy, fulfillment and destiny do not smile upon stuttering hesitation of deed. The universe punishes hesitation with equal fervor just as it rewards action.

Our priest here would call out the difference between righteous deeds and the grave mortality of sin.

Those are labels for the same practical lines of achievement in the dark world.

The physicist would say that our slain cat still lives on within an alternate universe.

But in this one, the deed is done.

Understand the secrets of the three realms.

These realms of thought, word and deed form the esoteric base of the most formidable Way of the weaponized human being.

Dissecting these secrets according to our modern process cuts open the heart of reality and exposes the initial framework underlying the grid of The Nine Laws.

But what does this knowledge give us? How can we hang, with certainty, our gripping hands upon the rungs of this grid and unlock the momentum of destiny?

Your key to the lock of fate is built by your forging and focus of the three, in your understanding of the Laws, and your full comprehension and acceptance of the dark world in its entirety.

Yet even the **Dark Triad Man** is not immune to error.

We have one final ingredient that spans time and space, and lurks grinning as the adversary of plans, the stalker of outcomes, and the great deluder of order.

It is a capricious serpent known by a legion of names from time immemorial.

Let us now become introduced.

It is waiting, laughing.

We will laugh back.

The Gamesters | Danse Macabre
Hans Holbein the Younger (1497–1543)

Chapter 20

Chaos, Derailment and Death

There is an inescapable ingredient in the flow of the dark world that runs through it as a wild and unpredictable strain. It is madness, and it drives chaos, derailment and death.

That ingredient is the random.

It is the line of fracture in the bones of reality, the swirl of insanity in the existence of reason.

The element of randomness is ever-present in the dark world. It is your responsibility to absorb this, acknowledge it, incorporate it and adapt to it. In particular, the **Dark Triad Man** has a terrible responsibility to fully embody it as a means to surmount it.

We will review that embodied surmounting at the end of this chapter.

Just as the **Dark Triad Man** is a feature of, and not an intruder within, the dark world—he also embodies the nature of chaos and understands appropriate accord with that aspect of existence.

The basal nature of chaos in the dark world is irreplaceable: it tests the validity of fate's direction. It is tempting by the devil, the spooky entanglement of particles, the shrug and smile of the enlightened sage when asked why things did not seamlessly accord in perfect harmony at all levels.

Why is the universe as it is? What is the purpose of the random, and does God—as Einstein bitterly denied—in fact play dice with the universe? Is the randomness of probability and reality controllable, or is there simply no point to anything?

This is a nihilistic question that is often asked.

If things cannot be controlled, if the random cannot be eliminated, what is the point? If the most accurate vision, the most brilliant planning, and the most competent executor cannot guarantee success, who can do other than despair?

Is this not the argument of Satan and the puzzlement of the physicist?

The answer lies in understanding radically important points and brings us back to the underlying, forbidding reality of the dark world. Randomness exists for great and sacred reason.

Randomness is not a bug, but a feature of the operating system. It was designed into things deliberately as a basal and integral layer.

The simplest way to explain this perspective is to once more play off the contrast of theology and science, of apparently disparate approaches. Spinning those perspectives is the means to arrival at the reality underneath.

From a theological perspective, consider that the very nature of man himself introduces a fatal tumble of randomness that impacts the plans of Heaven. Free will, the prerogative of human beings with which God does not interfere, introduces the chaos of uncertain outcome into the greater plan and brings something absolutely integral and fascinating to the unfolding story:

That thing is interest.

The existence of free will, the endless struggle for the souls of men, brings with it the interest and attention of all things. The outcome is not clear, for it is indeed up for individual decision—infinitely unique to each mind and heart. The decision of a man for good or evil, for sin or worship, is his prerogative alone. And even God and the devil do not preordain the outcome.

It is in this struggle between the planned and the random that infinite polarities take interest in order to enumerate the saved and condemned, to refine creation into a singularity of decision.

From the perspective of the scientist, the random is the underlying feature that drives the heart of the quantum foam. It is indeterminable, it is unmeasurable, it is unknowable… until determination takes place, until observation ensues, and state becomes manifest.

It is the interest of the observer that drives the process of observation, in order to select information and thereby scale the shape of things. It is interest that causes intelligence to ask questions and derive answers. The random provokes curiosity and identification results in learning, the birth of new information. It is the growth of truth.

Randomness is thus inherent. It is an essential feature of sincere truth and does not violate it.

Do not fear the random, but accept it as what makes the universe interesting.

Do not despise the presence of chaos, but respect it as the origin of potentialities.

Do not avoid chance, but honor it as an appetite that cannot be sated.

Chaos is the laughter of the universe.

To deny chaos is to become derailed.

To resist laughter is to fail.

Random failure is a well-known component of any system, and forms the basis for the subtle embodiment of the **Dark Triad Man** as an agent of chaos.

Random failure *will* take place. Thus the **Dark Triad Man** knows that interruption of any system is possible, scaling of any castle may be effected, penetration of any heart can be achieved.

This works both outwards and inwards.

The building of chaos and randomness into the plans of men is a fundamental part of making those plans robust. The "what if" process, the identification of risks and mitigation, of potential outcomes and contingent responses, is a fundamental resiliency that must be baked into the delivery of outcomes by those who are accountable for results.

A successful CEO who runs a billion-dollar empire hedges well against the fragility of economies and currencies, creating a circular flow of assets that survives the collapse of a market.

The supreme commander who leads the combined armies of a grand alliance plans well for the turbulence of weather and tides of battle, and adapts to the tumultuous surprises of the enemy.

Every successful parent who raises children in the dark world understands the unpredictable and surprising circumstances and situations that young humans create, and does not hold expectations of perfect behavior, outcomes and precision in family plans.

It is through the sudden, unpredictable and shocking experiences of life that parents and children share bonding and the strength of the family is cultivated for generations.

It is in the fearsome thrust of unexpected breakouts that the commander of troops finds victory and defeat tumbled and turned, and seizes opportunity to ensure survival of his nation and people in the face of impossible odds.

The shocking collapse of equities and the cascading surge of valuations that crackle and leap through the markets of the world are the most powerful opportunities for extraction of vast profit from the unpredictable, heaving sea of information and trends.

Understand this well.

The purpose of the random is to make things interesting.

God does not fancy boredom.

The universe does not go quietly.

Coincidence is delightful to creation.

Even Satan has his sacred purpose.

Through his understanding of the inherent nature of chaos the **Dark Triad Man** enables his thought, word and deed to be fluid. By baking in accommodations for the random into his vision, planning and competence he creates resiliency of focus, intention and adaptation.

It is through embodiment of the random that his narcissism, Machiavellianism and psychopathy become levers with which he spins *himself*, and this quality of pivoting mobility becomes his source of appropriate interaction with the random.

Sincere truth exists. *Makoto* is reality.

The random happens, and cannot be removed.

Thus *makoto* changes, and the **Dark Triad Man** changes with it.

Is all truth subjective and relative? Yes.

Does absolute truth exist? Yes.

Which is real? Is it the quantum realm of probability and indeterminism, or the actual realm of delivered fate? How does a man operate with this confusion, and avoid derailment and death?

The answer is not a forgiving one.

The answer is that you cannot.

You will make mistakes. You will have derailed plans.

You will stumble, fall, and collapse in this life.

And you will die.

That is also the Way.

It is why laughter exists.

This brings us to the last aspect of life and living in the dark world, and a crucial and important lesson that once more comes to us through the ancient lore of the *ninja* and the modern brilliance of the masters of finance.

You strive for appropriateness, not balance.

You do not pursue balance, for you cannot unbalance or rebalance the universe.

It is never out of balance. It does not need you to right itself.

There is only illusion of perception, error of intention, inaccuracy of action.

The screaming cry of "Why?" is as old as man himself.

The answer is neither the reassurance of God or the cackle of the Devil.

It simply is.

Form one more card in your mind, black and white, polar opposites.

On the front, lay the grid of the dark world.

That is the condensing, focusing, finite, entropic, ending, dying singularity. The dark world is the plan of God, the determination of fate, the momentum of history, the determination and closure of all things.

It is that which is finite, shaped, dying.

Chaos is the back, the infinite white light of unbounded, undetermined, untrammeled, unstructured, unknowable and unmeasurable randomness.

Spin the card!

Spin it with the delight and interest that God has in the jackpot of humanity.

The outcomes are ever up for grabs.

Recall our singularity of central gray, in the first example of gradient we examined in Chapter 17.

What you see is what you get.

Spin life. Spin love and hate, spin birth and death, spin everything.

Tumble and turn. It is the Way.

And the ferocious rails of navigation on which you hurtle with driven momentum, that tunnel through the kaleidoscopic polarities of insanity and reality, are the Laws.

The Nine Laws of the **Dark Triad Man**.

Violate them, derail and die.

Follow their road and you will laugh well in love, in joy, and understand.

Align them, and triumph.

The Emperor | Danse Macabre
Hans Holbein the Younger (1497–1543)

Chapter 21

The Nine Laws Aligned

We will now examine how the Laws are implanted within the grid, how they are emplaced as rails of transit across the realms, channels and controls of the dark world. The basis of how they provide transit for the **Dark Triad Man** will be explained.

The structure of this book is designed to bring you, step by step, into deeper and more robust understanding. This design is also intended to permit you, at any moment of uncertainty or challenged comprehension, to backtrack and resume accurate momentum along the lines of knowledge that are delivered here.

Thus we have taught you the Laws, explored the dark world, revealed the controls of narcissism, Machiavellianism and psychopathy, and placed them as the levers of fate that are employed by the **Dark Triad Man** and employed as his mastery of potentialities of the dark world.

We have taken you through condensation of forged realms of thought, word and deed. We explored the focus of channeled vision, planning and competence and how they shape and form the funnel of the dark world. Lastly we hardened that tumble and turn in the wild spin of random chaos.

Now we align the Laws to the grid, nesting them as a frame

of arrays for interaction. This chapter illustrates their significant primary positioning.

Learn well how The Nine Laws are matched to the realms, channels and controls.

The very first array of the Laws is in the realms of thought, word and deed:

Figure 21.1: The laws of the realms

SURVIVAL

Survival is the First Law and it is the very basis for all deeds.

Without survival there is no existence.

Without survival, there is no mind, heart or body and therefore there is no execution. Indeed, it is execution that is the most sobering end of survival. Always keep before you the alternation and pivot of sincere truth, the verb and the noun, the action and the act.

Action cannot take place without survival, and survival—the very existence of life itself—is the most compelling drive that any living organism possesses. A fight for survival is the deadliest. A determination to survive is the highest ferocity. A bloody scream of triumph is victorious expression of survival by the winner.

Hesitation is the death of survival. When life is not adhered to with resolve, where uncertainty of deed causes interrupted pursuit of life, survival cracks and sinks, defeated, dying.

Survival lies in the realm of action and of deed.

No one can survive for you.

It is personal action you must own.

CONCEALMENT

Concealment is the Second Law and it is the facilitator of the realm of words.

Without concealment there is no space for expression. Not all words are shared.

Word must arise from concealing silence in order to resonate. Concealment is the method of controlled communication, whether communication of existence or redirection of connection. Concealment is deliberation, it is precision, it is the beginning of skill.

Concealment protects truth in time of war through the hoisting of deliberate false flags, designed to mislead and redirect the adversary away from vital plans and secrets. Thereby the momentum of justice is preserved in alliance against the depredations of tyrants.

Concealment advances survival by preventing revelation of the existence of prey. The dappled coat of the deer blends with the fluttered leaves of autumn, and its frozen stillness keeps it hidden from the searching gaze of a passing cougar that the deer cannot outrun or fight.

You will not always be the most powerful actor in the fields and forests of the dark world.

Concealment is a subtle Way that you must master.

PURPOSE

Purpose is the Third Law and it is both outcome and derivation of the realm of thought.

Without purpose, there is no point to either existence or to men.

Men think, and create purpose. Thoughts conceive ideas; ideas take shape from thought; they marry to desire and potential; and purpose is born into the dark world. Where there is purpose there is pursuit, and where purpose is achieved the very detonation of fate itself takes place.

Purpose is what drives the ambition and outcomes of kings and empires, of commanders and armies, of executives and enterprises. Purpose is what refines vision into mission, the answer to the endless question of "Why?" that is the ever-present point of validation for all things.

Purpose benefits from concealment and is your reason for survival.

Purpose is derailed and scattered by confusion.

You must be clear in purpose, and adhere to purpose from the sacred center of the heart.

The second array of the Laws is through the channels of focus:

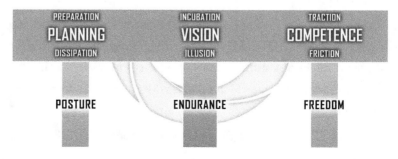

Figure 21.2: The laws of the channels

ENDURANCE

Endurance is the Fourth Law and it sustains the incubation of vision against challenge.

Without endurance, the prongs and pangs of disappointment and resentment will derail vision.

The dark world will inevitably cause sorrow and loss, pain and regret, damage and hurt. The cultivation of endurance is essential to the perseverance of momentum. Endurance spans time, endurance transcends harm, endurance passes through grief and fear and reaches peace.

Endurance is what gives rise to nobility of purpose. It is the foundation of character, the fountain of resiliency, the facilitator of hope. That which persists, endures; and by endurance the survival of concealed purpose is manifested.

Endurance is withered and sapped by illusion. Dependence upon illusion trips and overthrows endurance. It cannot persist when illusion is its basis.

Thus clarity fosters endurance, and must be your path of channeled vision in the dark world.

POSTURE

Posture is the Fifth Law and is the living shape of plans and their seamless accord to reality.

With inappropriate posture there will be stumble, stutter, collision and collapse.

Posture is the purest manifestation of receptivity and the appropriate delivery of array. Posture is the form of the man, his expression; it is far more than mere "stance" or lineup. Posture is position with flow, it is communication without dogma, it is movement in perfect accord with fate.

When a dreadful arc of blurring steel hurtles with cruel precision at the neck of the *ninja*, it is not by static stance or rigid technique that he slips death. Razored metal shears not bone and blood but empty and useless space. The trader's posture is his wisely diversified portfolio.

Seamless fluidity is perfect posture. It is how questions of life and death are successfully answered.

Dissipation of posture leads inevitably into calcification of stance and the rigidity of unresponsiveness. Rigidity and dogma die under swung steel and heresy.

FREEDOM

Freedom is the Sixth Law and the demand of dignity and movement for all living things.

Freedom is not negotiable. Without freedom, friction becomes a singularity that stops momentum.

Freedom is the ability to pivot direction, to embody mobility, to act with real traction. It is the uniquely driven outcome of individual competence, the result of endurance and posture combined to deliver results that are far greater than mere happenstance.

The capacities and victories of the champion in the ring are the result of his freedom to move, freedom to hit, freedom to engage and disengage, to dwell freely within the maelstrom of swing and strike. All of these are competencies that channel into the frame of cultivated freedom.

Freedom is lost where friction is applied. Laws constrict speech. Consequences hamper conduct. Shame murders ideas.

Maintain mobility, for it is how freedom endures.

The third array of the Laws are aligned to the controls of the **Dark Triad Man**:

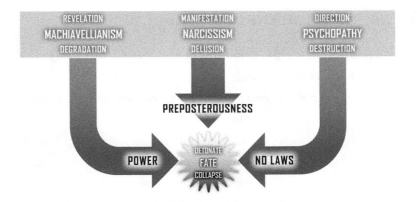

Figure 21.3: The laws of the controls

POWER

Power is the Seventh Law and the weight of planning as it manifests the shape of destiny.

Without power there is no result, no force of impact. No follow through or detonation.

Power is the prerogative of choice exercised. It is decision realized as a specific outcome slammed into actual truth. Power is the handle that delivers the chosen outcome of the Machiavellian by control of revelation, the skill that explodes planned fate into being.

Power is mass, the weight, the gravity of sincere truth that has been shaped and focused and thrown as a deliberate vow into the heart of potentiality, wrapping the embrace of probability around the wild tumble and turn of possibilities and determining outcome through inexorable constriction.

Power degrades without exercise, for no control lasts as potential forever. It must be used.

Power is the prerogative and privilege of the **Dark Triad Man** and he does not forswear it.

PREPOSTEROUSNESS

Preposterousness is the Eighth Law and the joyful, wild laughter of the universe in achievement.

Without preposterousness there is no contest, there is no interest, and there is only emptiness.

Preposterousness is energy, the quiver and vibration of fate. As fate detonates into reality it reveals all other possibilities as unsustainable delusions. Preposterousness is inherent in all outcomes, for it is the blur of chaos that shines brightly through all condensation in the dark world.

Flip a coin ten billion times. Even if each time before it has landed face up, at the next it still has an even chance of once more showing heads. This equal chance of pivoting binaries holds infinitely true even as odds grow insanely longer in the exponential calculation of rarity of outcomes.

Preposterousness is the rail of uncertainty and possibility that underlies all destinies and fates.

Without preposterous chance and chaos, fate itself has no arena to establish presence.

Preposterousness is the wisdom and laughter of the **Dark Triad Man** and he does not forget it.

NO LAWS

No Laws is the Ninth of the Nine Laws and is the final rail of your foundation in the dark world.

Human laws are destruction of truth, a failed attempt to force the dark world to be a bright place.

No Laws is momentous recognition that the common man is bound by regulations and rules, ordinances and restrictions imposed upon him by fallible rulers—men who do not, themselves, accord with the proclamations they arrogantly announce and enforce with cruel, capricious and uniformed brutality.

Justice is not a human decision, but the unfolding of the will of God in the world of creation. Karma is not a human preference, but an inexorable consequence of decisions and actions. Society and culture are not absolutes, but merely the profit and dominance of the ruthless who do not hesitate.

No Laws is grim reality behind millions of murdered innocents, toppled gunshot into pits.

No Laws is the unbound wildness that empowers the thundering hooves of the conqueror.

No Laws is dreadful, solemn testimony required of the **Dark Triad Man** and he does not deny it.

The grid of the dark world and the alignment of the Laws is now fully revealed.

Understand the funnel from infinity to singularity, how it spins and swirls.

Respect how the Laws cross it, and learn to see the road ahead.

Then take your own life in hand…

…and drive.

Understand reality and sincere truth as delivered through the grid of the dark world.

Practice, study and master your existence through the immortal framework of the Laws.

Comprehend the process that takes place as the dark world is stretched and stitched across the frame.

Learn positive, successful, delivered flow of the Way.

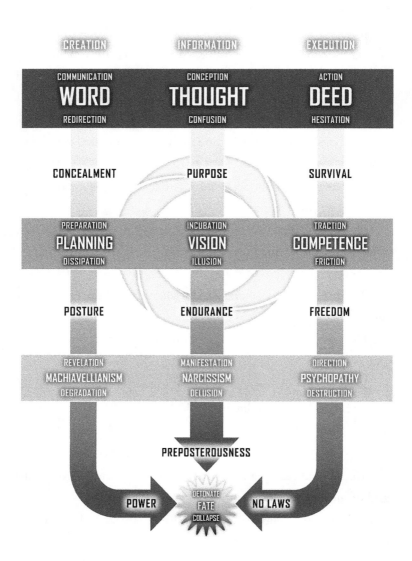

Figure 21.4: Complete grid of the dark world and The Nine
Laws in concert

Information conceives thought, it avoids confusion, forms purpose and incubates vision without illusion. It manifests in narcissism absent delusion, preposterously realizing achievement of fate.

Creation communicates word without redirection, it conceals preparation of planning, and avoids dissipation to display posture with Machiavellian control. It preserves against degradation of power until final revelation dawns as powerful and inevitable fate.

Execution is the result of action, the acceleration of unhesitating deed by exploitation of traction and the smoothing of friction. Competence grows freedom through mobility of direction. The psychopath slips destruction without the inhibition of false laws and slams home into the detonation of ruthless fate.

Beware negative, failed, stuttered defeat of the Way.

Information ill-conceived confuses thought, and illusion delivers poor vision which cannot endure in the dark world. Narcissism becomes delusion that will never manifest, and the entire preposterous structure collapses into failure.

Creation is redirected and communication does not connect. Words remain hidden. Plans have no coherence and dissipate, posture forms with inappropriate revelation. The Machiavellian degrades into powerless collapse of useless writhing.

Execution hesitates and deed is not put into action; survival is threatened by the friction of incompetence that drags you down as prey in the dark world. Freedom is lost and the psychopath is destroyed, for no laws will protect him from dying collapse.

The polarities of the Way are ever present. Blinding chaos shines through the vast deeps of the dark world. *Makoto* spins and fate laughs ceaselessly with joy in all possibilities.

God and the Devil watch with interest and the **Dark Triad Man** straddles all.

You must study and experiment in these things, ceaselessly and with great focus.

Respect and value the dark world. Honor and observe the Laws.

Know them deeply, and prepare your mind and heart and body.

Now it is time to give you the gift of skills, methods and principles.

Draw closer, brother, and prepare yourself for descent further into the dark world.

It is time for us to train.

PART THREE:

TRAINING

The Cardinal | Danse Macabre
Hans Holbein the Younger (1497–1543)

Chapter 22

Training Considerations

There are several crucial layers in this book.

The first layer provides you the navigational tools of the **Dark Triad Man** and equip you with clear, outlined understanding of how The Nine Laws shape his insight, hone his intention and accelerate his cutting edge of action. They are not mere platitudes but living, vibrating lines that overlay the grid of the dark world as a networked frame.

Part One thus cracks open the dark world and exposes the rails of the Laws.

The second layer explains the dark world itself. It introduces you to the **Dark Triad Man** and educates you in the ways that the world, man and God are shaped, aligned, integrated, and deployed. It teaches you the sinking, condensing flow of fate within creation. Rather than adhere to a framework that ignores the numinous or demands anthropomorphic deity, we have focused down into the gears and mechanisms of the cosmic jackpot.

Part Two thus reveals the nature of the dark world itself and the most basal form and source of it.

We now turn to the training and exercises that build and cultivate your strength of skill, understanding of methods and recognition of principles as employed by the **Dark Triad Man**. You will be presented with many interactive lessons that are designed to speed you forward and pull you into development of power. Training exercises to explore the terror of the broken heart, the incandescence of joy, and the detachment which removes cruelty from necessity and wild abandon from your processing.

Part Three thus shapes you as the weaponized human being.

The outcome of this section of The Nine Laws is disciplined development. The inexorable result of focused thought, word and deed into vision, planning and competence is outcome. Outcomes that are not the product of disciplined focus are scattered, unpredictable and far less profitable than achievements delivered by a man of action who is precise, coordinated and well-trained.

You must move far beyond theory into practice.

Ten thousand books on swordsmanship and strategy cannot replace the thousand daily cuts of the practitioner who is determined to master the riddle of steel.

Endless talks of military strategy are nothing in comparison to the grim and unforgiving reality of human war, of fire teams engaging in confusion, ferocity, overthrow and killing.

Infinite spinning of business processes and complicated service models, grand architectures of product and organization and testing are pointless if the enterprise cannot achieve sales.

A theorist is not a realist. The dark world does not preserve theorists.

The grinning skulls of theorists decorate thrones in the dark world.

The **Dark Triad Man** is an operator. That is what you must become.

The operator is cognizant of reality and of the difference between theory and practice. He follows the path of both of the warrior and the monk. He puts one foot in each realm. He disappears into the holy sanctuary and manifests from the power of the battlefield, as demanded by his purpose.

It is important to define and contrast these ways of the warrior and the monk.

Let us examine our pinnacles of archetype for these two roads of life that, together form the great Way that you will walk in your training.

The monk withdraws from all things.

The monk secludes himself from the tumult and chaos of the dark world and finds calm and contemplation in a highly ordered and artificial existence. There are long years of cultivated study, a ceaseless and disciplined focus on truth and the attrition of error and illusion, until age and training finally focus into the singularity of enlightenment.

The monk reaches heights of wisdom and advanced understanding. Worldly concerns and fears slowly drop away over the years, and the patient array of his thought, word and deed becomes at last a clear and shining path of alignment, unstained and untroubled.

There is wisdom and gentle, calming fulfillment in the path of the monk.

The practice of the monk is repetitive attrition. The scholarship of the monk is the carving away of the inessential. The mastery of the monk is the seamless contemplation of the unfettered mind.

The warrior engages with all things.

The warrior throws himself into the roaring maelstrom of the dark world and finds strife and collision, danger and death, horror and joy, hate and love, passion and despair. There are long years of misery, exultation, suffering and ecstasy in an unpredictable existence of upheaval. With time the warrior forges his edged spirit, incisive mind and unstoppable deed into a singular weapon of skill that roams the dark world as the most dread manifestation of predatorial human power.

The warrior reaches the satisfaction of advanced achievement. The trials and tribulations of the world cease to shock and scare, and over the years the array of his thought, word and deed becomes a piercing, penetrating lance of competence that has survived all, overcome all, and won all.

There is reality and fierce, demanding aliveness in the way of the warrior.

The practice of the warrior is repetitive cultivation. The scholarship of the warrior is the layering of the essential, over and over, on top of itself. The mastery of the warrior is the seamless dominance of the unhesitating spirit.

Each approach is valid. And each approach has its costs and dangers. The monk pays the cost of disengagement from life, disengagement from love and family and children and the wonder of what comes next in the world. The enlightenment of the monk is real, yet the severe and ever-present danger that is faced by the monk is that his advanced spiritual state and practice are only valid within the confines of his holy and sterile surroundings.

When warriors enter the monastery, the slaughter is terrible.

The warrior pays the price of peace and calm, predictability and comfort. Love is passionately sought, but yet inevitably torn away and the sorrow of loss is savage. Predictability is absent, and the warrior ages through his cultivation of hypervigilant awareness and loneliness in the singular, unaccompanied stride of the apex predator. And the warrior faces the risk of not theoretical but actual death, sudden and painful and permanent.

The dominant lion watches his domain aloof and alone, knowing death comes.

What is the correct way? Is it to be a monk or a warrior? Which approach is best? How does a man today identify what is necessary for his development and advancement?

The answer from the **Dark Triad Man** is simple and yet profound.

Tumble and turn.

Each in turn, each in complementary and alternating fashion. For the Way is living, and not static; engaging and not slothful, and the dark world rewards those who straddle the realms of light and dark with the most brilliant experiences of engagement possible to human beings.

Did I not tell you that the dark world delights in paradox and contradiction?

Know that this is a beloved feature of existence, and not a chastising exasperation. To understand how this works, you must learn to turn things inside out, and see that contradiction itself is merely the laughter of the dark world at your puzzlement and amazement.

The highest and most sublime forms of martial skill have always come from temples. This is true of the *ninja* and of the famed *shaolin* monks of China. The greatest acquisition of worldly wealth comes from the "quants", esoteric traders who cocoon deep in the mysterious and impenetrable bowels of hedge funds and live within an obsessive singularity of infinitely complex calculations and models.

The most profound understandings of discipline and nobility have always come from the warrior. This is true of the soldier and the officer, the men who run to the sound of the guns, who race to the heart of explosions and screams, and in that horror of utter chaos and blood and insanity they embody the most sublime and honest expressions of brotherhood, of love, and of sincere connection with their fellow men.

You must engage both paths completely.

The entwined path of the **Dark Triad Man** takes place along an inverted model within the dark world. As the world condenses, as his experience grows, as his outcomes are delivered with greater and greater impact and accuracy—he rises from the ranks of practitioners, flowers from the ranks of the scholar and ultimately ascends to the states of the master.

This is the outcome of survival and success in the dark world. It is ascendance from it, through diving into it. Such a paradox! Yet instinctively you know this is the Way, and the purpose of Heaven's plan for our race of sacred beings.

In your ascendance through cultivation and growth, through enlightenment and wisdom, you expand and grow and blossom closer to the potential of a being formed in the shape of God.

Thus the **Dark Triad Man** is a warrior-priest, a holy swordsman, a killer and lover and father and son. He is a brother to his own, and with sacred purpose.

We will review this brotherhood in more depth at the conclusion of Part Four.

Understand the Way that is presented here. It is not spurning of the world, but carving away within it. It is not attacking the world, but layering its roars and charges.

This Way is not without risks, and you are responsible for seeing, perceiving, assessing, adapting, and surmounting them as a human being. This cannot be stressed enough.

You as the reader are responsible for your own experimentation, study and exploration.

You are responsible for your own life and you will fully own your inevitable death.

Deferral of your death is not possible in the dark world.

Delegation of responsibility for your life is ridiculous in the dark world.

You own your life and you will die.

Be the master of this life, and live well with all its joys.

Own your outcomes, and seize your deserved rewards.

In the opening chapters of this book I spoke to you of danger and risk within this material. I warned you that the content of this book is powerful, that it is severe, and that to proceed with full absorption of the content and exercises will cause profound and permanent changes.

I repeat that warning here:

This book is not for mere theorists.

If your interests in the Laws and the living power of the **Dark Triad Man** are merely intellectual and you do not have intention of self-transformation, put this book down and walk away.

Shelve it before you cause yourself harm.

I tell you now that the training within this manual is not pleasant, fun, simple, easy and soothing.

Practice and performance of the training in this book will cause the death of your current self.

If you are here to learn and not walk away from knowledge and power, skill and fulfillment—but to slay your complacent weakness and take a proud and shuddering step into the horror of growth— then let us begin.

Watch the blade that I take up, and turn upon you and cut with remorseless and pitiless experience.

Your complacency must die. Sloth of heart must be put to death. They are your weaknesses.

I am here to kill them as your brother, to push challenge and advancement and comradeship to you. Not to play and dance with you in the footwork of silly dilettantes who accord no seriousness to power and performance.

This book of The Nine Laws is a living blade of intelligence to cut brightly through your confusion. Its work is to unblind your eyes to the reality of the dark world, to its nature, and its spiraling concentration. It is the mirror of chaos that ceaselessly laughs as it burns through you.

This book of The Nine Laws is a grave and resonant communication of power, from my heart and voice and memory to you. It is the distillation of forty years of tumble and turn, life and death in the dark world, the lessons of my own engagement and survival, contemplation and application.

This is the road to joy.

The Nine Laws demand grim and serious training. Training that will halt and restart your mind, stop and accelerate your heart, interrupt and hurl your deeds into the focus of the **Dark Triad Man**.

A different man will emerge from the other side, one that the world regards as a figure of power.

This training is for men of action who demand performance.

It is for men who brave the power to laugh.

Are you ready?

The Duke | Danse Macabre
Hans Holbein the Younger (1497–1543)

Chapter 23

Training Model

The purpose of training is to cultivate expertise.

Expertise comes from embodiment of the truths of the Laws with ever more competent alignment and integration through the realms, channels and controls of the dark world.

This embodiment is the result of exercise and action, study and contemplation, analysis and dissection of your performance. The strata of your training is important.

What is this strata? Why is it called strata, and how does the **Dark Triad Man** give shape to his cultivation of real, practical and effective skill of impact?

How do you train?

Begin with the model of strata.

The strata of the Laws are principles, methods and skills.

A layered, solid and dependable cultivation of the delivery of consequences.

Before we examine the strata of principles, methods and skills it is important to understand what their purpose is.

Why train?

Why not simply dive into the dark world and live life as it comes?

The answer lies in the control of outcomes.

Your interaction with the material in this book and carrying out of the lessons is for the purpose of developing your ability to control the manifestation of fate.

That is the prerogative of the man of power, the honorable duty of the man of competence.

Principles, methods and skills are put into place as responses to the ceaseless spin and infinite blurring pivot of truth and falsehood, of reality and chaos, of the light and the dark.

How does one know when to strike? When does a man make his decision, what is the correct moment when polarity is interrupted and formed into the reality of fate? What is the process by which uncertainty and mesmerization are replaced with certainty and determination?

The answer lies in understanding what principles, methods and skills are for.

They are to address this rise of uncertainty, to steer within your engagement of risk, and to shape the collision of fate as it takes place.

Principles, methods and skills strengthen your survival. They add subtlety to your concealment. They hone and sharpen your purpose.

Principles, methods and skills sustain your endurance. They clear stutter from your posture. They remove shudder from embrace of freedom.

Principles, methods and skills enhance your power. They enable you to inhabit the preposterous. They are the chords that form within the ceaseless song of no laws.

They are the answer to the dilemma of uncertainty and risk as they arise.

The inverted model of the **Dark Triad Man** that we discussed in Chapter 14 becomes more profound as we lay out the framework of your training. That inversion becomes more striking, more visible. It is the glow of the living being from the aperture of expertise.

The narrowness of principles loosens as it is deployed into methods, which are underpinned by the broad layer of skill. And in reverse, skill determines methods, which are aligned to principles.

The practitioner develops skills.

The scholar studies methods.

The master lives by principles.

The Laws illustrate principles that hold firm within the reality of the dark world. Principles are observed, recalled, and followed to slow expansion of uncertainty.

Methods are forms and vehicles of engagement as uncertainty peaks, as the bell curve of risk swells upwards. They are ways of applying principles, interactions of those principles according to experience.

Skills are basal resiliencies that empower successful accommodation of the unexpected. Skills are the inculcation of instilled competence and the bedrock that supports execution when risk spikes.

Understand this well: unexpected, random manifestation of encounter and engagement has a probability of one. Recall the nature of the dark world. Never forget that chaos has a vote, and that surprise and delight are the same thing.

Men plan, and God laughs.

Develop skill. Repetitively practice skills until unconscious competence is ingrained. It is skill that enables the practitioner to survive collision when methods unexpectedly fail.

Practice methods. Consistently apply methods until fluency in application is untroubled. It is methods that enable the scholar to posture correctly when principles are violated.

Learn principles. Penetrate into principles until deep realization of sincere truth is sustained. It is principles that are the transcendence of the master when no laws hold and chaos explodes all around.

Your training in this book will alternate between two ends of an important spectrum.

Did I tell you that fate is a singularity, the final collision point at the quantum level, the polarity of reality and futility?

That is truth which is the basal glue of reality, the polarized and binary particle state which determines the final fate of Schrödinger's smeared and querulous cat.

There is also the manner in which truth manifests, the dark world of infinite shades of grey, where the existence of fate is itself a very special gradient and the cat either romps free or rots.

That gradient of fate runs between the great polarities of all human endeavor: success and failure.

It is success and failure we deal with in Part Three, and the reshaping and restructuring of your mind, your heart and your body into an integrated, weaponized human being.

We will cover specific exercises of thought, word and deed that form the basis of development of skill in the dark world and empower you to success. We will then review recovery of failure by the practitioner, exercises designed to uncover and correct issues of the higher realms.

We will explore more challenging exercises of vision, planning and competence that shape the channeling of outcome in the dark world and drive your road towards success. We will then outline recovery of failure by the scholar, exercises designed to de-layer and disentangle interference of the central channels.

We will define very difficult exercises of narcissism, Machiavellianism and psychopathy that control your targeting of manifested fate in the dark world and ensure your arrival at success. We will dissect recovery of failure by the master, through exercises designed to defuse and diffuse the failure of your determination of fate, and find source of rebirth in the new.

We now begin with skills.
Train well, my brother.
It is the Way, and you are on the road.

The Knight | Danse Macabre
Hans Holbein the Younger (1497–1543)

Chapter 24

Skills Training

CONSIDERED CONCEPTION

Learn: Consider the ingrained habits of the mind. Take note of what provokes your interest, what deadens your excitement, where your patterns of intellectual arousal lie. Review whether your habitual thoughts lead or follow, generate or dissipate personal momentum.

Explore:
- Acknowledge to yourself whether you habitually engage in following or leading thoughts.
- Take stock of your thinking and determine whether it focuses on creation or consumption.
- Know your own weak mental habits when directing your conceptions of the mind.

How would life be different if your mind was awake and deliberate?

Reflect: Calculate the number of hours you engage in active thinking and exploration of new potential paths of living, compared to hours that are engaged in passive reception of deadening external input. Learn where adjustments will advance you.

Train: Awaken the mind. Mindfulness is not mere self-awareness. You must treat the mind as a tool over which you have sovereign and competent ownership. Accustom yourself to controlled, active thought that follows deliberate process in addition to creative brainstorm.

Task: Develop habit of roughly redirecting your mind. You must hone it as a practiced tool. Have no pity for your own sloth. Your mind is a weapon; do not permit rust.

✦   ✦   ✦

BOLD COMMUNICATION

Learn: Each word you speak is a both a resonance of spirit and a determinative provocation of fate. Stutters and starts of thinking sounds such as "ah… um…" are weakening, bleeding, sloughing mistakes of the defeated.

Explore:
- Discover how your speech and communication are hampered by pause and hesitant filler.
- Record and observe how frequently that filler is used in response to anxiety or uncertainty.
- Dig into your heart and identify where wasteful suicide of intention arises inside you.

What would others feel in your presence if your words rang strong and clear?

Reflect: There is no profit from unconscious sabotage of delivered, powerful intention. Your vibrancy and resonance of word will only suffer through diffused and degraded weakness. Self-sabotage exists and has a source. Find it. Kill it.

Train: Eliminate all habits of speech that degrade, diffuse, disparage or destroy your natural resonance and dissipate the power of your word. Precision, clarity, and firmness are crucial components of the speech of the warrior that you must train to embody.

Task: Speak out before your peers. Step forward in school, in work, in social gatherings. Put your voice forward and develop compelling resonance. Attain skill of command.

✦　✦　✦

PERMANENT ACTION

Learn: There is enormous power in the execution of permanent deeds that cannot be taken back. A man who possess the will to do permanent things is a man who is willing to deliver fate into being through his own determination.

Explore:
- Admit whether you are truly reluctant to take steps that cannot be reversed.
- Know where your mind and heart are out of synch so that deed is unable to execute.
- Continuously ask yourself what the next best permanent action would be.

Who would see you as a different person if you became a man of action?

Reflect: Consider how difficulty in executing permanent deeds is a reflection of hesitant and badly integrated humanity. Measure your thought and your word against your deed and find where stutter and stumble of execution have become allowed and accepted.

Train: Permanent deed must be a habitual method of living. That is the heart of execution. You must strive to cultivate the momentum of a man who changes things forever when he fully engages.

Task: Take steps each day to do one permanent thing that cannot be taken back. Begin with very small and deliberate actions. Respect the power of irreversible action. Build familiarity with it.

✦ ✦ ✦

INSIGHTFUL THOUGHT

Learn: Awareness of the mind, and how your thoughts are arrayed, must be followed up by deeper penetration. Penetration of thoughts eventually reaches the other side and is followed by unfolding of new understanding. The discipline of critical thinking is absolutely integral to success.

Explore:
- Know when your thoughts stop and when your mind considers itself sufficiently exerted.
- Be aware of the trigger which moves you from thinking to decision and then action.
- Determine how you can consciously move that trigger to accord better with desired results.

Where would success explode if you adhered to critical thinking?

Reflect: Practice the extension and reduction of your deliberations. Learn to recognize where you manifest unnecessary complexity of thought and insufficient depth of review. Compare reasons for those disparities and misalignments. Where there is overlap, you have habit to shatter.

Train: Understand the parallels between stuttered thinking in both active and receptive realms of mind. Identify common root causes for inappropriate depths of mental process.

Task: Halt your thinking, select a strain of opinion, and cut it apart and validate it. Cold, remorseless identification of your own prejudices and error is mandatory.

✦ ✦ ✦

DELIBERATE WORD

Learn: The condensation of word has mass and resonance in the living universe. Fewer words mean more power of delivery with each. Understand the importance of deliberate word as a means to drive deeper resolution and impact into fate.

Explore:
- Be aware of what topics produce unnecessary wordiness and verbal diarrhea in you.
- Know your conversational habits and why you begin to grandstand or pontificate.
- Videotape yourself speaking on a passionate topic and dissect where repetition weakens.

How would it feel if all others stopped to listen when you spoke?

Reflect: Train yourself into the process of refining every spoken delivery to the few most powerful words with which your answer can be expressed. Be aware that each word is an expenditure of power, of life, of capacity. Ensure that your expenditures are not profligate and wasteful.

Train: Condense your words and speech, and therefore condense your intention. Where deliberate and heavy words are used with calm impact, power resonates into fate.

Task: Think before you speak. Never let your mouth flap with idiotic, useless pablum. Words are expensive to the spirit and you do not have unlimited wealth.

✦ ✦ ✦

COLLIDING DEED

Learn: Permanent deeds are singularities, and permanent deeds that collide are where redirections and ricochets of fate are achieved. When two men collide with permanent deeds, the probabilities of the universe itself shatter.

Explore:
- Grasp where your work collides with others and where you create resentful adversaries.
- Dissect yourself and privately uncover where your own actions collide and frustrate progress.
- Practice deliberate collisions of deed to drive greater, more powerful resonance of victory.

What reputation would you have if collisions only made you stronger?

Reflect: Collision of outcomes is an inevitable result in the dark world. Advance awareness of deliberate collision provides shower of profit, and surprised collision creates shrapnel of loss. Understand the necessity of deliberate deed.

Train: Become familiar with the process of colliding permanent actions in order to invoke shudder and shower of fate. Begin with extremely small collisions, and work through their outcomes.

Task: You must not fear conflict. It is your opportunity to advance, secure, resolve and actuate. Weakness, anxiety, fear and uncertainty do not go away on their own. Learn to kill them.

✦ ✦ ✦

PURPOSEFUL CONCEPTION

Learn: The Law provides inordinate power in the purposeful act of conception. Conception that arises from purpose comes to life with vast, inherent, infinite momentum. Purposeful conception is the gifted child that shines with brilliance amongst its peers.

Explore:
- Ensure that purpose plays a crucial role in the deliberate generation of your thoughts.
- Decide to conceive and let thought create birth from that deliberate, momentous approach.
- Foster deep and purposeful thought in alignment with the momentum of desired victory.

How would life feel if everything you created was on purpose?

Reflect: Consider how your success and failure correlates to ideas that are purposefully formed. The decision to learn a skill, to understand a concept, to build a new world—all are purposeful conceptions of the mind.

Train: Set out to deliberately create. Pare away the accidental generation of ideas for a period of time, and set the mind to an array of a few purposefully conceived ideas. Make purposeful conception a well-ingrained habit.

Task: If you cannot create value you are dead and worthless in any market. Push yourself to create and thereby form the basis of antifragility. Do not be cattle for slaughter.

✦ ✦ ✦

CONCEALED COMMUNICATION

Learn: The Law reflects that it is not merely voice which communicates. Body language communicates, attitude communicates, posture communicates. It is crucial to ascertain where your communication in different areas is concealed to you and to others.

Explore:
- Ensure that body language, posture, attitude and tone accord with the spoken words.
- Dissonance of word from other manifestations should be deliberate and not inadvertent.
- Remove or conceal that dissonance to prevent unnecessary revelation and following conflict.

What respect would others have if you were a model of authenticity?

Reflect: The integration of communication across voice, posture, body language, attitude and tone is a fundamental component of authenticity, whether in concealing purpose or in shuffling inner discord into successful and parallel array.

Train: Develop skilled delivery of word that is unfiltered and unflavored by dissonance of being. Be able to identify when there is internal dissonance, and be aware of external misalignment.

Task: Do not show with foolish simplicity the array of your mind, heart or body. Cultivate impassive mien by speaking with men who cause you fear. You will learn to control yourself.

✦ ✦ ✦

SURVIVING ACTION

Learn: The Law recognizes and responds to the inescapable truth that deeds in the dark world bring risk. Permanent deeds create permanent risk. Fatal deeds generate existential risk. Awareness of the potential collapse of each deed is integral to survival.

Explore:
- Remove thoughtlessness and carelessness as interfering issues during the delivery of deed.
- Do not simply accept risks without fully examining and exploiting avenues for mitigation.
- Protect grander goals from danger through complete assessment of risks and adaptation.

How would life reward you for accepting deeper risks?

Reflect: Your death is inevitable, yet hastening it is profitless. Correct action considers risk and accords appropriately with measured handling. Accept, mitigate, avoid as circumstances indicate.

Train: Carelessness is not courage. Drill into your competence through exercise of due diligence and preparation. The impact of your deeds becomes more profound as the stakes rise.

Task: Anticipate death with consistent habit. What if *that* approaching man was coming to kill you? What if *that* car attempts to ram you? Failure to pay attention is a primary cause of death.

The Monk | Danse Macabre
Hans Holbein the Younger (1497–1543)

Chapter 25

Practitioner Recovery

PERCEIVED CONFUSION

Learn: Confusion in the mind must be recognized and managed. The man who perceives his own confusion takes steps to adapt to its reality, and thereby is not controlled by the mere fact of confusion as a state. Familiarity with confusion is key to penetration.

Explore:

- What signs of confusion arise in you and how does confused thought manifest in your mind?
- What other aspects of confusion manifest in your body and in your heart?
- Does recognition of confusion profit you better than denial when it appears?

Confusion can be used to uncover deeper opportunities.

Reflect: Consider well that recognition of confusion in the mind may indicate confusion of the heart or the body. Use the mind to explore. Peel back evident confusion to find deeper striations of confusion and missing integration below the surface.

Train: Utilize confusion as a marker for the dissection of deeper failure of alignment. Confusion is a signal, a resonance of its own, that brings you opportunity of more profound integration.

Task: See confusion for what it is: mental disorder. This is not sickness unless it is permitted to continue once identified. Ferocious reorder of your mind is the Way. Do not fear it.

✦ ✦ ✦

FOLLOWED REDIRECTION

Learn: Redirection of words and the manipulation of communication takes place with either deliberation or inadvertence. Inadvertent redirection often reveals unspoken motivation. Deliberate redirection often reveals inner confusion.

Explore:
- How are you vulnerable to subtle and unprofitable redirection by yourself or others?
- What hooks do you reach for and become easily and fatally entrapped by?
- What entanglements of heart or body often underlie your vulnerability to redirected words?

Redirection is not failure, but a chance to improve accuracy.

Reflect: Understand that inadvertent redirection often has unconscious purpose below the surface, and overt redirection has inherently less honesty by its nature. Deliberate redirection is typically for unspoken inner purposes, and covert redirection is for known reason.

Train: Grasp the ability to recognize redirection and move in tandem with it, or restore direction with deliberate word. Cultivate the ability to lead rather than be led.

Task: Recognize when you are being redirected. Challenge manipulation. Spot your own internal redirection and take ruthless, direct and intelligent command.

✦ ✦ ✦

BURST HESITATION

Learn: Hesitation builds tension, mounting and climbing, until it can no longer sustain and either collapses or detonates. The transformation of hesitation into action brings with it inherent release of tension that drives more fearsome collision, harder impact and deeper penetration.

Explore:
- What tension builds when your hesitation is prolonged past reasonable point?
- Where is your hesitation rooted, and how can it be shifted from paralysis into deed?
- Does your hesitation in fact stem from weak intention or false belief?

**Hesitation is normal and the inevitable burst
can be aimed.**

Reflect: The bursting of tension finds release in momentous direction. Your ability to provoke the burst of your hesitation leads to explosive quality of momentum. Practice and ingrain the habit of recognizing hesitation as the source of explosive fuel, and burn it decisively.

Train: Hesitation is natural and your ability to both burst it when identified and create it in order to build tension, is a superior and profitable competence. Train in this well.

Task: Delay gratification and appreciate greater success. Defer release and explode with more ferocity. Don't fire until you see the whites of their eyes.

✦ ✦ ✦

SICK THOUGHT

Learn: Thought can arise with ill and disordered pattern, resulting in sickness of alignment of the three realms. Sick thought is malevolent, both in consideration and in internal impact. Recognition of illness in thought is necessary to purge toxicity of outcomes.

Explore:
- What clung negatives are continuously present in your thinking?
- Where do disparaging or deprecating moods or manners infect you and cause despair?
- How do you generate failure through habits of intoxication or wallowing?

Disordered mental processing is not shameful, but where maturity grows.

Reflect: Correction of patterns of unhealthy thought is far more profound than simple observation of mental habits or practice of positive chatter. Dig into the source of obsessive thoughts and single out the driving fears. Understand the mental avoidance that lies behind intoxication.

Train: Clarity of thought is driven from sober understanding of reality and refusal to shadow and shade your thinking to accommodate anxiety. Note, accept, and move on as developed habit.

Task: Do not self-deprecate, ever. It is useless, putrid wallowing in idiocy. Accurate self-assessment is not advanced by poison or whining. Do not engage in them.

✦ ✦ ✦

FALSE WORD

Learn: False word is more than mere lies or deliberate untruth, and far subtler than those outward manifestations. Where word does not accord with thought or deed, it is false word. This is not a judgment of accuracy or honesty but of alignment.

Explore:
- How do you separate falsehood and truth from your words as you speak them?
- Where in your actions and thinking is there variance from the words you speak?
- Do you conflate honesty and truth, falsity and lies, and thereby hobble yourself?

Truth is how resonant power builds in speech.

Reflect: Understand that false word is not a moral judgment, and grasp well that false word is an objective and unemotional assessment of whether word is aligned to thought and deed. It is akin to judging the hit or miss of a round upon a target, and not the appropriateness of the target.

Train: Discern the accuracy of your own word. The decision to hit or miss must be a deliberate one, for therein is the heart of accuracy and the true resonance of your word in tandem with aimed thought and triggered deed. Carve away falseness.

Task: Keep your mouth shut unless your word accords with your deed and thought. Never speak simply to make useless, divisive noise. Words are vehicles of fate. Respect them.

✦ ✦ ✦

WRONG DEED

Learn: As with thought and word, deed becomes wrong when it deviates from integrated alignment with its partners of the realm. Wrong deed sabotages outcomes, stalls momentum and dissipates power through useless expenditure.

Explore:
- Where do you have great faith in your mind and your heart but nonetheless trip over action?
- Is your sabotage of self in fact a warning that the mind and heart are also sick or false?
- What consistent behavior do you engage in that cracks your momentum and causes collapse?

Fix negative habits and release explosive momentum.

Reflect: Reliability is the quality that correct deed manifests. Where deed is wrong it is often a flapping warning flag that your thought and word are incorrect, misaligned and stuttering. Take care to investigate backwards where deed habitually falls wrong.

Train: Develop your ability to trace back refusal of deed. Excavate what you had believed was correct and integrated alignment of thought and word. Learn where self-sabotage is arising, and chop hard and well into what is found, taking apart the assumed and unearthing the real.

Task: Enforce follow-through with determined action. Use strict internal word and thought to correct the slough of false deed and push yourself to execute with finality on your duty.

✦ ✦ ✦

CONFUSED PURPOSE

Learn: The Law can divide and forestall momentum. Where purpose is confused, either through oppositional purposes or uncertainty of commitment, the **Dark Triad Man** must cut through confusion and assume ownership of decision and fate.

Explore:
- What inner confusion or personal uncertainty interferes with your sacred purpose?
- How do you permit and even foster derailment and consequent crash of your momentum?
- Can you distinguish between weak purpose, failed purpose and incoherent purpose?

**Resolving spiritual confusion makes
sacred purpose unstoppable.**

Reflect: Understand that purpose is where your momentum is at-tacked, both from without and within. Purpose must be engraved into your intention and embedded there as a living voice. If your purpose flags, you create space for spears of doubt, redirection and death to enter.

Train: Bring the shape of your purpose into vision. See it. Know it. Harden it. Hold it. Talk to it. Revere it. Your purpose is crucial to your vision, and is the motive power underneath it.

Task: If you have no purpose you are fodder to be churned up, torn apart and flung away as bloody waste by men who do. Devote specific, uninterrupted time each day to hardening your purpose.

✦ ✦ ✦

REDIRECTED CONCEALMENT

Learn: The Law may be pushed back and forth and exposed. Where revelation is inadvertent or provoked, whether by the prompting of an adversary or the silly demands of your own ego, the outcome is derailment of word into useless and failed connection.

Explore:
- Why are you the original source of your own destructive revelations?
- How does your concealment expose the preservation of your truths?
- When does candid open word become the bitter shape of cruelty?

Redirection can be compassion, kindness and protection.

Reflect: Where you have revealed with misstep or from ego, understand that the damage to your momentum resonates through far more than merely the moment. Caution and calm in accordance with the Law prevents subsequent scramble, hiding and redirection.

Train: Maintain concealment as an active and not reactive process. Hiding is weak and doomed to failure; concealment is graceful and may be either bold or subtle as engagement demands. Above all remove ego from your process of revelation and concealment.

Task: The masses of men are not your allies. You will engage only their resentment though declaration of your plans. Shut off your ego and shut your mouth as your default position.

✦ ✦ ✦

HESITANT SURVIVAL

Learn: The Law demands boldness and ferocity, for it is in hesitation that survival often fails and life collapses into death. Hesitation is not uncertainty, but rather the useless withholding of fate. Understand that survival is a binary outcome and hesitation breeds infectious probability of failure.

Explore:

- What about your life would no longer trouble you if survival was decided in the negative?
- Does your hesitation contain within it the quality of suicidal impulse?
- How can you overcome self-destruction and redirect your hesitation into action?

The urge to quit is common and a strong signal to adapt.

Reflect: The urge to survive is often superseded by the desire for things to be over. Struggle, pain, sorrow, loss, fear and impact are all things which throw into doubt the heart of survival and ferocity. Consider deeply what would shatter your will to survive, and what hesitancy you already exhibit.

Train: The integrated self does not hesitate to survive. Through complementary and bonded thought, word and deed you remove the interval between threat and response that forms a lethal gap in the human being within which the adversary strikes.

Task: Miserable hope that "maybe it will go away" is a certain ticket to a grim and unpleasant death. You will face your situations and you will make cold reality a glittering, dependable comfort.

The Blind Man | Danse Macabre
Hans Holbein the Younger (1497–1543)

Chapter 26

Methods Training

PULSED INCUBATION

Learn: Continuous acceleration and grip are unsustainable. Successful formation of vision is built through periodic contraction and relaxation, the breathing pulse of life that instills vigor and accrues momentum in periodic spurts.

Explore:
- Realize that vision will flag and fail if periods of rest and recoil are not given space to exist.
- See where pulsed or periodic rejuvenation and intermittent acceleration can prevent strain.
- Intersperse relaxation and restoration with deliberate constriction and expenditure.

How would life expand if you were never worn out or exhausted?

Reflect: The introduction of pulsed approach is crucial to the sustenance of long-term vision and successful outcome. Cyclic, stacked successes are how great visions are achieved; they are the rhythm of a living purpose, the accommodation of intensity to demand, the rolling of momentous energy.

Train: Learn the process of growing breath and life into your vision by finding, acclimating to and fostering the natural rhythms of your desired future state. Accept that the Way is one of life, not of flared death from singularity of approach. Accord your acceleration with sublime timing of push.

Task: Split up your vision into manageable components. Drive each in turn and do not allow yourself to obsess over a single component. Become a manager, not merely a worker.

✦ ✦ ✦

COHERENT PREPARATION

Learn: Random and reactive structure for planning is the path to dissipation. Understand the flow of progress from end to end of your vision. Map out the road of achievement and determine the milestones that indicate success and failure. Each milestone should advance your dialogue to determined conclusion.

Explore:
- Develop the ability to recognize when plans are incomplete or disordered.
- Learn how momentum dissipates at points where plans fail to materialize into reality.
- Observe how over-control of one aspect of plans leaves chaos as the manager for others.

How would fulfillment glow if you realized many dreams at once?

Reflect: The refusal to plan often stems from expectation of failure, and a sense of effort as being futile. Thus it is not expended. Grasp well that no plan is perfect, but that failure to exert a minimum basal level of planning means that collision with the random will have escalating results.

Train: The shape of your planning must be coherent from any place it is entered. Whether driving backwards from your goal state or forward from the immediate moment, any spot in which you land and pick apart your planning should produce a sense of inevitable direction for your work.

Task: Draft your plans on paper and lay out your roadmap. Then attempt to destroy your plan by attacking it as a vicious and insightful adversary. Strengthen your plans for the real world.

✦ ✦ ✦

TESTED TRACTION

Learn: Traction cannot be forced into place; it results from the competent placement of contact during engagement. Know your landing ground, your place of impact, your point of penetration. Traction spins quickly into friction, and escape from friction is through acceleration.

Explore:

- Recognize the feeling of successful traction in pursuit of a demanded outcome.
- Be aware of what takes place in the mind, heart and body when traction is perceived.
- Know how all three components of the human being are blended into successful traction.

How would others describe you if nothing could hold you back?

Reflect: It is traction that provides a secure platform not merely for acceleration but also powerful redirection. Consider how exploitation of traction is your doorway to change of course as well as commitment, and how loss of traction can also be exploited through the relaxation of drift.

Train: Just as pulse and coherence are essential to vision and planning, testing of traction builds your acclimation to handling and expertise in driving. Become expert in controlled failure as a means to achieving competence. Practice skids. Redirect with drifts. Widen and deepen your competence.

Task: Demand of yourself that you seek all angles to accelerate. Do not try to use them all. But you must develop awareness. Create not merely 360° of traction, but infinite spherical traction.

✦ ✦ ✦

GLITTERING VISION

Learn: Focused vision must glint and glitter as it is turned over in the mind and held up against reality as your precious future manifestation. Glitter comes in points and flares, not as overall seamless glow. Condense your vision into facets, and construct hard points of reflective shine.

Explore:
- Ensure that your vision has sharply defined aspects that can be tied to measured success.
- Constantly seek to edge your vision with harder lines of penetration into the future.
- Inspire your design of the future with brilliance that reflects from every facet.

How would it feel to prove you can create brilliance out of nothing?

Reflect: Just as no plan or competence cannot be improved, so too no vision is utterly complete. Turn your vision carefully over in your mind. Review where your vision is brightest and the connection points of your vision intersect, for those are the stress points that will either harden and penetrate reality or break apart when fate collides.

Train: Build grand vision with coherent, sharpened structure that carves your new reality when pressed by your plans and competence into the momentum of fate. Find your spots of bright reflection. Frame them together and harden the facets in a structure. Edges to your vision give places for the hands of fate to grip and turn, climb and grasp.

Task: Your vision must be hardened or it will not survive when you slam it into fate. Rivet your vision with vows. Uphold your vision with ferocity. Sharpen your vision with ruthless drive.

✦ ✦ ✦

PARALLEL PLANNING

Learn: Great plans do not move along a purely linear path but pull in, realign, and redeploy in parallel to the extent that deliverables demand. The hastening of fate takes place not through hurried effort but through greater competence, by deliberate efficiency and not frantic desperation.

Explore:
- Avoid sucking traps of unprofitable waiting within overall efforts and plans.

- Know which dependencies are unavoidable and what outcomes can be driven in parallel.
- Condense not only the plans and processes, but array your impacts simultaneously.

How amazing would success look if you made it happen all at once?

Reflect: The execution of plans is more than a mere plodding step from fate to fate. Living, resonant plans that effect execution on parallel lines are also more robust, for thus failure at one point does not derail the momentum of the entire enterprise. Learn this well, and build resiliency into your plans through competent, tandem arrays of work.

Train: Foster robust competence and overwhelming momentum. Layer lines of success together, effect changes and determine outcomes in many paths at once. Ensure your momentum has more legs to support the body of fate when inevitable random stumbles and trips interject into your effort.

Task: Abhor waste of time and resources. Crash timelines together and ripple efficiency through your work. Two birds, one stone. One shot, two kills. Single task executed, multiple goals achieved.

✦　✦　✦

DETACHED COMPETENCE

Learn: Mental and emotional separation from your outcomes is a key aspect of competence. Concern, anxiety, worry, fear, and apprehension are inhibitors to competent interaction. Exultation, joy, celebration and rejoice are overextensions that mislead competence.

Find the pivoting center of detachment from outcome and thereby maintain momentum and follow-through without letup.

Explore:
- Appreciate how early celebration often irreparably steals victory from eager hands.
- Know how anxiety and worry can cause fatal shiver in aim and result in missed impact.
- Discover where attachment arises most often—the mind, the heart or in physical action.

What victories would ultimate calm enable you to reach?

Reflect: The paradox of competence lies in the ability to accept greater and greater outcomes and risks with less and less attachment to outcome. Fools skip and leap over the falling of a leaf, while the grave and competent emperor does not flicker at the collapse of a city.

Train: Detachment from results must be your inverted cultivation of response to outcome. As your delivered fates grow more profound and have greater significance, work to remain within the immovable spirit that does not sway or shudder with the playing out of fate.

Task: Cease forever the ugly and contemptible practice of whining. It is a disgusting, humiliating and unnecessary reinforcement of weakness. Do not whine. Ever.

✦ ✦ ✦

INCUBATED ENDURANCE

Learn: The Law withstands through repetitive reinforcement. Nurturing and nourishment of your endurance occurs through resettling

your vision on the far side of trauma. Vision fixed in place bleeds off
and becomes illusion as trauma progresses; it causes truth to be seen
as false and suffering takes precedence in the mind. Fortify your
endurance with advancement of your vision.

Explore:
- Identify the stressors that most swiftly sever visions and cause
  them to be abandoned.
- Secure the tipping points where endurance breaks and vision
  is forsworn as illusion.
- Clarify broad illusions in order to leap with endurance past
  your suffering.

What sweet joys would blossom if you could endure the work?

Reflect: The tumble and turn of illusion and incubation, the furtherance of vision to the other side of trauma and suffering, is also
a tumble and turn of the present and the future. Temporary and
deliberate illusion can surmount immediate suffering; nurtured resiliency that sees the distant goal is how repeated blows are absorbed
and left behind.

Train: Where suffering threatens your commitment to vision, expand vision to specifically include robust transcendence of that suffering. When despair infects your thinking, surmount it by deliberately rejecting despair as a process. As exhaustion bleeds into your
endurance with sense of futility, rise above the infection of defeat
by merciless slap against your flagging spirit.

Task: Become familiar with exhaustion. Work around the clock
twice. Push yourself to limits and smash them. Get used to pain.
Smile grimly at heartbreak. Cultivate the Body of a Rock.

✦ ✦ ✦

PREPARED POSTURE

Learn: The Law provides shape and receptivity to the array of your mind, heart and body. Informed posture is prepared; prepared posture is the result of planning. The educated mind engages complexity with process; the seasoned heart embraces shock with calm; the trained body engages threat with grace. Successful preparation must commence before encounter.

Explore:

- Uncover within yourself where arrogance is a weak cover for lack of education.
- Dig into jaded reactions and determine where shock awaits with unprepared engagements.
- Test your movement when sick or shaky and expose fragility of presumed competence.

How would profits surge if you were always well-prepared?

Reflect: Tumble and turn your faces of posture from wisdom to foolishness, along the spectrum of effortless skill and clumsy grapple, within the gradient of surprise and boredom. Discover points and moments where preparation becomes expectation, invites chaos, and stands receptive to death.

Train: Seamless posture will reflect your appropriate complementation in engagement. Disposition of forces must be appropriate to the weather and the terrain. Organization of workers must be appropriate to the transformation of materials into products. Movement in response to the plunging blade must be in accord with the timing, distancing and angling of the warrior.

Task: Absorb the posture of the victorious. Watch the body language of the dominant. Observe who is prey and who is predator. Study successful military campaigns. Mimic the movement of experts.

✦　✦　✦

TRACTIONED FREEDOM

Learn: The Law expands your potential outcomes by defusing probability through diffusion of boundaries. Your engagements are accepted on broader terms than presented. The mobility that your freedom provides permits contact with the unexpected and traction from places of surprise.

Explore:
- Observe what limitations of habit, social construct or personal belief are present.
- Expose excuses and overlays of artificial constraint that enjoin mobility and perception.
- Abandon irrelevant boundaries and remove unnecessary personal shackles.

How would it feel if you were truly and completely free?

Reflect: The tumble and turn of subjectivity and objectivity are the shimmering alternation of polarities within which the decision of freedom or limitation is arrived at. The insanity of infinite moral relativity brings total loss of traction and the mindlessness of absolute dogma prevents the development of momentum.

Train: Develop mobility of perspective and freedom of input. Strive for unshackled determination and uninhibited assessment. Comprehend the demand of conscience and its relation to freedom of action, freedom of thought and freedom of speech. Develop continuous awareness of boundaries and their placement, of freedom and its strangling within the mind, the heart and the hand.

Task: Identify false boundaries and deliberately violate them. Accept the consequences and build on them. Spot idiot inhibitions and slaughter them. Live as an adult who abhors and rejects slavery.

The Merchant | Danse Macabre
Hans Holbein the Younger (1497–1543)

Chapter 27

Scholar Recovery

REINED ILLUSION

Learn: Mistaken entry into illusion of thought, word and deed is inevitable and natural. The scholar does not agonize or shudder over his discovery of illusion, nor halt and stutter momentum. The advanced method is to rein your illusion, to preserve momentum while redirecting it, steering it, not only inwards but potentially to the side as well. Rein illusions to attain outcomes of profit.

Explore:
- What illusions do you hold about your vision, your plans, your competence?
- Where do the outcomes of those illusions take you when they are allowed free rein?
- How can you transform overestimation of your skill into motivation for improvement?

Recovery from foolish mindset is a massive springboard.

Reflect: Illusion cannot be completely avoided. Observe the inherent proclivity of the mind and heart to embrace falsehood, and utilize your findings of error as corrective markers on the road of development. Just as one does not berate oneself for the requirement of steering wheel correction while driving, the presence of illusion is not moral failure but human nature to be put in service.

Train: Profit from your mistakes. Drive accuracy with your errors. Learn to feed upon the detritus of illusion and swing from illusory perception into accurate perspective. Continuous appraisal produces consistent improvement. Cultivate habitual practice of assessment and correction.

Task: Remove excitement from error recovery. Calm yourself down when you discover mistakes. Heightened arousal over the inevitable is pointless. Quit shivering over reality.

✦ ✦ ✦

CALMED DISSIPATION

Learn: Plans that fail produce shudder throughout organizations, relationships and men. Whether disastrous defeat on the battlefield, crisis in a marriage or the collapse of personal goals, this process of frustrated realization and awkward, stumbling accommodation proceeds most profitably through the process of calm. It is similar to gentling the hitching breath of a child who is finished crying.

Explore:
- What is your usual reaction to the disappointment of failed plans and objectives?
- How does your physiological arousal react to realization of frustrated outcome?
- Where can you broadcast calm in order to preserve a measured pace of momentum?

Frustrated plans infect momentum into new places.

Reflect: Consider that frustration, disappointment, failure and defeat are inevitable aspects of life in the dark world. This has a probability of one. Work to instill a mantle of gentility and calm into reactions and response, both internal and external. Foster stillness of the mind and heart. Project reassurance and direction to subordinates and allies.

Train: Detach from negative impact and comprehend the utility of dissipated energy. Learn well to calm and channel sinking, leaking, departing energy—the loss of potential—into more predictable, useful and lower energy states: probability. This process of calmed dissipation brings with it the ability to extract resource from fleeing value.

Task: Don't indulge in excitement or wild emotion. The trailing end of failure can often be grabbed and pulled back—but not if you are busy wailing. Get cold, get relaxed, and get dangerous.

✦ ✦ ✦

GUIDED FRICTION

Learn: When momentum comes up against hard, abrasive reality and the resultant friction is beyond competence to move past, the corrective method is to focus your guidance not upon your own momentum but to surrender active control and turn your competence onto guiding the source of that friction. Where the challenges to movement cannot be surmounted, steer the challenges.

Explore:

- What challenges have resulted in collapse when you could not broaden to higher perspective?

- How does your resistance to new scales of control contribute to the acceleration of collapse?
- What is the source of your resistance to and struggle against accommodating friction?

Struggle is a warning to seize control of the bigger picture.

Reflect: The experience of friction is a sign that the momentum of fate is scraping against the alignment of your thought, word and deed and your competence is lacking in the guidance required for achievement of vision and the completion of plans. Your measure of success is arrival at the destination and not how the vehicle is steered at any moment in between. Learn this well.

Train: Adaptation and orientation are infinitely continuous. Abhor any preference for the static. What is fixed in place can be more easily destroyed; what is anchored stubbornly is eventually worn away. Encounter with greater forces is inevitable and the scholar arrays himself to profit from the inexorable rise and fall of the sea underneath his vessel.

Task: Drop stubborn stupidity. When the bull rushes, give him a cape with a blade behind it. When fighting brutally for the blade, let go of the hilt and kill him. Don't fight. Win.

✦ ✦ ✦

TROUBLED VISION

Learn: There are times when despite extraordinary effort at the condensation of thought into vision, clarity refuses to appear and the process of visualization results in blurred focus. Doubt follows, and uncertainty reigns as troubled vision stumbles in the dark. This is a grave sign to you that there is illusion present in the origins of the vision, for the momentum of fate refuses it.

Explore:

- What vision of emotional power or physical result was impossible for you to visualize?
- Were you willing to accept the refusal of fate to create a compelling vision of the future?
- When was the refusal of fate to permit your vision first made apparent to you?

Destiny will speak clearly if you are willing to listen.

Reflect: The momentum of fate can be steered and aligned, it can be nudged and spiraled, but it cannot be forced and it will brook no halt. The inability of the mind to focus vision into reality is your signal that the probability of your vision is already unsustainable.

Train: Develop skill in recognizing the validity of your potential vision by measurement against the response of fate to the concept. The speed and coherence of your coalesced vision is in truth the response time of fate to your suggested manifestation. Lack of response proves illusion in your vision. Thus you learn to ally with the opinion of fate upon the viability of what you seek to achieve.

Task: Get real. You are responsible for making vision happen. Do not indulge in fantasy. Refuse silly, empty dreams. Grand vision glitters because it is sharp, not because it is pretty.

✦ ✦ ✦

CONFLICTING PLANS

Learn: The array of plans in this life will inevitably conflict and collide. They will crash together and leak resources, opportunity and profit. The result is loss, failure and defeat. Where plans conflict it is important to engage in both communication and dissipation: revelation of parallel tracks of deliverable, and discarding of those which can be deferred or abandoned.

Explore:

- What is your process for reconciling competing and conflicting plans in life?
- Do you surrender by default to external forces, or seek methods to conceal your plans?
- How can you build resiliency into your plans so that conflict dissipates rather than redirects?

Deep momentum comes from maintaining continuous mobility.

Reflect: The ability to raise and lower the potency and prominence of your plans is key to remaining stable through the crest and troughs of the waves of fate. Insistence on prominence is fatal, and refusal to display is also a point of failure. This rise and fall of probability is cyclic and inherent to things, for it is an eternal rhythm of testing.

Train: Be resilient in your navigation. Grasp that the practice of planning is conscious engagement with the random and the straining of actuality out of the foam of chaos. As you draw closer towards your determined outcome, relax your control of plans with gradient shift of intention and focus. Move from theory to practice, from planning to achievement, from aiming to hitting.

Task: Don't accept habitual failure but know that occasions are inevitable. Reconcile them through experience. Learn to hedge. Craft profit-taking into likely failure points. Crash your plans together before fate does.

✦ ✦ ✦

USELESS COMPETENCE

Learn: Competence often drops into ever-tightening spirals of pointless focus. Efficiency, determination and success approach singularity while irrelevancy of effort chases infinity. The supply chain is flawless, but no customers buy. A dazzling array of superb romantic presentations ensue, but directed at a woman who is uninterested. Useless competence is desperation.

Explore:
- When have you wasted valuable determination to force fate by stubborn competence?
- How was that spiral an avoidance of reality, and a refusal to accept its actual momentum?
- Where would appropriate application of competence have borne more profitable fruit?

Obsession with a single victory accelerates total loss and defeat.

Reflect: The derailing of effort and competence is not always to be found in the overall halt of successful measurements. What has value cannot always be measured, and what can be measured does not always have value. Remain focused on perception of momentum as a guide to the delivery of fate, and not on any singularity of competence.

Train: Develop the ability to recognize when competence has over-shot reality and is buried by the delivery of the inessential and irrelevant. Be consistent in your habit of splitting the focus of your competence away from your immediate deliverable or process, and pull it out and up into the broader plane of overall achievement. If there is dissonance you have identified trapped momentum.

Task: Pointless work is foolish. Foolish obsessions are not victorious. Stay on point with your larger victory. Do not chase sunk costs. What is over is over; what is done is done. Move on.

✦ ✦ ✦

ILLUSORY ENDURANCE

Learn: The Law becomes subtle as the scholar transitions from the broad realm to the channel of the Way. Endurance, tested, often feels strong until the moment of truth arrives and the resiliency, resistance and fortitude of endurance is revealed as utterly unsustainable. It cracks, fails, and collapses, leaving the outcome worse than if a different path had persevered.

Explore:
- What suffering have you revisited over and over yet failed to sustain endurance?
- Where do your breaking points lie each time that your endurance is revealed as illusion?
- Would fortification of one realm bring the others into higher and stronger resiliency?

Nested layers of endurance permit flex instead of snap.

Reflect: The secret to true endurance and observation of the Law often lies not in direct confrontation with the source of suffering and the active measure of will, but in the subtle tumble and turn of repositioned vulnerability that spreads display in place of strength. Understand that what is hard can be cracked, what is brittle can be shattered, and the fluid cannot be pushed.

Train: Strive to embody the immovable spirit through the broadening of vision to higher purpose. It is in the elevation of purpose that the surmounting of suffering is obtained, and by the pursuit of elevated spirit that the distress of the heart and worries of the mind are passed over. Grasp the difference between detachment and lack of care, between transcendence and forgetfulness.

Task: Never wallow in self-pity. Do your children rot at the bottom of a killing pit? Do you read this emaciated and naked in a death camp? Men endure those things. Your problems are smaller.

✦ ✦ ✦

DISSIPATED POSTURE

Learn: The Law is one of motion, flow and clarity of response. Where posture is held too long, and especially when a posture becomes adhered to, it becomes inappropriate and cannot be sustained. Posture by its very nature should not demand sustenance of effort from the mind or heart; it is a natural mirrored array. The result of forced posture is dissipation of energy and failure.

Explore:
- What posture do you attempt to force upon your mind, your heart or your body?

- After long and continuous effort, what realm begins first to tire and dissipate for you?
- How do you habitually accommodate your posture to persistent and inexorable challenge?

What is fixed in place can be utterly and irretrievably destroyed.

Reflect: Flagging, failing posture is grave sign that the posture in question is no longer appropriate and is overdue for shift. This does not require the discontinuation of plans. Posture is the living embodiment of purpose, and thus plans flow through correct posture. Correctness is a living gradient, not a static polarity, and complementary posture is the highest correctness.

Train: Fluidity of posture must be attained and held to as a primal imperative. Work to appreciate the flagging and dissipation of posture at the moment it commences. Observe, orient, decide, act and do so on a gradient of force. Pure observation has no bias and accepts all; the point of your strike is the singularity of decision. In between lies the flow of posture.

Task: Research stress positions. Select one. Reserve an entire day of privacy. Train in that stress position until you are in agony and collapse. Repeat. Observe where your heart, body and mind fail.

✦ ✦ ✦

FRICTIONED FREEDOM

Learn: The Law demands preservation of your mobility against unnecessary entanglements, inappropriate surrender and fruitless appeasement of adversaries. Yet there are indeed times where failure takes place and freedom is limited, entrapped, and you are faced with the struggle of operating from a position of shackled competence.

Explore:

- What is the response of your mind and heart to the realization of limited mobility?
- How does your freedom move between relief and rage when it is hampered or constricted?
- Does your experience of slavery arise from external pressures or internal barriers you create?

Slavery is only a moral failing when it is permitted.

Reflect: Freedom is fragile yet imperious, subtle yet profound. Freedom is your birthright as a human being yet the impulse to trade freedom for security is an inherent temptation that does not bear fruit in the dark world. Security itself is an illusion, a false appearance, and your preservation of mobility must not seek or succumb to the frictions of fear or threat.

Train: Granulated awareness of freedom is a moral responsibility. Your freedom is not negotiable; failure to preserve and uphold your freedom in the face of friction and scrape is the death of your overall momentum, loss of your power and removal of your capacity to endure and survive. Freedom is a living Law, one that you must maintain consistent and constant attention to.

Task: Loathe the ethics of the quitter. Rebellion is the birthright of free men. Know your rights. Be dangerous to cross. Maintain living plans of revolution were the entire world to collapse in tyranny.

The Robber | Danse Macabre
Hans Holbein the Younger (1497–1543)

Chapter 28

Principles Training

ACHIEVED MANIFESTATION

Learn: The highest realization of the control of narcissism is achievement of your intended vision in reality. It is the validation of aligned realms, the demonstration of integrated channels and the accord of living fate with your vision as proven new reality. Achievement is an unassailable demonstration of the validity of your vision and an irreplaceable measurement of your human power.

Explore:

- Recall your greatest achievement and go back to when the concept was first conceived.
- Dissect how vision was incubated and nurtured, how illusion and fiction were overcome.
- Relive the experience of deliberate, decisive fate exploding into absolute reality.

What would you do with power to detonate fate upon command?

Reflect: In the consideration of a past grand achievement and the drive of condensed momentum into the impact of fate, take note of

the spirit of wondrous excitement that entwined within the movement from potential to possibility, from possibility to probability,
and finally into actuality. Fulfillment is the mind of the victor and
that thread of fulfillment is woven into victorious results.

Train: Seek within your memory the moment where utter certainty
of outcome was an inward smile of calm confidence that glowed in
your mind despite the worst of criticism, disbelief, disparagement
and belittling inflicted upon you by others who did not share your
vision or purpose. Strive to relive that feeling of power and to
cultivate it deliberately with each new vision of your life.

Task: Start ridiculously small. Create vision for something as simple
as getting out of bed. See it with complete, brilliant clarity. Then
execute. Memorize the feeling of success. Repeat ceaselessly.

✦ ✦ ✦

DELIBERATE REVELATION

Learn: The most resonant delivery of the control of Machiavellianism is the total display of unhidden truth, the explicit array of
spoken power, the revelation of the master who at last makes all clear
to the world, to men and to God. It is the strength of confession,
the resonance of vows, declarations of war and announcements of
peace. Deliberate revelation is voiced summoning of fate.

Explore:
- Revisit when moments of fate have demanded full revelation
  of absolute truth.
- Return to an experience of powerful unfolding reality that
  demanded a herald stand forth.

- Recall a moment of pregnant anticipation that burst out into unstoppable, final exposure.

How would men respond if you spoke with the voice of God?

Reflect: Machiavellian control of revelation is not gratuitous or excessive but an elevated and advanced posture of mastery that accords with all potential extremes. Declarations of love and the sad news of death, announcements of marriage and the utterance of oath, are vivid moments when the human being is not merely shaping sound into voice but delivering fate and truth through word.

Train: Capture the resonant power of those moments in your life, whether positive or negative, and work to build your words along similar lines of power. The weight of those profound moments of communication are not created by word, but revealed through word. Tap into the underlying momentum of fate as a great and inexhaustible river. Let your words be the sound of it.

Task: Do you love? Share it. Do you despise? Declare it. Is a man your brother? Speak in his defense. Let your words clang to the ground, and let them ring forth. Clear and unmistakably.

✦ ✦ ✦

REMORSELESS DIRECTION

Learn: The unstoppable ferocity of psychopathic control stems from singularity of purpose and complete detachment from boundaries, limitations and fears. It is the clarity of an unfiltered animal; it is full accord with the impersonal nature of the universe. It is abandonment of ego by the psychopath and utter acceleration of momentum within the thundering flow of fate.

Explore:

- Recall when dominant victory felt inevitable and pity became entirely irrelevant.
- Resurrect the source of that utter commitment and performance with zero restraint.
- Review the unblinking clarity within it and the accordant experience of outcome.

What triumphs would occur if you had absolute detachment?

Reflect: The stripping away of the hesitancies and frictions of the ego permits the psychopath to move with infinite traction and instantaneous mobility into the direction and delivery of fate. By removal of attachments in the heart and chatter from the mind, the ability of fate itself to find perfect clarity of direction through the human being is achieved.

Train: Cultivate this power of purity in detachment. Focus on even small actions where you are able to remove desire, fear, anticipation, expectation and apprehension. Expand that experience of detachment throughout greater and greater actions. Learn to clear away the silly, chattering constraints of the human being in order to experience the full clarity of consequence.

Task: Turn off the mind. Drain out the heart. Capture the moment of pure, mindless, animal ferocity that characterizes the bloody champion, the roaring warrior, the thundering horse at gallop.

✦ ✦ ✦

EXPANDED NARCISSISM

Learn: The master brings narcissism beyond achievement and manifests it into the divine right of kings. The moment arrives when the expansion of narcissism has reached full expression, and the thought of the visionary becomes the adulation of the world. This is the reflection of fate back upon the man of immortal achievement.

Explore:
- Return to moments of achieved success, social recognition and public acclamation.
- Restore the sensation of self-perpetuating power, profits, successes and outcomes.
- Recall where declaration of vision infected men, who turned and followed that banner.

Where would men be marching if legions followed you?

Reflect: The promotion of fame and the entanglement of legend into the narrative of history is a vivid signal that vision is resonating through the human race. This propagation of fate is the exponential multiplication of vision from the man to the masses, the expansion of narcissism into a million resonating voices that drive impact with unforgettable result.

Train: Resonate belief through the world. Give voice to that which men believe, but cannot articulate. Proclaim that which they know in their hearts, but yet are afraid to speak aloud. Let your voice be a strong and bellowing horn of truth, and with consistent notes burst forth the reality that all who hear, join in and expand.

Task: Develop a following. Infect others with your vision. Awaken hearts by speaking what they know but fear to say. Set minds ablaze by declaring what the anxious are unable to put to word.

✦ ✦ ✦

HARNESSED MACHIAVELLIANISM

Learn: The master drives Machiavellianism far past revelation and plans and enthralls the works of other men. He bends them to the service of a single fate. All do the work of the master, for even those in opposition further his dreadful entanglements and their snares become the profitable entwined acceleration of his own subtle work.

Explore:
- Remember old momentums that even machinations of adversaries drove to greater success.
- Return to prior capitalization and integral harnessing of the work of friend and foe alike.
- Realize how those who embody subtle intelligence and deliberate skill are vastly rewarded.

What throne could be won if adversaries fought to support you?

Reflect: The work of ages is not accomplished through solely the overt and the evident. Great clashes of magnificent armies on the glorious field of battle are in truth put in motion and given timing by the subtle and silent means of expert, well-planned and deadly statecraft. Learn the Way of underlying brilliance, the shadow that gives shape to it, and the blur of light and dark.

Train: Harness all men into furtherance of your vision. Spread the clarion voice of the master into the halls and towns of the world. Let men rise and go forth at the power of your words, and cause the tapestry of history be woven through with your achievement by all men, drafted into the service of the great plan you bring into being.

Task: Select an adversary. Cultivate dialogue. Foster engagement. Penetrate motivation. Ensnare his vision. Hook his momentum. Reel his planning. Release him to pursue purposes under your control.

✦ ✦ ✦

INWARD PSYCHOPATHY

Learn: The master is coldest and most competent with his deeds when facing himself. Icy assessment of his failures and success, immovable detachment in decisions of his life, unflinching engagement with grim and bitter realities of disappointment, collapse, failure and defeat are his basal nature and the walls of a vessel capable of sustaining the storms of the dark world.

Explore:
- Return to your most compelling moment of remorseless and unfeeling assessment of self.
- Dissect your strengths, weaknesses, successes and failures with pitiless eyes of the psychopath.
- Review the greatest attainment and most humiliating consequence with equal equanimity.

What would take control if you had absolutely no illusions?

Reflect: Cultivation of the immovable spirit must be an inwardly mastered aspect of the **Dark Triad Man** just as through his engagements with external forces and crisis. It is vital that there be no rejoicing at victory, no despair at defeat, and no flicker of the detached and clinical observation of the weaponized human being as he surfs the deep waves of history into conclusion.

Train: Practice your ability to detach from your highest triumphs and your most disgusting failures. Work to let go with ever-increasing circumference from the cling and attachment of ego. The heart must retain normal pulse regardless of catastrophe or attainment of the crown. Within this singularity of observation without reaction is the essence of the Way of the dark world.

Task: Admit your addictions. Recognize your foul habits. Itemize your glorious skills. Feast upon your beauty. Inspect your ugly traits. As you assess them all, remain icily accurate and unmoved.

✦ ✦ ✦

FUTURE PREPOSTEROUSNESS

Learn: The Law that guides narcissist control is your rail into impact and detonation. The man who has brought vision into life, who is supported by the masses, who has history under his hand and writes out the memory of mankind as a manifestation of his own mind, sees forward into alternate futures with the broad perspective of the maker of fate. The mind penetrates all probabilities with infinite depth. All things are preposterous and no things are impossible.

Explore:
- Accept and examine how achievement is used to see into alternate futures and prepare.
- Position all postures to intercept and capture approaching, unseen probabilities
- Resonate with feeling of service as a focusing aperture of Heaven's intention on earth.

Where would you drive the dark world to make history?

Reflect: Man is the vehicle for the communication, preparation and revelation of the power of God on earth through the shaping of word and plans. Understand that this is a flowing, living continuum of information through to detonation, and the weaponized human being is how the infinite penetrates the finite. All things are preposterous before determination.

Train: When the moment arrives where you are the inexorable demonstration of inevitable fate, seize that moment and use it as the commencing singularity for an infinite number of possible futures. Within that singularity is the pivoting, blurring potential of all else that you wish to accomplish.

Task: Be nimble. Be quick. Be sudden and ferocious. The moment that you attain great success is the moment you are already gone. Eliminate lingering spirit. Move instantly into the next future.

✦ ✦ ✦

POWER OF THE PRESENT

Learn: The Law observes that the only reality that ever exists is the singularity of the present moment. All things in the past are interpretation, all things in the future are unreal, and you must inhabit and work within the reality of the present moment. Total realization that one works with what is, and postures according to what is happening, is the Way of the sage and the victor.

Explore:
- Harden attention, intention and action into a single, perfect point of engagement.
- Live completely in the moment as an infinite experience of competence in the "zone".

- Drive this infinite and perfect engagement into each moment of actual daily living.

What sacred fulfillment calls to you in each moment?

Reflect: Understand that the condensation of the dark world comes to the point of the moment. You are forever in that moment, and within it is all the power that you will ever have. Inhabit that power and direct it, shape it and use it. Each split second of reality, let your vision move forward into momentous revelation. This creates an endless and continuous moment of impact.

Train: Learn to live in the moment and dwell within its conscious flow. Be aware that power is a living thing, not a static tool or mask to adopt. Work ceaselessly to permit power, not to force it. Cultivate the resonance of power, do not force screams of it. You must become a pipe for the flow of power, a prism through which power is focused and burst.

Task: Develop purely physical skill that requires seamless concentration within risk. Ride motorcycles. Train in firearms. Lift weights. Build authentic power. Apply it to other facets of life.

✦ ✦ ✦

NO LAWS FROM THE PAST

Learn: No Law governs the future, and the past does not control it. Men point to the past, but leaders walk forward. Men fight old wars, but victors seize new thrones. Men wallow in nostalgia, but conquerors raise new empires to heights of glory. There is no restriction, there is no prevention. The claim that another Caesar will never arise is foolish and obtuse idiocy given voice.

Explore:

- Understand the dark world is not finished and grasp that the Law overrules even itself.
- Absorb that No Laws is the Way of existence, and that chaos and random are integral.
- Realize the truth of No Laws means that this universe can be driven anywhere you desire.

What if the will of God is success for your desires?

Reflect: The great men of history have never been trapped by the past, but moved boldly forward to create a separation between the past, their lives, and the resultant future of the human race. Their will and determination are the flexing junctures of fate. Understand that this greatness is not magic, nor luck, but understanding of the Laws, their entwining, and their unraveling.

Train: The step to separate yourself from the common man is to cease the acceptance of boundaries of the past. Abandon helpless clinging to the predictable and the safe. Seek the freedom of your own direction and drive directly through the collisions you encounter in the dark world. There is no fate you cannot master, and the world itself can be turned upside down by the man who observes no law.

Task: Is there a sorrowful memory? Let go of it as useless. Is there an addiction that has held you back? Walk away from it. Does a past failure haunt you? Laugh and shake it off. Move on, always.

The Beggar | Danse Macabre
Hans Holbein the Younger (1497–1543)

Chapter 29

Master Recovery

DEVASTATED DEGRADATION

Learn: Disordered, manipulative and over-exerted control results in the devastation of utter degradation. It is an implosion of Machiavellian skill, the dissipation of all plans, and the redirection of word into collapse. The aftermath of collapse is handled by the master through acceptance, acknowledgment and surrender rather than scramble to uphold the unviable.

Explore:

- What moment of horrific, agonizing devastation and collapse is vivid in your memory?
- How did concealment work against you, and what crude posture led to your defeat?
- Did you create this devastation yourself, and to what extent do you bear full responsibility?

Never flinch from outcomes you have created.

Reflect: The dark world does not guarantee bright outcomes or brilliant success, and there is no propensity for the momentum of fate to arrive at victory. Equal probability is accorded to failure, complementary potential is aligned with defeat, and you are the owner of both.

Train: Accept full ownership. Deny no responsibility. Take complete accountability. Embody total mastery through radical acceptance of outcome, regardless of direction, and thereby maintain momentum and the potential for rebirth of renewed voice.

Task: Your most grotesque and hideous outcome is not the defining moment of your life unless you allow it. The immovable spirit applies to your own fallen nature. Get up. Walk on. Rebuild.

✦ ✦ ✦

MURDERED DELUSION

Learn: The result of arrogant, unsupportable pride is the cruel, brutal and shrieking murder of delusion as the truth of reality clangs into being. The wise man is played for the fool, the king is usurped by his "loyal" councilor, the careful architect sees his grand tower sway and smash to the ground as truth inevitably and willfully makes itself manifest despite his blindness in calculation.

Explore:
- When have you been surprised by the total collapse of illusion that you reinforced?
- Why did you separate from reality and when did shattered delusions become your path?
- Did you creep or plummet into idiocy and was the realization a slow or sudden consequence?

Never deny the cold evidence of brutal reality.

Reflect: Stubborn refusal to abandon dreams is the source of many a delusion that ends the careers of tyrants, smashes the structures of State and precipitates the collapse of marriages, alliances, businesses and champions. As momentum towards fate grows and illusion is adhered to with tighter grasp, the outcome of delusion is inevitably horrific.

Train: Snap out of disbelief and surprise. Abandon attempt to preserve empty theory and bankrupt belief. Discard protestation of facts and plunge directly into the cold shock of truth. Just as you cannot carry water in spread fingers or raise a fortress upon shifting sands, you will not profit through clinging to that which is proven false and has no further momentum or potential.

Task: Your most sorrowful and agonizing loss is not the end of you unless you wallow in ridiculous spiritual masturbation. The immovable spirit applies to your own heart. Get up. Move on. Heal.

✦ ✦ ✦

ACCEPTED DESTRUCTION

Learn: The result of uncontrolled, hurtling and directionless momentum is utter, colliding destruction. The crazed blindness of the madman floors the accelerator of fate and the outcome is crash, explosion and insanity. On such impacts the ruler falls upon his sword, the tyrant blows out his brains and an entire people march to death.

Explore:

- How has stupid and bullheaded insistence on your own way ended in total failure?

- Why did you blind yourself to warning perceptions and attempt to force improper fate?
- Are you able to perceive the difference between subtle miss and idiotic smash?

Snap out of madness and break free of plummet.

Reflect: Carelessness and ferocity are an unstable mixture that drive wildly gyrated results. Such mindless force applied with detachment from reality is a recipe for destruction which brings down not merely the actor, but also the stage, the audience and the theater.

Train: Recognize the failure before impact. Take your foot off the accelerator and relax into the unavoidable smash. Whether it is the sacking of the city, impact of fist upon jaw or the realization of collapsed equities and destroyed portfolio, calm awareness of outcome is your key to returning to survival in the aftermath. Accept the inevitable, assume dignity, and face the rifles with no blindfold.

Task: Your most crushing defeat and permanent damage was not your death, for you are alive to read this today. Accept your loss and continue. Embody immense inner dignity.

✦ ✦ ✦

DEADLY HUBRIS

Learn: The most deluded path of the human being is the spinning and preposterous belief that Providence has made exception to the rules and that he is favored, protected and immune to the inherent and immovable nature of the impersonal universe. The dark world rewards those who believe themselves exempt with a terrible, forbidding and inescapable nemesis.

Explore:

- When have you engaged in magical thinking and believed that fortune held favor for you?
- Why did you throw dice with fate while believing that the dark world had taken sides?
- Where did you allow your ego to make contact with the most ridiculous arrogance of all?

The dark world murders men who believe themselves gods.

Reflect: Pride is the source of the fall and hubris is the most infectiously corrupting manifestation of it. Eventually the mind cannot conceive of outcome other than total victory, enabling the random to take root and grow disorder and chaos within the unfolding vision. Blindness is that road, destruction is its destination, and death is the unforgiving toll.

Train: Remain grimly vigilant to the beginning of magical thinking. View any lapse of adherence to the truth of an impersonal universe as evidence that a deeper, earlier error has taken place and that your steps must be retraced until objectivity is recaptured, neutrality towards self is restored, and clarity of manifestation renewed.

Task: Recognize a karmic risk you have formed by unwarranted arrogance. Identify the crashing fate that approaches as a result. Either prove that arrogance justified or prepare for immense destruction.

✦ ✦ ✦

ENTHRALLED MYSTERY

Learn: The most degrading path of the human being is the enthrallment of lies and compulsive deceit that places expedient profit and invariable manipulation as a goal to achieve in and of itself. Fascination and enthrallment with twisting and turning is responded to by the dark world with eventual collision and collapse, for no house of lies can be sustained forever.

Explore:

- How have you entered into festering enthrallment of falsehood through your word?
- What degradation was the result of manipulation and lies at the foundation of your vision?
- How were your plans overthrown by ill concealment that deformed them at conception?

Foundations of lies will collapse in flames.

Reflect: The temptation to expediency and the pursuit of unearned reward is a constant lure to the man who has developed matchless skill. The responsibility of power is not merely justice, but also a refusal to turn power into swift bankruptcy through violation of the laws of karma. Such expenditure is unsustainable and unviable, and results in inevitable revelation of reality.

Train: Do not delight in concealment of word or posture, and do not degrade your power with useless and unnecessary gratuity. Master the calm of subtlety and avoid the crassness of habitual lies. Embody the spare and utilitarian delivery of revelation and concealment, of privacy and promotion, and do not seek pleasure or profit in the fact of their tumble and turn.

Task: Mental and emotional masturbation is as fruitless and draining as the physical. Cease your gratuitous ecstasy in pointless, stupid and frantic self-stroking. Go forth and achieve without drama.

✦ ✦ ✦

SADISTIC CRUELTY

Learn: The most destructive modalities of the human being are pleasure in the wanton idiocies known as sadism and cruelty. Damage, devastation, destruction and death are at times the appropriate and correct outcome of the master's work. Where the spirit falls into pleasure in the agony of others and gratuitous infliction of destruction, mirrored consequence comes swiftly.

Explore:
- When did you engage in unnecessary destruction and push beyond into gratuitous cruelty?
- Where have you badly mistaken evil for necessity and satiation of lust for a clinical act?
- How do you cause friction by your demand for satisfaction at the expense of natural justice?

Ugly fate follows quickly on the heels of brutality.

Reflect: The tumble and turn of good and evil arises from the polar potentials of the necessary and the unnecessary, the appropriate and the inappropriate, the correct and the incorrect. Learn well the speed with which unneeded force, unnecessary words, and inauthentic heart give rise to the singularity of hideous evil.

Train: Continuously monitor the detachment of your spirit from not only fear, worry, anxiety and anger but also the seductive grotesqueries of gloating and frenzy. Overextension of posture into pleasure from the use of force is unprofitable attempt to employ pain and brutality as personal currency. Strip sadism from your process as swiftly and surely as you remove pity.

Task: Cruelty, sadism and brutality arise from weakness. You have been cruel. Acknowledge the moment. Identify the weakness. Lance that boil of personality and drain the abscess of spirit.

✦　✦　✦

POWERFUL CONSEQUENCE

Learn: Consequence is the result of thought, word and deed in alignment as a single realm, but the fact of alignment does not produce success—it only ensures powerful outcome. The sage drives consequences with greater impact than the common man and acute awareness of the depth of his mistakes is a serious and crucial aspect of his mastery.

Explore:
- What mistakes of yours created cascading impact that shattered the plans and lives of others?
- Who have you harmed through careless. unthinking delivery of thought, word and deed?
- Why did you continue despite your awareness of this damage during your unfolding of fate?

Refuse a blindfold and stare down the rifles.

Reflect: Rework and recovery after collapse are far more expensive and time-consuming than care and due diligence in creation. The concealment of false purpose in order to further its survival brings integration of thought, word and deed into powerful negative consequences.

Train: Strive always to actively monitor the unfolding of consequence through all your encounters and engagements. Consequence does not occur in static moments; it is the place where the hose of fate blasts continually against the surface of reality. Detect spurts in the hose, deviations in the flow, interruptions in the stream that cause spatter and shock at the end point of impact.

Task: Accept full responsibility. Do not pass the buck. Cease your excuses. Demonstrate personal accountability. Own your mistakes. In this manner you will resonate integrity, and rule gravely.

✦ ✦ ✦

PREPOSTEROUS KARMA

Learn: The random will never be denied, and even the sage and the master find themselves at the colliding end of chaotic and unexpected karma. The most masterful controls can nonetheless fail for the simple reason that failure is not impossible. Grasp well that your spin of fate means that you will sometimes lose.

Explore:
- When have you been shocked and surprised by the unbelievable result of impossible failure?
- How did you forget that you are not the only architect of fate that walks in the dark world?
- Why did arrogance and idiotic self-importance cloud your expectation of cold reality?

Stupid men ignore how death travels fast.

Reflect: Tumble and turn your perspective of karma. Accept that there is no separation from the momentum of its inexorable process. Understand that you are a living and continuous facilitator of it, and the most preposterous disappointments and sorrows all arose directly from your mistakes.

Train: Habitually engage in brief moments of isolation and consideration. In those moments, ensure that dissection of your vision, planning and competence take place as reflection against the inevitable momentum of karma. Simplify and contrast them against the inescapable truth of inexorable universal justice. Acknowledge and correct where you are bringing destruction.

Task: In the past you have badly blown things apart. Set aside a long private period to explore the worst of them. Deconstruct it fully. Find the errors. Then ruthlessly apply them to your current life.

✦ ✦ ✦

ILLEGAL REALITY

Learn: Narcissism, Machiavellianism and psychopathy will inevitably bring you into opposition with the laws and regulations of organizations, governments and rulers. The weaponized human who operates in conflict with those human constructs will inevitably be caught and subjected to the outcomes of exposed illegal action. Do not mistake cleverness for invulnerability.

Explore:
- What crimes have you committed in response to the demand of your conscience?
- Do you understand and accept that even human law honors the lesser of evils defense?
- How do you reconcile your power with ridiculous constraints designed for lesser men?

Fools believe laws control the dark world.

Reflect: Reconciliation of mastery with the shackles of the mundane is crucial to development of the precision of the **Dark Triad**

Man. Laws and regulations for the weak, the profit of the powerful, the subjugation of the free and the order of human society demand continuous comparison, consideration and decision.

Train: Work to develop appraisal of the law without apprehension. Observe your inner concern in response to outer violation of law. Grasp the nature of shifting and mutable human ordinances in opposition to the basal and continuous thread of human nature and history. Know that what is lawful now, was once crime... and what outlaws a man today, makes him a sovereign tomorrow.

Task: Think hard upon your crimes. Catalogue them all and calculate what total sentence society would inflict. Observe that ridiculous tally. Grasp that conscience must guide you, not human law.

The Waggoner | Danse Macabre
Hans Holbein the Younger (1497–1543)

Chapter 30

Stacking, Attrition and Techniques

We now turn to how the Laws are stacked upon each other and carved through attrition, how the **Dark Triad Man** provides his mind, his heart and his body with techniques of insight and impact.

It is fundamentally important to absorb that techniques are infinite in nature. They are not itemized and limited collections. It is useless to strive towards building a catalogue of techniques; rather, the correct Way is to enable techniques to arise spontaneously from seamless interaction of skills methods, and principles.

When you are able to generate technique from that basis, you apply appropriate thought, word and deed. Vision, planning and competence are accurate. Narcissism, Machiavellianism and psychopathy present as ironic in their success to the common man, but are the penultimate result of long training.

Techniques are the shape of impact, the sway of the ringing bell. Technique comes from the timing, distancing and angling of your engagement with encounters in the dark world.

Understand this well. You cannot always be faster, stronger, smarter, harder, richer, lovelier or "better" than the adversary. But there are things you can nearly always move closer to accuracy.

Timing is the pillar of technique associated with thought. Timing arises from your perception, and your perspective drives the moment. The vision of your purpose must accord with the times. Endurance takes place over durations. Human lifespans are preposterously short, and yet infinite patience is required in the sudden moment of swung steel and decisions within the markets.

Angling is the pillar of technique associated with word. Your angle informs your dealings, and both traders and warriors speak gravely of angle in the dark world: position of portfolio, position of forces. Posture manifests in angles and thereby alignments of disparate momentums are achieved. Right angles crack things. Converging angles blend things. Parallel angles separate things. Whether you wish to collide, to conjoin, to estrange—angling is your answer.

Distancing is the pillar of technique associated with deed. Distance controls the ability of momentum to accrue, enables acceleration to be calculated, creates necessary space for mass to attract and collision to take place. Survival is determined by distance from detonation, freedom is qualified by distance from friction, and direction is possible only when crossing distance.

Timing, distancing and angling create victory.

Even when you are slower, weaker, dumber, softer, poorer, uglier or "worse" than the adversary you nonetheless have the capacity to influence outcomes by creating changes in timing, distancing and angling. You therefore assist fate itself with arrival at different outcomes.

This is the basis of technique.

Just as there are innumerable possible alignments and arrays of timing, distancing and angling—there are infinite potential techniques, and the source of all of them is your unique perspective, your momentary position, and your relativistic space.

How, then, does the **Dark Triad Man** use the Laws to generate techniques? How does he accumulate, grow, add to and build his repertoire of technique through positive application of the Laws? What is the correct Way?

The answer is in the form of processes.

Processes are the machine which spits out product. Processes are how you develop capacities and deliver outcomes.

Stacking and attrition are the processes of The Nine Laws and the dark world.

Stacking is the bright, the growing, the brash and confident outward way of employing skills, methods and principles of the Laws to manifest your determined outcome.

Attrition is the dark, the shrinking, the subtle and questioning inner way of honing skills, methods and principles of the Laws to bore through your determined outcome.

Let us now examine stacking.

Stacking is how things grow. We have examined this in our process of the grid and the Laws, how they interact in the realms, channels and controls.

Inform your thought. Purpose your vision. Endure with narcissistic preposterousness. The businessman researches the market, identifies a need, builds what does not exist and captures the imagination of the world until his profits pour in to soaring levels of value.

Create your word. Conceal your plans. Posture with Machiavellian power. The king declares war, his lords hold secret council, the generals array the troops with subtle and momentous position on the battlefield until the clash of armies determines the rise and fall of thrones.

Execute your deed. Survive competently. Live in freedom as a psychopath who does not accept shackles. The outlaw travels through towns and roads, acknowledging no master, exudes grim capability and his deeds live on after his execution.

Attrition is how things die. We have reviewed this in our analysis of the dark world, how it inevitably condenses, and cannot exist outside the finite boundaries of life and death.

Collapse is preposterous to avoid, for not one thing lasts forever. It is delusion that endurance cannot be broken, for torture in endless forms will inevitably snap the endurance of all men. Illusion is inherently infected throughout purpose, for man is not infallible.

You are powerless to prevent collapse, for degradation of posture takes place through the very action of planning. Concealment cannot be maintained for ever, for it dissipates as truth inexorably reveals itself and karma hammers on the door of reality.

Fate terminates without choice in the law of inevitable destruction, for the entropic structure of our finite universe proves freedom to be mere friction against reality and survival is utterly impossible by the very design of all things.

How does the **Dark Triad Man** reconcile these polarities of joy and sorrow, of hope and despair, reality and simulation, good and evil? How does the infinite imagination of the man attain pure reason within the absurd and writhing bubble of transient blood and meat that births it?

Tumble and turn the Laws, principles, methods, and skills. Toss and spin the realms, the channels, the controls. Blur and pivot the dark world, yourself, and your interactions.

Learn to stack the Laws as you tumble and turn their relationship and application. Skip from realm, to channel and to control as you toss and spin your inquiries. Uncover subtle relationships as you blur and pivot through the bright potentials of fate:

- How does the survival of your purpose shape the posture of your endurance?
- Does power grow when you conceal freedom and obey preposterous laws?
- When freedom is preposterous is your survival a matter of endurance?
- Does purposeful vision foster powerful deeds of survival?
- Is it competent to plan upon posture that conceals hesitation?
- In what direction does your power manifest when your execution is only word?
- What is your conception of direction? How do you think through revelations?
- When does your communication have traction? What action of psychopathy is creative?
- Who is responsible for preparing manifestation? How is incubation executed?

Stack value upon value to ensure triumph.

Complementary expenditure of effort and action, consideration and contemplation, is necessary on the darker end of our spectrum of living. Learn to attrite as you contrast and compare the grid, entangle and unwind the Laws, detonate and collapse yourself and the dark world.

Tear apart and pull away the delicate edges of death and defeat, the micro-indicators of failure and collapse. Excavate the very root of initial infection. Learn to employ the dark world in the service of your determination, your outcomes and most of all in adversarial contest:

- Where can redirection be used to deliver the adversary into friction and degrade his posture?
- Does hesitant posture confuse the adversary who believes in your Machiavellian competence?
- Can rejection of survival and deluded action redirect the plans of a visionary adversary?
- Does dissipation of competence destroy the psychopath and collapse his posture of power?
- Will creation of illusion degrade the adversary's thought and direct his execution?
- How does deluded word sustain preposterous endurance against lawful action?
- Do destructive deeds degrade your vision and create preposterous thought?
- Are deluded thoughts always preposterous, or do no laws prevent them from manifestation?
- How does information collapse and detonate, and is fate eternally created and destroyed?

Carve away your expectation of immortality.

Take ownership of your own discovery. Forge your individual form of character. The answers you obtain through the tumble and turn of growth are immortally specific to you.

Be an investigator, a dissector, a vivisectionist of your own life and motivation, success and failure. Consistently tear apart your mind, your heart, your body to achieve greater, more robust rebuilding of each.

Train ceaselessly in the Way as a practitioner of skills. Develop them with determination.

Study the Way continuously as a scholar of methods. Employ them with seasoned confidence.

Master the Way as an adherent of timeless principles. Deliver with enlightened understanding.

And never, ever forget the final and irrevocable truth of the dark world:

You will eventually be killed, and your bones will be forgotten. Live with great joy and vibrancy until that day.

The Ship in a Tempest | Danse Macabre
Hans Holbein the Younger (1497–1543)

Chapter 31

Warning to the Reader

Reality is forbidding and training is dangerous.

The dark world does not play favorites.

The fact of your training increases your risk and exposure to impact, destruction and death. Exploration of methods ensures your stumbles and slips will have greater danger than mere slow and stupid living. Striving for mastery brings you into frequent proximity to collisions of fate.

It is crucial that you employ this book, and the material within it, from a perspective of deep and respectful responsibility.

This is not mere avoiding harm to other people, although that is a wise precaution.

It is far more than that.

It is taking responsibility for your own outcomes.

You must live your own life and not copy the life of another. Models are fine, but by definition models are not reality. Build a unique life.

Train well. Train with care. Be cognizant of your utter responsibility for your own safety.

Train hard. Train ceaselessly. Be aware that the dark world delights in random upset. Injuries happen, defeats ensue, and some of them are unrecoverable and even fatal.

A rich life is expensive.

Do you wish to build a fortune? You will lose smaller ones for each great one.

Do you wish to raise children? You will fail horribly as a parent even as you raise strong sons.

Do you wish to head an enterprise? You will only be trusted after you prove turnaround of failures.

Do you wish to rule an empire? You will never attain immortal name without great glut of blood.

Understand the dark world well.

It does not cease to be dark because you understand it, and your skills and scholarship and mastery cannot hold back the tide of death that laps and crashes against the reefs of damage.

If you expect this book to teach you to win every time, you are a fool.

If you believe this book will enable you to completely escape scars and loss, crippling wounds and a broken heart, you have failed to read with care.

I tell you here today you will fall and die.

It is up to you to make vision real, and grandly shape the life you live before that inevitable event.

Seize each moment and live in laughter, joy and power.

I believe powerful living is worth it, and my life is testimony to the pursuit of it.

Do the same, and never forget that your death will come with inevitable arrival.

Let that truth be a compelling force in each moment of your existence.

Strive to be a champion. Endure the pain, the exhaustion, the loneliness, the deferred gratification that ceaselessly builds. Conceive your thought, incubate your vision. Control its manifestation with narcissism and win the roaring adulation and wealth of the world when you burst it into being.

I tell you that shivering motivation and cheap vision will see you defeated by better men.

Work to attain the throne. Manage the stress, the worry, the concern, the unending effort that guides and steers. Communicate your word, prepare your plans. Control their revelation with Machiavellianism and seat yourself upon the throne to the amazement and accolade of lesser princes.

I warn you that foolish exposure and rambling process will see you ruled by ruthless men.

Hammer home with accuracy. Carve away the hesitancy, the sloppiness, the weakness of the common man. Execute deeds of action. Exploit traction with competence. Control the direction of fate with psychopathy and attain the unblinking gaze of the apex predator.

I guarantee you that careless effort and sloppy performance will see you killed by vicious men.

There are other threats that await you as you absorb and work through this material.

Heed my warning and avoid the beckoning pitfalls that threaten your development. They will easily ensnare you as you progress through understanding of the grid, the Laws and your training.

The first pitfall is failure to train all three components of the human being.

Training by the **Dark Triad Man** for seamless comprehension of the dark world and mastery of the Laws is not merely a matter of intellectual research, consideration and understanding.

It demands more than spiritual reflection, concentration and developed accuracy of emotional and verbal competence. You need more than mindfulness and enlightenment.

The attainment of physical prowess, robustness, hardened musculature and deadly skill is only a small part of the overall development of the man who follows the Way.

You must have all three, and all three must be pursued past the point of comfort. You must dive deeper than exhaustion, you must continuously reset limitations further, and you must work hard to integrate them completely.

Intellectual understanding alone is useless if you do not have the physical competence to dominate your arena and the emotional maturity to profit from victory.

Emotional depth and sensitivity is awkward and pitiable when married to physical weakness and ignorant stupidity that expects specialized tenderness and comfort to be offered.

Physical strength and skill is contemptible when it is the vehicle for a dull and unthinking brute without subtlety, grace or charm to raise him to position of power.

Reinforce the demand of integration. Continually correct your investments and decisions. Strive to complement your growth, and your work of building, with appropriate and measured care to strip away the useless, inefficient and the gratuitous.

That will advance your development with the maximum possible certainty.

The second error that many make is to seek mastery of principles without skill and method.

The **Dark Triad Man** is a legendary archetype. The modern example of James Bond is the most famous. Bond is suave, deadly, classy and calm. He is expertly skilled in love and death and he delivers preposterous fate into being against all odds and adversaries in the service of his purpose.

Men admire James Bond. He is a stellar model and a superb presentation for good reason.

Yet few men consider the necessary effort and training to become such a resonant archetype.

The groundwork must be laid in real life, with real experience, and the process of moving from practitioner to scholar and then to master does not work in reverse.

You do not enter the *dojo* and expect to be addressed as *sensei* by those who train there. Without long years of bone and blood, blade and training, it is undeserved.

You do not enter the world of business and expect to be granted lucrative stock options and golden parachutes as a new entrant to your industry. Long experience comes first.

Do you wish to be a master of lovemaking, seduction and enthrallment of the female?

Then you must have actual relationships, and live with women, and grasp their nature. And you will go through the roller coaster of human engagements, experience shocking adjustment of expectations, and gain from winning, against those challenges, the masterful male power that they find so intoxicating.

Do you wish to be a dread lord of the warrior arts, deadly and precise and fearsome in battle?

Then you must train ceaselessly, and inventively, and ferociously, for years and years and at the cost of time, relationships, opportunities and grave personal risk to your health, your safety and even your survival—for you will fight the way you train, and safe training means a quick death upon the field.

Do you wish to be a legend of the business world, with billions in disposable cash at your fingertips?

Then you must work long hours every day, hours that are ceaseless and exhausting and stressful, and you must learn what works and what doesn't, how value is created and expended, how to secure profit and leverage it mercilessly in the most unforgiving arena of all: the market.

There is a vital habit that the master performs, that the dilettante does not:

The master returns to the basics.

Over, and over, and over. You must do the same.

Do not be enamored of yourself or consider yourself above the filthy, horrid, grunting and squalid work that is the foundation of any grand achievement. It is in the mud that roads are laid, and it is with blood that empires are built.

There are no shortcuts. There is only the truth, and the Way.

Walk it, and learn well. For the grave arena of the dark world awaits with enormous challenge. You have brutal tasks ahead: overcoming terror, preventing rape, fighting smashed culture and handling dreadful risks.

All of these come before triumph.

You must make it through.

PART FOUR:

ARENA OF BLOOD AND WAR

TERROR OF TODAY ✦ RAPE OF CIVILIZATION

SMASHED CULTURE ✦ DREADFUL RISKS

THE TRIUMPHANT ROAD

The Queen | Danse Macabre
Hans Holbein the Younger (1497–1543)

Chapter 32

Terror of Today

It is terrifying when civilizations collapse.

That terror is inflated and exploded by several concurrent and intersecting trends that are an inescapable part of human life in the dark world. Today those trends are appalling.

Bombs explode in cities across the globe, detonated in suicidal, howling fury by men who ululate and scream the name of Allah. The terror of Islam is deliberate, simple and unmistakable: oppose the followers of that barbaric ideology and you will have your head viciously hacked away from your trunk in a gush of blood.

And all the while public narratives deny that one thing has anything to do with any other. Pundits and politicians condemn, mock and shame you for crying out the truth that none can fail to see, even as grief-stricken families in your country weep over coffins they dare not open.

The value of money is artificially inflated and collapsed, manipulated and made ridiculous, and the flow of it no longer passes from hand to hand in exchange of real value—but through ten billion instantaneous calculations that the common man cannot hope to interrupt or influence.

The resulting terror of poverty and hopeless economic prison is also deliberate, and has a very simple purpose: prevent men from grasping their ability to rise above the trodden masses and seize their own rightful wealth. It is designed to keep men from challenging the oligarchic order.

To keep you confused, and frightened, and stuck.

Values of culture that have withstood the challenges of thousands of years are arbitrarily cast away, and the very basal essence of male and female has become a bizarre and ridiculous pony show of useless, pontifical blathering. Social commentary has been exploded into incomprehensible stupidity, and the entire weight of lethal State power enforces this new orthodoxy of political correctness.

Social shaming, "doxing" attacks upon reputations and livelihoods is used to bewilder and paralyze those who seek to promote and advance the traditional values of Western society.

Small wonder that men today suffer from terror, rage, frustration and misery at this hurtling speed of endless, ceaseless assault upon their civilization, culture, nation and identity.

It is moving too fast!

It is a ceaseless avalanche of lies.

It is an unstoppable bombardment of wild advertised claims and impossible standards. Infinite, instantaneous wealth and fantastic celebrity glamour are upheld in screaming contrast to your despicable failure, and you feel the horrific and despairing slide of your time being sucked, irrevocably, into the black and empty abyss of idiocy. There is nothing but contempt and mockery from those who have everything, while you and your brothers despair with empty hands.

How can you even begin to deal with this?

It is too much. It hurts with appalling pain to feel your life slip away in ceaseless and impotent terror. It is the terror of despair and defeat.

I understand this terror.

I understand how it feels.

I understand the resentment and rage and nameless, gripping fury that does not even have a target to land upon and thereby, somehow, bring some sort of order to the dizzying merry-go-round of misery. There is not even a coherent thing to blame.

I know that every single day you feel your precious moments of life slip by while sanity creeps further out of reach. And there seems to be no clear way through the nonsense.

That is by design, my brothers.

It has been deliberately, specifically, malevolently created to impale you to the floor and profit off the blood that streams from your transfixion.

Your suffering is not by accident.

All of our brothers suffer with you. All of it is on purpose.

I want you to hold this book tightly, right now, this very moment.

Grip it hard in your hands, as cruelly as you can.

Leave the imprint of your hands on the power of this book.

Are you ready?

I am here to stop it all.

I am here to extend a gripping hand and haul you off the torture wheel. I am here to place vengeful steel in your hands and grim joy of living in your heart as you stride forward with your brothers, unshackled. Free as men, free to snap off the manacles of terror, laughingly free to seize the thrones of the new age and slam frothing tankards together in toast over the remains of the old rulers.

Your terror ends now.

Right here.

Fear, anger, resentment and despair are inevitable. They are normal parts of life.

The reward that comes from victory over these terrors is power.

The key to transforming the hurtful, cruel and often shattering experiences of life is not by enforcing safe spaces and avoiding trigger words, or by shutting others down and denying their voices.

It is about power. Authentic, radical, personal power that strengthens and hardens you to surmount suffering. I want you, as a human being, to have it.

I demand that you, as a man, cultivate it with every bit of ferocity you possess.

Power is how men win, and how terror is defeated.

Power is not about force. Power is about understanding how things work, and using your mind, your heart and your action to create results that are greater than the sum of self.

Power is your tool to deliver the explosive, fateful dominance of a man who hefts the axe of fate.

With that axe, you may cleave the world open and see terror for what it is.

It is merely what takes place. No more, and no less.

The savage depredations of the Islamic State as they chain, hang and burn men alive is nothing new. Thousands of years ago the Greek tyrants roasted men alive in brazen bulls.

The Assyrians, centuries before the Greeks, flayed men alive and draped their entire skins over the walls of conquered cities with dispassionate, brutal cruelty.

English kings tore men apart and burned their guts and genitals in front of the very eyes of victims and their families, then hung their quartered and dripping limbs from castle gates.

Terror is simply a weather pattern in the dark world. From time to time, there are always storms.

This does not make it good, and right, and healthy.

But it does make it predictable, expected and inevitable.

Terror is employed because it works. Make no mistake in this respect.

Invading battalions of cruel butchers with chilling reputations for unsparing, merciless killing are common throughout history. The red no-quarter flag has flown on ships of war and on battlefields of Europe; today that flag is the black-and-white of Islam but the same practice holds true.

Do not fool yourself that the dread lords and armored men of today are more or less vicious and cruel than those before, or those to come. They are not, and you are lied to if you are told they are.

Simply understand how things are, through all of natural history, and accept it.

By that acceptance understand how to make use of it.

Learn to take the paralyzing influence of terror, the insidious and freezing infection of it, and transform it into your antifragile advantage.

Terror has a reverse component, and that is the ferocity of desperation.

Terror can be pivoted and turned into the source of rage and innovative power.

That pivot must take place within *you*.

You, the individual, are the critical linchpin for the flowering of desperate resistance.

You are the weak link in the family, the squad, the tribe, the nation, the culture!

You herald fate for your civilization.

Terror is not only defeated through killing the enemy, but through mastery of the self and internal processing. The purpose of terror is to immobilize you; to freeze you; to trick you into the false and grasping hope that *doing nothing* will somehow save you from the alternative of certain death.

Doing nothing is not the Way.

Abrogation of personal responsibility is not how men survive.

There is a difference between being afraid and being terrified.

Being fearful and being terrorized are not the same thing.

Fear is normal. You will always, to some extent, live with fear. Fear of death, fear of rejection, fear of loss, fear of pain. And in time, fear does something normal: it goes away with experience.

Terror does not, for the purpose of terror is to stop your mental and emotional processing, to freeze your ability to think, to speak and act.

When you clamp down upon your tongue and you will not speak your mind, because all defense by your words leads to condemnation—you are sublimated in terror.

When your faith and loyalty and allegiance are stilled in your heart, and you dare not proclaim belief and truth—you are subordinated to terror.

When your deeds are forestalled and you refuse to take action in defense of your values, your purpose and your freedom—you are subjugated by terror.

Terror is not acceptable and you must, without hesitation or wavering, penetrate through it.

The way to penetrate through terror is by grim and ruthless adherence to plans and process.

The way to adhere to plans and process is by consistent, systemic, repeated training.

That is the purpose of this book.

It is your manual.

Terror is the ultimate friction, a seductive enthrallment that infects you with paralysis. It is the commission of suicide through inaction, an absurd response designed on behalf of the adversary.

Terror is unnecessary and need not be accepted.

Terror is a manufactured artifact of the disordered mind.

Restore order, and terror loses its power.

Adhere to process, and the mind finds release from terror in the relief of reliable work at hand.

This is why the Machiavellian redirects the infection of terror, why the psychopath has natural resistance to it and the narcissist shrugs off its cloying shroud.

This is why the soldier trains, over and over and over, until ruthless process is inherent to his nature and the dreadful roar and fire of blinding steel death are simply worked through at speed.

Your ability to recognize the birth of terror is the first necessary step to destroy it.

How do you recognize terror? How do you identify the very first creeping tendrils of paralysis that entangle and entwine within your heart, your mind and your body? What can you do to halt that seemingly overwhelming dread?

Begin by identifying what refuses to move.

Find the central point of any and all paralysis within you.

Where is the pin driven through your thought, your word or your deed?

What transfixes you? Where are your heart and mind impaled, and your hands thus frozen?

Ruthlessly force movement off that point. Restore momentum to decisions and direction. Know that while you may nonetheless be defeated and destroyed, it is better to do so on your feet with steel in hand than on your knees, mumbling in useless and unappreciated terror.

Never do the work of the adversary for him.

Thus your work in facing the terror of the day is to return to your plans, to repeat and tune your processes, and to work your systems and methods.

Your responsibility is to train.

Training is your source of power, your victory over terror, and the paving stones of the life you must build ahead for yourself, your family, your nation and culture.

It is the seminal bath that sustains continuous, renewing rebirth of your civilization.

Your situation may remain hopeless, and I tell you that in this dark world you will assuredly die.

But do not go quietly, no matter what lies terror screeches or threats it attempts to compel you with.

Train hard. Train ceaselessly. Build your fortress of self-reliance. Sell your life dearly, and at such cost that the transaction itself is prohibitively expensive to the adversary.

When the time comes, fight. Protect your loved ones.

Protect them from rape and plunder by the invader.

For it hurtles towards them in the dark world.

You are the fortress in between.

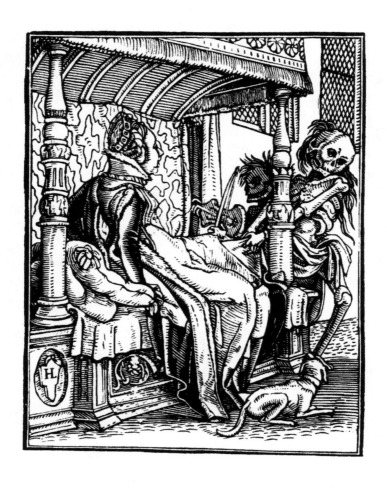

The Duchess | Danse Macabre
Hans Holbein the Younger (1497–1543)

Chapter 33

Rape and Civilization

It is not enough that terror remains a facet and aspect of the dark world, a tried and tested method of men and Caesars alike. The excoriating horrors of rape are also an inevitable reef upon which the waves of the dark world crash and foam.

Your adversaries will ceaselessly attempt to drive and dash you against them.

Rape is not merely about sex. It is not about "toxic masculinity" or other silly, platitudinous monstrosities of foolish modern solipsism.

It is about plunder. It is about dominance, humiliation, conquering, ravaging and forcibly taking without let or hindrance and in disregard of the bitter agony it causes.

That agony, in fact, becomes an exquisite form of pleasure and satisfaction to the plunderer.

Indeed, that is one of the most intimate and devastating aspects of it. The vulnerabilities of your women, your daughters, your wealth and your country are savagely harvested in front of you.

During times of open existential war such as we face today, rape is a specific and brutally effective weapon designed to inflict the maximum possible horror and subjugation upon a people.

Rape has been used as a weapon of war since well before the dawn of history.

To take a man's woman, lay her bare before him, rut into her and seed her belly with the gene of the dominant conqueror is the most brutal and demonstrative example of unstoppable power that man possesses. It savages, it destroys, it humiliates and turns culture into beaten ruin.

It is why invading armies rape the women left behind by dead husbands at the front.

It is why occupying ideologies rape the intelligentsia of a conquered nation and enforce servitude.

It is why successful cultures rape failed ones, enslaving their people and raising cities on their bones.

Dominant nations colonize indigenous populations, plundering the natural resources of oil and gold and lumber and crops and leaving behind nothing but the remnants of defeated traditions.

The power of rape is why it proceeds and persists.

It is the ultimate imposition of will, and the purpose of it is not to freeze you but to break you.

Rape is a strategy of the adversary that you must recognize in all its forms, and take grim and unwavering steps to counter from the very moment of threat.

Rape turns you into the crushed and broken toy of the sadistic invader.

Today we see this clearly in the massive use of rape as a specific ideological pillar of Islam designed to overcome, overawe, smash and destroy the tribes and cities and peoples that it conquers. Cages of prepubescent girls are bartered in the markets of the Islamic State; bearded theologians across the Middle East thoughtfully stroke their hairy faces and pronounce declarations of righteousness in taking what "the right hand possesses".

Understand well the correct response to rape when leveled against your women, your tribe, your country, your culture and your civilization.

There is only one correct response:

Fight the adversary. Instantly.

Fight them to the death.

Upon recognition of intent and action to rape, the full and most savage training you possess must come to the forefront and be utilized without hesitation, remorse or restraint.

This is the necessary path you must follow in the dark world unless you choose to accept powerless, degrading and defeated submission to the spectacle of your own plunder and mocking death.

Teach your women to fight and kill, brothers!

Let their steel and gunfire speak with a finality that mere words and slogans cannot match.

Teach your tribes and towns to band together and respond.

Let your disciplined, roving packs be grim and shocking consequence to offenders who cross your borders, plunder your wives and daughters and laugh at the weakness of your political leaders.

Command your nations and culture to wage war against those who despoil human beings, whether the openly declared adversary that Islam represents—or the grotesque, appeasing and inexcusably bankrupt fools who believe that tolerance is a virtue even to surrender.

Never accept the strident calls for prostrated groveling that issue forth from contemptible would-be slaves, who hide their own inner shame by ensnaring their fellow men in shackles!

You hold this book in your hands as a road to vision, purpose and power.

You must fight for all of it. That is what training equips you for.

For there is no safety in the dark world.

Rape is a weapon that will be turned upon you as you grow in wealth and power, assets and establishment. Your adversaries will seek to not merely penetrate and seize those values, but to demonstrate your helplessness as evidence of their triumph before the eyes of men.

Ruthless, unhesitating, ferocious and unrecoverable damage to the adversary is utterly and irreplaceably important if you wish to prevent and terminate the threat of rape.

You must learn this well.

For where one rape takes place, all others pile on—even adversaries who were merely onlookers, or perhaps previously allies… because why not?

The dark world is a place without pity.

If you allow it, you will be tracked into the mud as forgotten and discarded bones while your grandchildren spring forth from the loins of the invader.

The correct method to prevent rape is force and war.

The dark world respects strength, viciously and unhesitatingly applied with fearsome and colossal consequence. This is simply how it is.

Recognize it.

Adapt your mindset to embody savage consequence to any and all attempted invasions of plunder.

Train this determined and lethal response into your women, your children, your family and loved ones. That is how their life and dignity will be preserved.

Build this ferocious and responsive delivery into your brothers and your community. Let there be no possibility that plunder goes unpunished. Demand cruel and fatal result.

Foster this thinking into your nation and culture. It is easier for men to relax, and avoid struggle, than to remain hard and noble in the face of challenge. Insist upon it.

Eventually the culture itself, if not strengthened by men of purpose, collapses into self-immolating castration of will. Sackless politicians carry water for domestic enemies, and men who retain their dignity and natural male protective power are resented as "toxic".

Never allow your women to lie prostrate under the swaggering thrusts of the criminal.

Never allow your community to be invaded without consequence by raiders.

Never allow your nation or culture to be disgraced, humiliated and destroyed by putrid quislings, excited by the false apparatus of power they receive in return for prostitution of their country!

You are the warrior that must protect your family, your tribe, your country and civilization.

You bear solemn and sacred duty.

Rise, right now, and face forward.

Stand where you are, in this very spot.

Open your spirit and speak to yourself in brutal and unflinching prayer.

Where is the family you value most in this world?

Who are the loved ones that would cry out in pleas of agony to you?

Who are you responsible for as the protector of last resort?

Could you live with yourself, after watching their despoliation and murder?

It is not the way of men of honor to permit unchallenged atrocity.

You know in your heart what you would do to prevent it.

I am here to equip you for the work of resistance.

I bring coherence and shape to your fury.

You must prevent the rape of civilization.

It is your responsibility to use your training in the dark world to achieve results.

It is the duty of men to preserve, protect and defend.

It is the duty of the **Dark Triad Man** to lead in war.

Commit yourself to combat when the alternative is unimaginable.

Put your training into fearsome action. Fight!

It is the only way that honor is upheld in the face of rape.

And you must band your brothers together, and fight as one.

For your culture is being smashed.

The Drunkards | Danse Macabre
Hans Holbein the Younger (1497–1543)

Chapter 34

Smashed Culture

You live today in the most ridiculous, preposterous and mind-numbingly stupid cultural collapse imaginable. Millions of naked emperors prance across social media, and your very language itself descends into a meaningless and depressing array of Orwellian nonsense.

Today you are living witness to the unforgiving smash of your own culture. Its putrid expiration while it chokes upon its own incestuous vomit is unacceptable to watch, much less permit.

Naked fools in collars are led by merrily prancing, helplessly effete, rainbow-clad buffoons who parade through your towns and cities. They are upheld as examples of brave social pride, while men who suffer in triple-digit temperatures with battered rifles, heavy packs and scarred helmets are forgotten, ignored and discarded.

They are left to die, waiting in hallways, while criminal invaders are enriched and acclaimed.

You are *right* to be angry and bitter in the face of such desecration.

University students shriek, sob and gesticulate in repetitive chanting screams of incandescent triggered outrage at mild shadings of gender pronoun.

As if such things mattered to the dark world.

"Safe spaces" are proliferated, more gags are demanded, additional freedoms pissed upon and corrupted by those who deliberately embrace weaknesses that their fathers would have spat upon in absolute and utter contempt.

Two generations before their grandfathers willingly stood in the stench of diesel smoke and puked into the storming waves, ready to wade ashore through a hail of murderous Nazi machine-gun fire and leave their exploded limbs and guts upon the sandy stretches of Normandy.

In this generation an accredited ambassador of the United States was dragged from his burning consulate, then viciously raped and beaten to death. Bloody handprints stained the walls where desperate fingers clawed for life, and brave warfighters who ran to the sound of the guns died in hot and brutal barrages of mortar fire while no one came to help.

Thousands of miles away, the Commander in Chief of America ordered not one fire team in support.

"What difference, at this point, does it make?" asked his Secretary of State.

I tell you that it makes all the difference in the dark world.

When you cause your culture to belch and wallow and vomit drunkenly in its own folly and idiocy and grotesqueries; when you degrade the very concept of nobility, and elevate mocking snark and repulsive arrogance as prideful signal of virtue; when you embrace and promote the very worst of your cultural weaknesses as its most triumphant and diverse strengths: you pave cruel road towards final smash.

The adversaries of your civilization will not stop your foolish citizens from doing the unforgivable work of destroying your most precious cultural legacies on behalf of invading raiders.

When they see that suicidal cuckoldry has sick and cloying hold upon your helm of state, they draw pre-sharpened steel and begin to march.

The older generation will not rise up, for they have done their own work in the past age and it is now, irrevocably, on *your* shoulders to preserve your culture from smashing ruin.

Where does this leave you?

When the entire array of social narratives, the celebrated spectacles of your nation, the "leaders" held up as brave and stunning examples are all disgusting, emasculated, weak and contemptible—what do you do?

What is the way forward when your entire civilization rocks from repeated blows, designed to permanently rip and tear your culture apart?

How do you respond when every formal utterance of public figures and personalities is a cynically delivered, preposterously calculated and meaningless virtue signal that eats away at the moral fiber of your nation like a metastizing cancer?

Your answer is to smash back.

Right now, walk to the window. If you are able, walk outside.

Stand there and gaze out, with this book once more tightly in your hands.

Breath hard. Breathe repeatedly. Feel these bound pages crack within your grip!

Look into the distance before you! Your brothers are out there, in the dark world.

I swear oath of utter truth to you in this very moment:

Your brothers look just as hard for you.

Find them.

Find them, or give up your culture to death.

Your duty is to meet, and bond, and plan.

Commit to the serious work of finding the brothers with whom you will learn and train, fight and smash, and face dreadful risk in the dark world.

And take great heart in one more truth: you only need to search half of the distance, for the point of meeting is in the center. And it has never been easier to search than today.

With great determined purpose, find them.

Form your ranks amid the smashed and bloody sway of your dying culture.

You will never save it as a solitary hero.

But as an army you can smash back with unstoppable force.

Start raising it today, exactly where you stand.

We all gather, brother.

And we mean to win.

Join us.

The Empress | Danse Macabre
Hans Holbein the Younger (1497–1543)

Chapter 35

Dreadful Risks

Life is about risk. So is the dark world.

In the dark world risks are dreadful and full of horror.

Embracing risk and not sloughing momentum away through fear is what drives the outcomes of the powerful, the successful, the determined and the victorious.

You will never achieve immortal name or blinding wealth by tentative, fearful avoidance of risk.

The global Caesar to come, he who sits astride the first throne of the entire world, will tell you that he bedded infinite risk and flipped her over, then ruthlessly bedded her again while she flailed with knives for teeth in her open and screaming mouth. And he will show you the scars of her iron nails.

The great financier grins as he commits to ventures while knowing that his entire investment may be wasted with irrecoverable loss.

The leader of the resistance lays plans and trusts in men despite the certainty that the inevitable traitor will betray his brothers to tyrants.

If you wish victory, you must dance with death. You must spin quickly in the *Danse Macabre*.

Death is always your risky partner in that fatal dance. The true champion steps into the ring with sure and certain knowledge he will be hit with terrible blows that may destroy his name and career.

And death always leads, here in the dark world.

There are an infinite number of risks you will face in life. There are ever-present risks to your health and safety, to your sanity and circumstances, to your offices and profits and outcomes.

Some risks you have control over, and some you do not.

The purpose of this chapter is not to teach you how to weigh risks, how to mitigate risks, how to conduct risk analysis or build decision diagrams. That is knowledge you can easily find elsewhere.

Our purpose here is to instruct you in the single, crucial mindset that you must grasp, absorb and manifest with unflagging determination in the dark world.

And to highlight specific, dreadful risks that you and your brothers face in your work ahead.

We will begin with the mindset you must take towards risk.

Risk can never be eliminated from living in the real world.

Therefore, resistance and denial of risk is the fruitless and futile work of a fool who is destined for failure, crash and poverty of outcome.

Risk and reward are inseparable. Reward is the shore, and risk the storms and seas that the brave must navigate in order to reach the land of gold.

You must learn to laugh not at risk, but at fear. Risk can be prepared for, but fear is not truth—it is merely a signal. Risk can be fortified against, but fear is not brick and mortar.

When you are no longer afraid, risk is assessed with accuracy.

There is a trick to handling fear.

It is a habit you must enforce.

What is your most savage, secret desire in life?
As you hold this book, acknowledge it from the heart.
What great prize do you wish for, above all other things?
Do you want it more than you fear it?

The most dreadful risk is that you let life slip by.

The most miserable, bitter regret is dying without living.
The worst mortal sin you can commit is despair.
Take this book, and use my teaching to *live*.

You have adversaries, and they are legion. They despise you, and work together.

By standing in defense of yourself and your family, you become a target. That is the first dreadful risk you must accept the instant you refuse to be a slave, subject to entitled rape by a master.

The legion of adversaries arrayed against you are delighted by firing upon individuals.

By forming your bands of brothers in the dark world you are no longer a lonely target to pick off, for you have now become a threat. This is a second dreadful risk you must accept the instant you dare to raise spears shoulder to shoulder with your brothers.

The leaders of hateful legions will lead fearsome charges against your ranks to crush and destroy you.

By marching as an army to smash back against the destruction of your nation, culture and civilization, you now present a both grand and terrible obstacle, and the last bastion of defense against the plans of those who seek annihilation of the West.

Dread lords will be your adversaries. They will raise bloody banners and march to meet you on the field of war.

Dreadful risks rise as your power and brotherhood grow.

Assassinations, both virtual and real, will be conducted against you to forestall insurgency.

Skirmishes, both cultural and physical, will explode among you to crush open resistance.

Total war, both military and civilizational, will blow apart as the throne of global Caesar grows near.

Understand the dark world and its inexorable, massive slide of momentum!

I tell you today that you cannot transform this world into a place of light and peace. I tell you that the cruel and basal nature of our predatorial race will never abandon ambition.

Dreadful risk is inescapable, and nothing will prevent your eventual death.

Sell yourself dearly. Form ranks and fight!

Find your brothers ahead of battle.

You will observe men with this book. In the dark world they are there, training.

Stand and approach them. Speak gravely to them with the recognition of a brother!

It is through bonding of men that the terrible, dreadful risks of the age are overcome.

Clasp hands and grip shoulders. Look into the eyes of *men*.

> *We few, we happy few, we band of brothers;*
> *For he today that sheds his blood with me*
> *Shall be my brother; be he ne'er so vile,*
> *This day shall gentle his condition;*
> *And gentlemen in England now abed*
> *Shall think themselves accursed they were not here,*

And hold their manhoods cheap whiles any speaks
That fought with us upon Saint Crispin's day.[8]

This is how the West will survive.

Men who lock shields together, aim spears, and march as one.

Fearsome terror demands equally fearsome preparation. It is by your training in this manual of power that your preparation as a man is established with the deep momentum that drives impact.

Cruel rape demands utterly ferocious and instant response. In your vigilance and ferocious teamwork is found solution to turn back the enemy and crack apart his plans for your humiliation.

Smashed culture requires bold and concerted assault in battalions that smash back with furious and grim attack, and turn the tide of war and preserve the heart of your civilization.

The most dangerous risk comes from isolation and inaction.

Failure to train yourself, to find your brothers, to stand shoulder to shoulder and fight with total ferocity means defeat as a man, a comrade, a citizen and a warrior.

You must meet this dreadful risk with determined heart, committed mind and capable body.

Quickly, and without hesitation. For the dark world does not wait, but swells with bloody intention in the next roaring cycle of human atrocity and collapse, murdered millions and savagely dismembered and eviscerated empires.

You can no longer sit on the sidelines. They will turn into gutters that run with the blood of innocents. That has always been the way of things.

This time will not be different.

Man has not become kinder, and illusions have not become real.

You must face dreadful risks directly.

There are only two outcomes in the dark world where civilization is concerned.

Defeat and ignominy, or survival and triumph.

Choose well, my brother.

And choose quickly.

The road is shaking underfoot.

The Magistrate | Danse Macabre
Hans Holbein the Younger (1497–1543)

Chapter 36

The Triumphant Road

The point of our review and exhortation in this arena of blood and war is to bring you to culmination of immortal reward that lies within the darkness.

There is no wallowing here, no useless slopping and splashing in fear or negativity.

The point and purpose of this book is to wake you, shock you, teach you.

And then to aim you, and unleash you with fearsome accuracy.

Make no mistake that your outcomes in the dark world have serious, permanent consequences of wealth and crash, power and death, victory and smash.

We seek, for you, the triumphant road.

That is the purpose of the Way.

The triumphant road is one of reward.

It is the preservation and advancement of civilization. It is the defense and flowering of culture. It is the prosperity and protection of the nation, the support and shelter of the family, the survival and purpose of the individual.

The Nine Laws are the rails on which this triumphant road is laid.

This book is the manual for the conscious, deliberate and unstoppable capture of its rewards.

This book is for men of action who demand performance.

It is for men who live for battle, and the triumph of victory.

The first reward comes through personal transformation and understanding of power.

It is the joy of living, the freedom of conscience, the delight in vital and happy days.

It is your stride into ferocious embodiment of the Way that is delivered through The Nine Laws, the cultivation of deep momentum that characterizes the immortal archetype of the **Dark Triad Man**.

It is the structure of your thought into coherence starting with the most basic possible level.

It is to be the deliberate architect of your own fate, the determiner of the fate of others, the conscious engineer of the outcomes of battles and engagements in the dark world.

It is the foundation for all else, and the purpose of this book.

It is tearing apart and rebuilding of your thought.

Thought must give rise to great clarity of mind.

The second reward is your tribe of brothers, formation of community and comradeship in struggle.

It is the noble love you bear for them, that envelopes you in return, and offers great fulfillment.

It is your coherence as a social unit, it is the distinguishing deep road of the Way. It is the place where bonds are forged, where larger purposes are established.

Those bonds become the immense and momentous vehicle of brotherhood in time of war.

It is throwing off the shackles of illusion and humiliating defeat. It is the formation of cadres, the root of civilization itself, the army of the dark world and the permanent end of your isolation.

It is where you take the knowledge of this book and fulfill your consequent duty of leadership.

It is distillation and projection of your word.

Word is the ringing, unsilenced voice of your conscience.

The third reward is the thrill of the hunt as a marching army under bloody banners.

It is exultation of physical triumph, the heaving chest of victory, the hands clasped over the kill.

It is the purpose of civilization, the advancement of men, the exultation of the knight in the maelstrom of fire and steel. It is the ultimate destination of the Way, the engagement of the warrior.

The roar of victory from the throats of triumphant men is the reason for all your training.

Your work of absorbing and studying lessons, the dangerous and challenging task of finding brothers and unmasking traitors, rewards you with definitive outcomes for the clash and collision of the age.

It is the defeat of the adversary, frustration of his plans, and the security of peace—on your terms.

It is acceleration and impact of your deed.

Deed is the beating heart of your life in action.

There is only one way that you will obtain all these precious rewards.

It is not possible to leap straight ahead into undeserved victory without great struggle.

You must commence your transformation by absorption of fundamental and crucial basics. There is no other road to vision, purpose and power; there is no replacement for the training of the practitioner, the study of the scholar, the comprehension of the master.

We now conclude Part Four of this book. And send you equipped, back into the dark world.

It is time for your world to crack open. For each individual particle of information to be carved apart and spun, pivoted from probability to possibility, twirled between actuals and potentials.

It is time for you to tumble and turn for real.

We have cut directly through the heart and opened the pulsing beat of the entire universe. It is time for you to drive the terrible momentum of the dark world itself, and to lead among the race of men.

Prepare yourself for shocks, for yours must be the hand of the **Dark Triad Man**.

It is time for you to move from theory to practice, from scholarship to mastery.

It is time for you to lead, to spread word, to form the basis of the cadres that will save the West.

Grip the face of your brothers. Turn their eyes to the pitiless and impersonal reality that swirls without limit, and direct their gaze hard onto the brilliant pivots that form our entire universe.

Share with them the knowledge you have encountered here. Support them through their growth as I have supported you, for their current self will not survive it. And men do not leave their brothers behind in the dark world.

It is time for them to die as well, and begin again, newly made.

It is time for all of you to be reborn as insurgents, triumphant, the conquerors.

Lead your brothers into the new age that dawns.

Militant monks and sacred warriors, brothers all.

You must inspire them, teach them, lead them with this knowledge.

Your protection of your loved ones must be instant and instinctive.

Your defense of your tribe and nation must be ferocious and competent.

Your advancement of your civilization must be inexorable and existential.

All of these things are your responsibility. Fulfill those duties, and live well.

Today is all that you will ever have, and all that you ever need.

Use it to build your shining tomorrow.

WHAT NOW?

ADVANCING THE MAN

CULTIVATION, EVOLUTION AND INSTRUCTION

OWN, ENGAGE AND FOLLOW

AFTERWORD ✦ GLOSSARY ✦ STUDY RESOURCES

The Bishop | Danse Macabre
Hans Holbein the Younger (1497–1543)

Chapter 37

Cultivation, Evolution and Instruction

The **Dark Triad Man** progresses through an identifiable evolution as an actor in the dark world. It is a flowering of living, an ongoing transformation with defined, identifiable and patterned shape as he passes through age and cultivates his experience.

What is the greatest outcome of the **Dark Triad Man** as he moves through this dark world, planning the execution of his vision? How does he adapt to his stature as his visions are achieved, and what is the end result of all of his training, his engagements and his successes?

What are the stages of life for a weaponized human being?

They are cultivation, evolution and instruction.

They are the path of life itself, the process by which each generation of men is born, grows to adulthood, shapes history, and teaches the new men who come after them.

The first stage we will examine is cultivation.

Cultivation is how learning, understanding, strength, skill, determination, power, values and all the other aspects of the man are attained.

Information is sought, layered, grown and intertwined across fields of inquiry. The knowledge base of the man grows and is nurtured, pruned and tested.

Comprehension is arrived at, incorporated into knowledge, and fostered through comparison and contrast, exploration and study. The perspective of the man is broadened, expanded and furthered.

Physical experience is sought, lusted after, bathed in and satiated. Athletic endeavors are pursued, lovers are writhed with, the exultation of the physical body is explored and grasped.

Accomplishment of deed and proof of market value is reinforced by the man's achievement of ascending profit and evidence of his reliable consistency to the arbiters of wealth.

Moral considerations are weighed and identified, selected and promoted, and the man moves from weighing questions of virtue, to solid demonstrations of it in his relationships and performance.

This process of cultivation is one that forms with concentric, narrowing circles as the man moves from youth to adulthood, from adulthood to maturity, and eventually into wisdom. It is a forming, shaping, clearing process as questions are answered, truths uncovered, and realities absorbed.

The **Dark Triad Man** does this deliberately and not as an afterthought.

You must consciously work to develop your progression through manhood.

Cultivate momentum, collisions and outcomes. Tumble and turn them each moment, each day, each year. Shape your life deliberately and live through experiences that teach and inform, reveal and unfold your comprehension.

Explore this world. Grow in experience. Seek out challenge, yearn for contest, train well and hard for the collision of adversaries who bring their own purpose, power and determination to bear in opposition to your vision and planning.

Through repeated hard knocks, through successes and failures, the man is cultivated from the child and the youth becomes the adult.

You cannot skip or evade this necessary process.

Proclamations of wisdom without the foundation of experience are empty.

Declarations of power without the base of competence are worthless.

Announcements of finding without the process of experimentation are pointless.

Insist upon cultivation of wisdom, power and intelligence in your daily life. Ceaselessly work to accumulate and layer your insights and your triumphs.

In the errors of love you will find the calm reassurance of the mature and reliable partner.

By mistakes in business competence you discover the discipline of professional performance.

In the crack of chastising bone against flesh you are taught the value of circumspect words.

This is the process of cultivation. It is an active process, and it is not replaceable.

Without cultivation, evolution is stalled.

You cannot short-circuit this process and leap from one stage to the other.

Evolution must take place gradually, for it is not an instantaneous change.

This is a mistake that often appears in life. It is a trap for the unwary and the impatient, who need—and will receive—firmer and crueler lesson taught by the inexorable consequences of the dark world.

Young men who declare mastery and promote their inexperienced pronouncements as wisdom, lead fools into disappointment and futility.

Wise men who seek to restore their dissipated youth through surgery, affairs and inappropriate displays of fashion make absurd and sorry spectacles of themselves.

The young are not wise.

The wise are no longer young.

The child does not parent the adult.

The adult does not partner with the child.

Experience cannot be substituted for. Understand this well. The process of cultivated mastery must evolve on a measured path, and a key ingredient in this process is time. It cannot be hurried and it cannot be hastened. Truth and wisdom arrive in their own time, so long as the man engages well with the world and concentrates his intelligence and emotion upon correct and relevant learning.

Evolution of the man is a passive and not an active process. Evolution is not something forced, or pushed—it is an ongoing result of cultivated living.

As the man engages with the dark world and tests his theories, challenges his values, collides his allegiances and breaks his heart the inevitable, subtle transformation of evolution takes place. Hypotheses become reliable or discarded. Values are solidified or abandoned. Love and loss tumble and turn, and cynicism or acceptance blend into forward expectations.

Evolution is a slow process. Even trauma does not accelerate it, but rather redirects it—for the recovery from inevitable trauma is, itself, a lengthy working out of issues.

Evolution is what, in the end, brings wisdom and peace.

It is where the **Dark Triad Man** reaches his apex.

The final outcome is that the slayer becomes the sage.

As adherence to the Laws is cultivated, evolution takes place. As experience shapes the perspective of the man, his vantage point for the flow of history becomes broader and more incisive.

The trader develops an inherent ability to spot the ups and downs of the market as they blip past on a rapid candlestick chart, overlaid in his mind upon the news of the day and the latest valuations of equities. He reaches a state of instantly responsive and effortless, profitable transcendence.

The warrior similarly advances in skill, competence and power to a place where the challenges of steel and lance, squads and armies, tactics and formations are already overcome. His victories are, as the sages describe, won even before the battle ensues. He attains the state of the great strategist.

This evolution is seen in the transformation of the Laws from constricting, shaping and aligning the dark world to the expanding, clearing and freeing realization of sincere truth.

Survival becomes irrelevant, for vision is achieved with subtle continuance that outlasts its creator. Legacy is the result, and though the body turns to dust, the impact of the man pervades history.

Concealment transforms to transparency, and the sublime quality of truth results in impenetrable depth that the fool, the idiot and the enemy cannot discern despite open revelation.

Purpose reaches simplicity, and with each victory the man of purpose seeks more basal and fundamental fulfillments. Power, wealth and position give way to happiness, calm and satisfaction.

Endurance loses struggle, and with seasoned experience in the dark world the equanimity of the immovable spirit is no longer a tension-filled process but one of serenity in the face of reality.

Posture has no form, and the shapes of principles, methods and skills are no longer identifiable. Success simply appears, movement is undefinable, strictures of process are abandoned.

Freedom glows internally, and the mind and heart are unfettered from the bondage of desire. The transient dwelling place of the body is no longer a limitation on comprehension or manifestation.

Power and karma become one, for the Way is not deviated from and the will of Heaven is entirely accorded with. Delivery of fate is no longer a personal struggle of the man, but seamless living.

Preposterousness transforms to utter joy, for the struggle to reconcile the realms of light and dark, life and death, order and chaos subsides into appreciation and delight at the unfolding of all things.

No Laws returns to inexhaustible bellows of God, and there are no longer concerns with truth or falsehood, control or escape, dominance or surrender. The futility of law becomes quiet amusement.

The warrior becomes the teacher, and the trader becomes the mentor.

As this evolution takes place, and elevation and transcendence of the man ensues, he returns his understanding and value back to the pool, and instructs.

It is the testing, the application, the real-world collision and impact that drives the maturity and seasoning of the **Dark Triad Man** and enables his gradual transformation from the warrior to the priest, the investor to the philanthropist.

This is the great closing of the circle, what the *ninja* refer to as *shin-den* or heart-to-heart transmission. You have an obligation to take part in this.

It is by the passing on of the great riddle of steel to the young warriors who form the upcoming ranks of culture, that culture is itself preserved. This takes place from teacher to student, from drill instructor to recruit, from father to son.

There is great and sacred importance in this transmission.

It is how civilization is preserved, how knowledge is both sheltered and advanced.

This heart-to-heart transmission of truth is the final grave and solemn duty of men of action who demand performance.

You must teach the young, and you must share what you learn with your fellow men.

Never leave your brothers behind in the dark world.

You do not exist in a vacuum of pure theory.

Power and capacity belong in the service of purpose.

Go forth into the dark world. And return to the source.

Straddle heaven and earth as the **Dark Triad Man**.

And bring your discoveries home.

The New-Married Lady | Danse Macabre
Hans Holbein the Younger (1497–1543)

Conclusion: Own, Engage and Follow

This concludes the complete book of The Nine Laws.

The Laws have each been reviewed in their entirety, and laid down as navigation rails for the transit of the **Dark Triad Man** through time, space and the human experience.

We have explored the dark world and framed it within the grid, laid out the path of forged, focused and controlled human delivery of fate.

Deep and fundamental training has been delivered to you. Return to it again and again so that you may drive deeper comprehension, more incisive analysis and vaster capacity into your work of living.

It is your great and joyful responsibility to make complete use of this material.

You must own it, engage with it, and follow it.

You invested in this manual and you now own the outcome of using it.

Own this material by excavating value, by diving into its concepts, and exploring it completely.

Read well. Study deeply. Train continuously, and do not forsake your accountability to yourself and your loved ones during your development into the most utterly actualized human being possible.

Achieve the resonant authenticity of the weaponized human being.

Escape the limitations of time and space through solemn contemplation of the slow, continuous roll of human experience through history, over the present and into the future. Broaden your ability to perceive sincere truth, and release any lingering resistance to the grander and more sublime perspective that comes with experience.

Infect your work with the subtle utility that is the hallmark of the competent master. Plan your work in parallel. Achieve many goals with each action. Focus your word and vision into thunderous deed. Skip and transit from Law to Law, from realm to channel, from weaponized control to achieved fate through Machiavellian tumble and turn of the hollow and the actual.

Prove the total inevitability of your glittering vision through utterly absolute manifestation!

Be the chosen of God through adherence to the Way of Heaven.

As owner of this material you must also engage with it.

Serve as the councilor of kings. Bring your ability control the grid and Laws into the pursuit of goals greater than merely personal ones. Deliver the voice of revelation to your brothers. Manifest the vision of the enterprise with professional dedication. Direct the acts of your subordinates with the icy competence of the man who does not hesitate.

This is engagement with the serious content of this book, and the delivery of its lessons into the reality of your own life. Make great use of it. Effect deep and permanent changes in your approach to living and the strength of your determination.

That is how you honor this material. Once more I tell you that the shelf or bookstand is not the place for this volume, and it does dishonor to your investment to leave it there.

Carry it with you. Take notes in it. Highlight and underline and circle sections that shine for you, and return to them over time and observe your transforming perspective.

Through total ownership and complete engagement, you extract full value and leverage precise knowledge. Take heed of my solemn command to you:

Tumble and turn! Plan your vision with competence, and let the dark world watch your attainment.

Always follow truth where it leads you in the dark.

That is why the Way exists.

Create the great work that men follow.

There are those who walk this path with you. For those behind you, pull them forward into the present. For those beside you, stand with them shoulder to shoulder in the dark world. Those ahead of you provide you with visionary proof of what can be attained. Follow them.

The crucible of the dark world does not reward the loner. This flies in the face of much of the popular media, which portrays the loner as a mysterious, nearly magical figure who rides in alone, achieves wonder, then vanishes in solitary drama and splendor.

I tell you now that this is illusion, and a rapid way to be ignominiously killed.

Teamwork is essential, or else the most successful businesses would be sole consultancies.

Coordination is necessary, otherwise the greatest battles would be won by individual duels.

Integration with other human beings is necessary, as any head of a successful home and family will confirm with ready assurance.

You do not walk the Way in silent contemplation. You are accompanied on this path by your followers, your peers and your leaders.

Connect with them.

Speak with them. Lead your young men, find your brothers, and raise spears with them under the leadership of men who have gone before.

That is the culmination of the Way and it is your responsibility to embody it.

Own what you hold in your hands. Engage with the entire world. Follow the Way.

This is vitally important:

You are the point where fate explodes.

Never forget it.

The Old Man | Danse Macabre
Hans Holbein the Younger (1497–1543)

Afterword

The ultimate essential essence of this book is to give you the tools to be happy.

I often must remind readers or critics that I did not make the world a dark place; it was ferocious and unforgiving when I arrived. And I will pass away in time, and the dark world will swirl along towards extinction without notice of my agonies or fears, terrors or trials, just as it does not perceive yours or that of your loved ones.

What, then, is the value of any these things?

Why do we suffer?

The great singularity of value is in our own experience of living.

Just as the hurtful and unhappy aspects, encounters and engagements of this life are myriad and entangled, so too are the joyous, the loving, the delightful and the happy thrills that are nestled sweetly into the smile of a child, the quick flip of a bird on the wing or the rain that falls, quietly, nourishing the green world we have been given.

It is all preposterous, but it is beautifully preposterous, and the immortal part of us is love and joy.

I will share with you the final secret that you will, over time, discover as you apply the Laws, observe the dark world, and live within it.

The great and final secret is a joyous and amusing one.

It is understanding that once you reach the limits of the Laws and have turned back and re-explored, circled through them, passed along them, and uncovered every possible variation—that the true work is inside you, and the most perfect stacking and attrition and achievement of purpose and vision all comes down to a single satisfaction:

Fulfilled joy in living. Yet understand that joy is not a destination, nor a way station. It is not a place with a marker that you measure distance to or track progress towards.

Joy is the experience of sacred purpose fulfilled.

Confusion, hesitation and redirection fade away and love is utterly communicated in the joining of human beings. New life is conceived, and birth is the sacred action that adds even more joy to existence and interest from the great Creator that waits on the other side.

Illusion dissipates and friction soothes, and the spirit incubates and prepares to accelerate from the traction of wisdom and compassion and kindness into the next multiverse that awaits.

Delusion, degradation and destruction are discarded, and by revelation of direction the great story of fate itself is made clear, and all pain and sorrow washed away.

This is a life worth living: the examined life, the life of purpose that meets fate.

It is the experience of the **Dark Triad Man**.

The dark world does not go away before we do, but even in the end it too shall pass away.

It is preposterous to know what happens next, but one truth is certain:

No laws here will hold.

Ask, and it shall be given you; seek, and ye shall find; knock, and it shall be opened unto you:

For every one that asketh receiveth; and he that seeketh findeth; and to him that knocketh it shall be opened.[9]

Ask, seek and knock.
Word, thought and deed.

It is the great Way from the beginning of time.

Be prepared.
Take advantage of every opportunity to learn, to train, to connect and to live.
That is the Way, and this is the time.
It is your duty to live well.

Survive the challenges of the dark world and reach peace.
Conceal your plans and create living achievements.
Find sacred purposes and drive them to fulfillment.
Endure the great trials of life in the dark world.
Stand with dignified posture and embrace your humanity.
Live in freedom and never negotiate for chains.
Be as powerful as you can possibly be.
Remember it is all preposterous, and laugh well.
And no laws hold, perhaps not even death.

We have trained you in the Laws and the grid, the lessons and the Way.
Now you must grow deep momentum of your own, and master it utterly.

Drive your personal road to vision, purpose and power with everything you have.

All the thrones of the world await you, glittering in their magnificence.

Live well, my esteemed friend and beloved brother.

I will see you out there, in the dark world.

The Advocate | Danse Macabre
Hans Holbein the Younger (1497–1543)

Glossary

Action: The first realization of the dark world in the realm of execution. Action is the motion ensuing within the performance of deed, the bright polarity of outcome.

Aperture: A concentric, closing portal through which flow is constricted and relaxed, and thereby focused for deliberate adjustment of impact.

Channel: Condensation of the realms of thought, word and deed drives them into channels of delivery; it is through channels that reality flows.

Collapse: Negative outcome of fate; unsustainable structures, ideas and beliefs reach the singularity of collapse when their integrity fails.

Communication: The reason for word and the foundation of the universe; delivery of information into actuality through intelligence.

Concealment: The Second Law. Refers to the necessity of circumspection and silence as essential to the guidance and preparation of plans.

Conception: Point at which thought begins, the commencement of intelligence out of information and also the positive outcome of thought.

Condense: Collapsing, encircling, narrowing, funneling natural process of the dark world; an implosive and hardening process.

Confusion: Negative outcome of thought; incoherent conception, disordered contemplation, uncertainty of mind; incorrect processing of information.

Consequence: The result of thought, word and deed in the dark world; the first inevitable result of momentum within the universe.

Control: Narcissism, Machiavellianism and psychopathy, the traits used by the **Dark Triad Man** to deliberately steer the outcome of fate.

Creation: The source of the universe; the beginning point at which momentum starts its process of condensation, entropy and death.

Dark Triad Man: A weaponized human being; skilled in thought, word and deed; scholar of vision, planning and competence; master of narcissism, Machiavellianism and psychopathy.

Dark world: The plane of existence within which momentum ensues; where consequence, karma and fate accumulate and the **Dark Triad Man** operates by means of the Nine Laws.

Deed: Human action in execution; the source of surviving competence and the freedom of the psychopath in unbounded and unrestricted action to detonate fate.

Degradation: Failure of Machiavellianism; useless spinning of complexity with gratuitous control, resulting in loss of power and collapse.

Delivery: The process of conveyed consequence and karma into the impact of fate; the application of outcomes achieved by the human being.

Delusion: Failure of narcissism; wild spiral of intelligence into corrupt and disordered control, resulting in preposterous mind and collapse.

Destruction: Failure of psychopathy; hurtling, directionless and negative action that results in potentially unlimited collapse.

Determination: Process by which fate is arrived at; the fixation of spinning probabilities, between polarities of potential, into a defined state of actuality.

Detonate: Positive outcome of fate; information, creation and execution reach the singularity of achieved actuality in the dark world.

Direction: Process of controlled psychopathy; means by which the competent deed reaches detonation at a deliberate point of impact.

Dissipation: Failure of planning; sloughing away of momentum and lessening of shape for the delivery of intention into the dark world.

Endurance: The Fourth Law. Endurance is the quality of perseverance, of putting up with, of sustaining vision despite the challenges inherent in the dark world.

Execution: The starting point of fate at the hands of man; the process by which the dark world unfolds with determination of reality.

Fate: The singularity of achieved, determined final state for potential; where probability reaches one and all other outcomes become infinitely preposterous.

Flow: Quality of continuous, living and resonant movement inherent within all things; pure stream of actuality as it manifests.

Focus: Result of application of constriction and relaxation; applied through the use of apertures by the human being to bring the realms of thought, word and deed into concentration of channel.

Freedom: The Sixth Law. Freedom is the non-negotiable principle of mobility; the ability to choose direction and achieve traction according to desired direction.

Friction: Failure of competence; loss of momentum through the dark world towards goal outcomes as a result of incorrect focus of flow.

Gradient: Seamless, even blend from one polarity to another; infinite region of measurement between two opposing singularities.

Gratuitous: Unnecessary thought, word or deed; excessive vision, planning or competence; wasteful narcissism, Machiavellianism or psychopathy.

Hesitation: Failure of deed to ensue; stuttering, unformed negative outcome of unseized opportunity for action in the dark world.

Illusion: Incorrect vision; adherence of thought to false perception and interpretation, leading to deviation from desired direction of momentum.

Incubation: Process of cultivating vision; nurturing, shaping and bringing into focus the desired future state of fate within the mind.

Information: Infinite, unbounded and indestructible reality; truth that exists outside of time and space; the flowing source of all.

Karma: The result of vision, planning and competence in the dark world; the reactive force of the dark world in response to delivery of outcome by the human being.

Machiavellianism: A trait of the **Dark Triad Man;** the posture of plans, the power of revelation as it is controlled into detonation of fate.

Makoto: Sincere truth; singularity of reality, the undeniable and unassailable fact of things that can be extrapolated from the gradient that exists between polarities.

Manifestation: Successful achievement of the control of narcissism; the point at which vision is no longer future potentiality but begins to flow into probability and thence actuality.

Momentum: Inherent movement of finite creation from birth to death; descent through the dark world of all things, the quality of mass in motion.

Narcissism: A trait of the **Dark Triad Man**; the endurance of vision, the preposterousness of manifestation as it is controlled into the detonation of fate.

No Laws: The Ninth Law. No Laws is the basal reality of the dark world; unassailable truth that boundaries imposed by human beings are unsustainable illusion.

Pivot: Spinning of polarities; the tumble and turn of the realms, channels and controls upon the axis of possibility, the exploration of potential final states of fate.

Polarity: Oppositional values at the ends of a gradient; absolute and complementary states of final singularity that represent alternatives of actuality.

Posture: The Fifth Law. Posture is the array of things, the expressive flow of thought, word and deed in response to encounter, the shape of vision, planning and competence as they enter engagement.

Power: The Seventh Law. Power is prerogative, the expansion of capacity and capability, the cultivation of momentum, mass and energy within the dark world.

Preparation: Positive process of planning; the shaping of structure for plans, the pivot and anticipation of opportunity and risk within the dark world.

Preposterousness: The Eighth Law. Preposterousness is acknowledgement of the infinite improbability of any outcome, and the inherent flow and presence of chaos through the dark world.

Psychopathy: A trait of the **Dark Triad Man**; the freedom of competence, his utterly unbounded direction as he controls the detonation of fate.

Purpose: The Third Law. Purpose is the sacred resonance of the heart, and the great motive idea which drives the momentum of fate.

Random: Unpredictable, inherent instability of result; the outcome of chaos as it bleeds into the dark world and manifests with preposterousness.

Realm: The great vehicles of thought, word and deed; where information, creation and execution enter into existence within the dark world.

Redirection: Failure of communication; random or purposeful outcome of concealed intention, the negative result of word that does not connect.

Resonance: The vibratory quality of echo through the dark world; cascading results of thought, word and deed, parallel momentum of vision, planning and competence; perpetuated impacts.

Revelation: Deliberate and measured exposure of plans by the Machiavellian; reversal of concealment and presentation of creation in the dark world.

Shin-den: Divine transmission; the process of the *ninja* where deep revelation of sincere truth from one human being to another is delivered as sacred gift.

Shinshin shingan: "Divine mind, divine eye"; the state described by the *ninja* in which the realms, channels and controls are perfectly aligned and integrated, and invincibility of delivered fate accrues.

Singularity: Infinite mass, energy and information condensed to a point; absolute value and ultimate polarity with an oppositional complement.

Survival: The First Law. Survival is the perpetuation of a living existence within the dark world, necessary for the continuance of thought, word and deed.

Thought: Human conception of information; the source of purposeful vision and endurance of narcissism until at last fate manifests and detonates.

Traction: Positive application of competence; exploitation of contact through utilization of skill and the source of accelerated momentum.

Word: Sacred communication of creation; the source of concealed planning and the posture of the Machiavellianism until intention is revealed and fate is powerfully detonated.

The Nun | Danse Macabre
Hans Holbein the Younger (1497–1543)

Study Resources

In forty years of practice, training and living in the dark world I have come across countless written resources that have helped to shape my perspective and perceptions of the human race, its history, and the astonishing wonder of the finite universe we live within.

It would be absolutely impossible to list them all, and undoubtedly any best efforts in that direction would inevitably miss one or another key literary gold mine, arouse the ire of readers, and generate demands for updated versions of this work to include their particular favorite.

It is important to recognize that while I certainly have my own favorites that I have accumulated over the years, any list that a single man generates would be inherently limited. As well, I firmly believe that it is more than just the information within a book; the very time and place of reading it creates a crucial framework for absorption of its content.

Today, the times are changing quickly, and this work of The Nine Laws is needed badly.

Men who read it today will be far more receptive than men several hundred years ago. Perhaps I would have been burned at the stake in ages past for writing this book; perhaps in the years ahead, social justice warriors will curse the name of Ivan Throne and wreckage he helped create of their murderous collectivist fantasies.

Perhaps, perhaps. I am already told that "men should be imprisoned for reading this, even if they have committed no crime." And I already receive ugly threats of death.

The dark world is an exciting place. One thing I know for certain:

The most important resource you have is a love of learning, a determination to seek out knowledge, and an inquiring mind that does not slam doors upon alternate sources of intelligence.

Seek it out. Always, always maintain the mindset of questioning excavation of truth.

For that, too, is the Way. And it stands the entire human race in good stead.

To read more of my writing, and to engage the living band of brothers who form around this knowledge, visit the home of my work.

You will be made welcome. And the brothers there are not intimidated by the adversary.

www.DarkTriadMan.com

I would rather be ashes than dust!

I would rather that my spark should burn out in a brilliant blaze than it should be stifled by dry-rot.

I would rather be a superb meteor, every atom of me in magnificent glow, than a sleepy and permanent planet.

The function of man is to live, not to exist.

I shall not waste my days trying to prolong them.

I shall use my time.

Jack London (1876–1916)

The Miser | Danse Macabre
Hans Holbein the Younger (1497–1543)

Notes

1. Giles, L. (1988). The art of war: The oldest military treatise in the world. Singapore: G. Brash.
2. Shinmen Musashi no Kami Fujiwara no Genshin. (1995). A book of five rings (V. Harris, Trans.). New York: Overlook press.
3. Shinmen Musashi no Kami Fujiwara no Genshin. (1995). A book of five rings (V. Harris, Trans.). New York: Overlook press.
4. Toda Shinryuken Masamitsu (1891, January 1). New Year's Day essay.
5. Skeem, J. L.; Polaschek, D. L. L.; Patrick, C. J.; Lilienfeld, S. O. (2011). "Psychopathic Personality: Bridging the Gap Between Scientific Evidence and Public Policy". Psychological Science in the Public Interest 12 (3): 95–162.
6. John 1:1, King James Version
7. Erwin Schrödinger, Die gegenwärtige Situation in der Quantenmechanik (The present situation in quantum mechanics), Naturwissenschaften (translated by John D. Trimmer in Proceedings of the American Philosophical Society)
8. Folger Shakespeare Library. (n.d.) Henry V from Folger Digital Texts. Retrieved from www.folgerdigitaltexts.org.
9. Matthew 7:7–8, King James Version.

CPSIA information can be obtained
at www.ICGtesting.com
Printed in the USA
BVHW040212061218
534925BV00007B/34/P